THE LIFE OF
OLIVER ELLSWORTH

Da Capo Press Reprints in

AMERICAN CONSTITUTIONAL AND LEGAL HISTORY

GENERAL EDITOR: LEONARD W. LEVY
Brandeis University

THE LIFE

OF

OLIVER ELLSWORTH

BY

WILLIAM GARROTT BROWN

DA CAPO PRESS · NEW YORK · 1970

A Da Capo Press Reprint Edition

This Da Capo Press edition of
The Life of Oliver Ellsworth
is an unabridged republication of the
first edition published in New York in 1905.

Library of Congress Catalog Card Number 76-118028
SBN 306-71940-1

Published by Da Capo Press
A Division of Plenum Publishing Corporation
227 West 17th Street, New York, N.Y. 10011

Manufactured in the United States of America

LIFE OF OLIVER ELLSWORTH

OLIVER ELLSWORTH.

From a portrait by an unknown artist, probably made in Paris.

THE LIFE

OF

OLIVER ELLSWORTH

BY

WILLIAM GARROTT BROWN

AUTHOR OF "THE LOWER SOUTH IN AMERICAN
HISTORY," ETC., ETC.

New York

THE MACMILLAN COMPANY

LONDON: MACMILLAN & CO., Ltd.

1905

Norwood Press
J. S. Cushing & Co. — Berwick & Smith Co.
Norwood, Mass., U.S.A.

TO

W. P. F.

PREFATORY NOTE

I DO not think it worth while to list all the authorities which I have used in this work. The footnotes contain specific references for all important statements of fact. Whatever contributions the book may make to the knowledge of Ellsworth's life have been drawn chiefly from certain unpublished sources — letters of Ellsworth, and manuscripts relating to him, of which the most valuable are two by Oliver Ellsworth, Jr., his son, and two complete biographies, one by Hon. Joseph Wood, his son-in-law, and the other by Rev. Abner Jackson, sometime president of Hobart College, who was married to his granddaughter. Wood's work was used by Flanders and others who have published accounts of Ellsworth. So far as I know, Jackson's has not hitherto been used at all.

For procuring me this material, and for help rendered in many other ways, my thanks are due to various members and connections of the Ellsworth family. To Mrs. F. C. Porter of New Haven, to Mr. W. W. Ellsworth of New York, to Mr. and Mrs. W. Irving Vinal of Washington, to Mrs. P. N. Nicholas of Geneva, New York, to Mr. G. E. Taintor of Hartford, and to Mrs. Elisha Geer of Windsor, I wish to make a particularly hearty acknowledgment of my obligation. Many other persons have assisted me with information or suggestions, — among them, Professor A. C. McLaughlin, Hon. H. C. Lodge, Professor F. B. Dexter, and Mr. Cephas Brainerd. The officials of the New York Public Library, and those of the libraries of Harvard, Princeton, and the Massachusetts and Connecticut Historical Societies, have courteously favored me with access to material in their several collections.

W. G. B.

CAMBRIDGE, MASS.,
October 1, 1905.

CONTENTS

CHAPTER I

PAGE

A COLONIAL BOYHOOD AND YOUNG MANHOOD 1

CHAPTER II

THE BAR AND THE ASSEMBLY 30

CHAPTER III

THE CONTINENTAL CONGRESS 53

CHAPTER IV

THE GREAT CONVENTION 107

CHAPTER V

THE SENATE 177

CHAPTER VI

THE SUPREME COURT 238

CHAPTER VII

PARIS 282

CHAPTER VIII

HOME 327

APPENDIX A 347

APPENDIX B 350

INDEX 361

LIST OF ILLUSTRATIONS

OLIVER ELLSWORTH . . . . *Frontispiece*
From a portrait by an unknown artist, probably made in Paris.

OPPOSITE PAGE

OLIVER ELLSWORTH 180
From a miniature by Trumbull, now in possession of Yale University.

OLIVER ELLSWORTH AND HIS WIFE 258
From a portrait by Earle.

ELMWOOD, ELLSWORTH'S HOME AT WINDSOR 330
From a photograph.

OLIVER ELLSWORTH

CHAPTER I

A COLONIAL BOYHOOD AND YOUNG MANHOOD

AMERICANS nowadays display but little fondness for
the earlier periods of our national history. Perhaps
one reason is that along with our astounding growth
in territory and power and wealth there has grown up
in us a pride of mere bigness that makes us irreverent
and impatient of the little things it all began with.
Another reason may be that we have wandered so far
away — and more ways than one — from those ideals
which the founders, whenever we turn back to them,
seem to be forever holding up to us, not without an
effect of warning and reproach. But I think that
many of us may also be rendered shy of Revolutionary history and biography by our distaste for the
kind of fervor with which they are commended to us.
The zeal displayed in celebrating the founders is too
often merely partisan, or merely academic, or merely
antiquarian, — or merely feminine. Of late, a journal-
istic impulse has set some rather clever pens to work,
revamping our oldest stories, upsetting our most dignified traditions, and disturbing our reverence for our
greatest national characters. But this brisk icono-
clasm reflects too clearly the commercial motive which
is now so dominant in all our journalism to take strong
hold of any but a rather shallow class of readers.

In one way or another, however, by partisans or anti-
quaries, by learned professors or by clever space-writers,
by pious descendants or by women's clubs, all but a
very few of the leading actors in our earlier scenes
have been from time to time sufficiently, if not always
quite fittingly, bewritten and belauded.   John Marshall's fame is still, it is true, for want of a competent
biographer, one of the vaguest of our national possessions; and even of Washington there is not yet a
written life of a preëminence comparable with that of
his career and character.   But I think no other in the
whole list of revolutionists and founders is at present
in quite such danger of losing his right place and rank
as Oliver Ellsworth of Connecticut.   Historians apart,
and a few lawyers with a historical turn of mind, the
chances are that not one in a hundred of his countrymen knows to-day a single fact about him, save that
he was once, for a little while, Chief Justice of our
highest court.   Two accounts of him were published
about the middle of the last century, but both belong
to series of lives of the chief justices, now but little
read.

Yet the truth is that if any one man can be called
the founder, not of that court only, but of the whole
system of federal courts, which many think the most
successful of the three departments of our government,
Ellsworth is the man.   In the famous Convention which
determined the entire framework of the government,
he was one of the members whose names should always
be associated both with the general character of the
Constitution and with important specific clauses.   To
scholars it is known also, though the evidence is somewhat vaguer, that he had already done good service in

the Continental Congress. In the first half-dozen years of Congress under the Constitution, when it was almost constantly engaged in constructive legislation second in importance only to the Convention's, his influence was so great that if any man could be called the leader of the Senate in that period, it was he. His, also, was the leading rôle in one of two negotiations with foreign powers on which, even more than on domestic controversies, the safety of the young republic seemed for a long time to depend. For more than a quarter of a century, beginning with the nation's birth, he was, with scarce an interval, engaged with great affairs and in high places. That he was for a few years the head of the judiciary, before its work attained a very great importance — this is by no means his chief title to remembrance. It is, rather, the most factitious of his claims. But if, on the other hand, it is not a mistake to count the founding and the working of governments among the noblest of all mundane enterprises, other and more solid services to his country demand for this colonial lawyer greater honor than has ever been his portion since his life-work was finished — now nearly a century ago.

I do not wish to anticipate the reader's judgment of the career I purpose to relate; but a word at the outset concerning the probable causes of the neglect of Ellsworth — if it be indeed decided that he was deserving of more honor than he has received — may not be amiss. If the accidental plays a part in life and in history, it plays at least an equal part in biography and historiography. Students of the history of literature know well enough how hard it is to secure for the contemporaries of the greatest masters

their just award of fame.   If Shakespeare had not lived
when he did, a dozen poets and dramatists would doubtless be esteemed more highly than they are.   In affairs,
the misfortune of the second bests is quite as great.
The contemporaries of Washington and Hamilton and
Jefferson, or of Lincoln and Lee and Grant, lose by
obscuration more than they gain in reflected lustre.
In nearly all his memorable activities, Ellsworth was
the associate of very famous men.   In the Continental
Congress, he was often detailed for special services
with Hamilton and Madison.   In the Constitutional
Convention, none of the younger members could hope
to make such a figure as Washington's and Franklin's,
while the actual lead in the debating fell most naturally to Madison and Randolph and Morris and Wilson.   When Ellsworth became a senator, his real
leadership was never clear to his contemporaries, for
the debates were secret, and men like Robert Morris
and Richard Henry Lee were once again his fellows.
As Chief Justice, he followed Rutledge; but Rutledge's
service was so short that Ellsworth might as well have
had John Jay for his immediate predecessor; and his
immediate successor, who held the place a third of a
century, was probably the greatest judge in the whole
long history of English and American jurisprudence.
Turning his hand to diplomacy, Ellsworth negotiated a
very important convention with France.   But Jay's treaty
with England, negotiated but a few years earlier, had
become the target for the opposition's fiercest attacks ;
it attained, therefore, by party controversy, a celebrity
which neither Ellsworth's convention nor any later
treaty could rival.   Even in his capacity of Connecticut leader and representative, Ellsworth was again

and again the colleague of Roger Sherman, an elder
if not a better statesman.

That he belonged to the little colony of Connecticut
may also not unreasonably be set down as a sort of
mishap to his fame. He himself was very far indeed
from thinking it a misfortune. " I have visited several
countries," he said, when he was growing old, "and I
like my own the best. I have been in all the states
of the Union, and Connecticut is the best state.
Windsor is the pleasantest town in the state of Connecticut, and I have the pleasantest place in the town
of Windsor. I am content, perfectly content, to die
on the banks of the Connecticut." [1] But it is no
controversion of this loyalty to hold that from the
banks of the Charles or the Hudson or the Potomac
he might have found a shorter path to eminence
among his contemporaries and to the reverence of
later generations. If he had lived in any one of the
bigger colonies, leadership in continental assemblies
would doubtless have been easier to win. A New
England worthy, he would have stood a better
chance of competent literary celebration if he had
belonged to Massachusetts. Americans from all
quarters have long been content to learn their country's history from a group of writers who, since their
own homes have been in eastern Massachusetts,
have taken care, with a zeal that ought to be emu-
lated rather than reviled, to guard from oblivion the
great men of their own famous commonwealth.
Had Ellsworth been of these, he would doubtless
have found a competent biographer among the men

[1] " An opinion handed down by Oliver Ellsworth," which hangs in a
frame beneath his bust in the drawing-room of his home at Windsor.

of letters of Boston and Cambridge. But Connecticut, colonized in large part from the slightly older
province, has too often been content to accept the
place which the people of the Bay Colony assigned
her, and to figure in history as a kind of *hinterland*
to Massachusetts. In later years, her nearness to the
still more populous and wealthy state of New York,
and to the greatest of our cities, has affected in much
the same way the popular notion of her importance.
Referring to this disadvantage of her geographical
situation, more than one Connecticut orator has compared the state to Issachar, "A strong ass crouching
down between two burdens."[1] To many of us, therefore, Connecticut still remains, in history as in
geography, a little state between New York and
Massachusetts. Ellsworth also remains what at one
time, occupying a compromise position, he probably
seemed to his contemporaries, — an obscure figure of
a statesman, between, let us say, John Adams and
Alexander, Hamilton.

But there is much in the past of Connecticut, and
particularly in her career as a colony, which is eminently deserving of our interest, quite apart from any
connection with either Massachusetts or New York.
No trained student of our institutions will lightly
dismiss any reflection of the late Alexander Johnston,
and it was his opinion that Connecticut had so good
a government as a colony, and had progressed so far
in the experiment both of democracy and of the
federal principle, that when the time came for our

---

[1] Wadsworth, in Connecticut Assembly, reported in *American Museum*,
October, 1787; Ellsworth, in Convention to Ratify the Constitution.
Elliot's *Debates*, II, 186.

greater national experiment she presented the best of all the object lessons which the founders had before them.   He holds, accordingly, that to the general scheme of our government no other state contributed so much of what was new, of what was American.[1] Her constitution of 1639 he deliberately pronounces " the most far-reaching political work of modern times." Such a claim, from such a source, is enough to arrest one's attention, even though the varied chronicle of Massachusetts distract from one side, while on the other side there bulks the central importance of the greatest of our states and cities.   Every day, hurrying in swift railroad trains from New York to Boston, or from Boston to New York, hundreds of people thunder across the entire east-and-west extent of the little intervening commonwealth.   From north to south, an ardent pedestrian has walked across it in a single day. Most travellers, passing over it, leave it still unvisited. Yet if one pauses for a closer view, there is much worth seeing in Connecticut.   Though the visitor knows already the New York Highlands and the Hudson River about West Point, even though he also knows the charm of Massachusetts' landscapes and the rugged splendors of her northern shore, he will wonder why one hears so little of the beautiful valley of the Connecticut.

For any one who cares to look into Connecticut history, there are equal surprises.   There is in it the very essence of those New England ideals, the full-

[1] Alexander Johnston's "Connecticut," Preface, and pp. 322–325.   But in the *American Historical Review* (IX, 480, note), Mr. Max Farrand has pointed out that the evidence is wanting to prove that the Constitutional Convention of 1787 ever did take the Connecticut system as a model in any portion of its work.

est exhibition of those New England characteristics, for which we oftener look, instead, to Massachusetts. The ancient town of Windsor, a few miles north of Hartford, is at the centre of Connecticut's most charming stretch of country. It is the centre also of what is best and strongest in the traditions of the little commonwealth. "Ancient Windsor" now, the place was at least old Windsor to the generation that fought the war of independence. Along its main street, which follows for some miles a slight ridge or "sand bank," parallel to the broad and straight Connecticut River, scores of colossal elms, and an extraordinary number of good colonial houses behind them, bear witness to its age. It was, in fact, one of the three towns with which Connecticut history began; and throughout the colonial period, the Revolution, and the early years of independence, it contributed to the service of the colony and the state a long list of honorable names. They are, with very few exceptions, names which indicate that the original source of the first immigration was the great middle class of English society. The only perceptible admixtures were Scotch, or Scotch-Irish, and Huguenot French. On the gravestones of the old Windsor burial-ground one finds the epitaphs of generation after generation of Allens and Allyns, Bissells, Browns, Cookes, Drakes, Edwardses, Egglestons, Ellsworths, Enoses, Filleys, Fitches, Gaylords (originally Gaillard, and French), Gilletts (originally Gillette, and also French), Grants, Griswolds, Haydens, Loomises, Mathers, Newberrys, Phelpses, Pinneys, Rockwells, Sills, Stileses, Stoughtons, Thralls, and Wolcotts. The same names have appeared and reappeared, at frequent intervals, for two centuries and a half, in the public records of the town, the colony, the state. Several have risen to high places in the lists of the servants of the nation. Generals and judges and admirals, inventors and men of letters, leaders in great business enterprises, congressmen and senators, and at least one President, have traced their descent from men who came to Windsor when the country all about it was a wilderness. The two Windsor names which emerged into the clearest light between the settlement and the Revolution were those of Edwards and Wolcott. In that part of the town which lay to the eastward of "the great river," Jonathan Edwards was born; and for a hundred and fifty years there was scarcely a single Windsor generation that did not look to a Wolcott as the foremost citizen.

The first of the Ellsworths came about the middle of the seventeenth century. Whence he came is not precisely known; the best-derived conjecture is, from Yorkshire, where the name is still quite common.[1] Neither is it known precisely when he came, but the town records show that in November, 1654, he was married to Elizabeth Holcomb, and that, the same year, he bought a home in that part of Windsor which lay to the south of "the little river," as the Farmington was called, and to the west of "the great river." Ten years later, however, he moved across the Farmington to North Windsor, and made his home on a plot of land which for two hundred and thirty-nine years remained in the hands of his descendants. From the

[1] Henry R. Stiles's "Ancient Windsor," II, 208–210; Ms. notes by Mr. W. Irving Vinal; two Ms. Lives of Ellsworth, one by his son-in-law, Joseph Wood, and the other by Rev. Abner Jackson, president of Hobart College, who married a granddaughter of the Chief Justice.

town and church records we learn further that he was
made a freeman in 1657, a juror in 1664, that in 1676
he gave three shillings for the relief of the poor of
other colonies, and that when he died his estate was
valued at £655, which was no mean sum for the times
and the country. A curious list of taxpayers,[1] made
in 1675, shows that for substance he ranked with the
first of his contemporaries. There were five classes in
all, and the highest class, of which each member possessed " a family, home, and four oxen," numbered but
twenty-nine. Ellsworth was of these. His gravestone
adds to these proofs of good standing a military title
somewhat more distinguished in the seventeenth
century than it is in the twentieth. The inscription
reads : —

> Sargient
> Iosiah [2] Elsworth
> Aged 60 years
> He Dyed August ye
> 20th Day ; Ano. 1689.

Nine children were born to him, and the graves of
his descendants are clustered thick about his own.
Many of these are marked with gravestones, bearing
each a title or a pithy record of some good work done,
or at least some honorable place held, in the little community. The sixth child and third son of the immi-
grant is designated on his gravestone simply as " Mr.
Jonathan Elsworth," [3] but it is otherwise known of him

---

[1] Stiles's " Ancient Windsor," I, 88.

[2] The first name is sometimes given as " Josias." For most of these
facts see *ibid.*, II, 210.

[3] But in the family Bible of Chief Justice Ellsworth his name is given as
David. This is puzzling, for all the other records name him Jonathan.
The best conjecture I can make by way of explanation is that by a slip of
the pen the Chief Justice wrote his father's name for his grandfather's — a

that he was born in 1669, that he died in 1749, that he was a successful storekeeper and tavern-keeper, a man of good sense, including a sense of humor, and that in person he was tall and strong. His wife was a Grant.[1] Their seventh child and fourth son, born in 1709, was christened David, and it is " Capt. David Ellsworth " (this time with two l's) on his gravestone. The title was not an empty one, for he served in the War of the Spanish Succession, known in America as the Old French War, and in 1745 commanded a company from Windsor at the famous siege of Louisburg. Returning in safety from that expedition, which was by no means a holiday affair, he lived to the eve of the recognition of the colonies' independence, and nearly all his life he was selectman of his native town. In-heriting a hundred pounds, he had the industry and the shrewdness to accumulate a considerable estate, and to win the reputation of an excellent farmer. A grandson has recorded that he had much " cunning, or quick-turned wit," and " sound judgment." His wife, who was Jemima Leavitt, of the neighboring village of Suffield, is rather formidably described as " a lady of excellent mind, good character, and pious principles."[2] Surviving him, she was married again, at the age of sixty-three, to a wealthy citizen of East Windsor.[3]

The highest and stateliest of all the monuments in the Ellsworth family group, rising up from the rear of

strange mistake to make, it must be admitted, and a stranger still not to have corrected. Oliver Ellsworth, Jr., a son of the Chief Justice, refers, in a Ms. that is still preserved, to " Jonathan, my father's grandfather."

[1] Stiles's " Ancient Windsor," II, 210–211 ; Ms. notes in the collection of Mr. W. Irving Vinal.

[2] Ms. of Oliver Ellsworth, Jr.

[3] Stiles's " Ancient Windsor," II, 212.

the pleasant little burial-ground behind the old First Church, and overlooking the little river, marks the grave of Oliver, the second son and second child of Captain David and his wife Jemima. He was born on April 29, 1745, and belongs, therefore, to the generation that came to its prime about the beginning of the War of Independence.

It is necessary to be brief with his childhood and boyhood, for little or nothing is known of his life in this early period. A farmer's boy in a provincial country town, he was doubtless accustomed to frugal fare, simple amusements, and hard, wholesome tasks.[1] Beyond question, he was made familiar from his childhood with the doctrine and observance of the Congregational Church—the established church of the colony. Since Connecticut from a very early period had maintained an excellent school system, supported by taxation, and Windsor was an old town of considerable wealth, it is also reasonably certain that his early schooling was as good as could be had anywhere in the colonies. But what sort of a pupil he was, or indeed what sort of a boy he was, we do not know. One fact, however, may be taken to indicate that he was thought a boy of promise. His father early set about to prepare him for the ministry; and in colonial New England the ministry ranked so high among the professions that only a boy of promise would be brought up to aspire to it. With that career in view, he was sent to the Rev. Dr. Joseph Bellamy of Bethlem, a

---

[1] He told his son that when he was a boy there was but one carriage in Windsor, and most people ate their food from wooden trenchers; that the life was hard, and manners simple to coarseness. Ms. of Oliver Ellsworth, Jr.

friend of Jonathan Edwards, famous as a preacher throughout New England, and known by his writings even in England and Scotland. Dr. Bellamy prepared the boy for college, and in 1762, at the age of seventeen, he entered Yale.

But it was twenty-nine years before he got a Yale degree, and then it came to him, not as in course, but *honoris causâ*. He remained at New Haven only to the end of his sophomore year; and there is reason to believe that either he or the authorities of the college, and not improbably both, would have been better pleased to close the connection even sooner. He entered, it seems, at a time of undergraduate discontents, such as all colleges now and then have to weather. The long administration of President Thomas Clap was drawing to a close, and his headship of the still struggling seminary, though admirable for vigor and devotion, had been growing too arbitrary to please the student body. There was much complaint also of the tutors; and it is hardly necessary to add that the students held the immemorial undergraduate conviction concerning the food which was served to them in the college commons, and that they did not forbear, when occasion offered, to make their disapproval known. It must be confessed that even a moderate epicure could have found a trifle to criticise, now and then, in the college fare. According to a set of regulations in force about this time, breakfast for four was one loaf of bread. Dinner was more substantial; but supper, also for four, was an apple pie and one quart of beer.[1] If young Ellsworth had made a request for-

[1] F. B. Dexter, "Yale Biographies and Annals," 2d series, 141. Daniel Butler on the Yale Commons, in Kingsley's "Yale College," I, 297–306.

ever associated with his Christian name, he would doubtless have won distinction earlier than he did.

The intellectual fare was, it would seem, neither more abundant nor more tempting. At Yale, as indeed at all the colonial colleges, the curriculum was a hard and fast and uniform programme. "In the first year," so the laws read, "They Shall principally study the Tongues and Logic, and Shall in Some measure pursue the study of the Tongues the Two next Years. In the second year they shall Recite Rhetoric, Geometry and Geography. In the Third year, Natural Philosophy, Astronomy and Other Parts of the Mathematicks. In the Fourth Year Metaphysics and Ethics. . . . But every Saturday shall Especially be allotted to Divinity."[1] It was useless to ask for more, or for any variation in the programme. The teaching force was too small to give well even what was offered. Each of the two or three tutors was responsible for *all* the instruction, in all branches, that was given to the class or section under his especial care.

The year before Ellsworth entered, there had been so much disorder that a petition, prepared, no doubt, by enemies of President Clap, had been presented to the General Assembly of the colony, asking an investigation. "There has been a tumult," a trustee wrote, "the Desk pulled down, the Bell case broken, and the bell ringing in the night, Mr. Boardman the tutor beaten with Clubbs"[2] —which was clearly contrary to rule, for Penal Law No. 19 expressly provided: "If any Scholar shall make an assault upon the Person of

[1] Laws of Yale College, 1745.
[2] Dexter, "Yale Biographies and Annals," 2d series, 682.

ye President or either of the Tutors or shall wound, Bruise or Strike any of Them, He shall forthwith be Expelled." Similar disorders arose from time to time until, in 1765–1766, the climax came in a practically unanimous signed petition of the students for the removal of President Clap. During the last term of that year, not more than two-thirds of the student body was in attendance. It is not surprising, when one remembers that this was the time of the struggle over the Stamp Act, to find the state of affairs in the college attributed to the spirit of resistance to arbitrary rule which was rising throughout the colonies. General Gage, at Boston, referred to Yale in 1765 as a "Seminary of Democracy."[1] Young Roswell Grant, of the class of 1765, wrote home to his father at Windsor that he would be very glad of a cheese, but added: "Shall not want that Cherry (Sherry) you reserved for me before vacancy, as all the Scholars have unanimously agreed not to drink any foreign spirituous liquors any more."[2] It is clear that undergraduate Yale was at least as patriotic as it was rebellious.

Ellsworth's share in these activities, patriotic and rebellious, cannot now be ascertained. He appears, however, in at least two cases of discipline on the records of the faculty.[3] His prime offence in the first case, in July, 1763, was the puzzling misdemeanor of joining with ten others, in the *evening*, "to scrape and clean the college yard"; but a second count arraigned him and his comrades for "having a treat or entertainment last winter," and still a third count set forth

---

[1] Dexter, "Yale Biographies and Annals," 3d series, 170.   [2] *Ibid.*, 94.
[3] Transcripts from the Faculty Records, which were kindly made for me by Professor Dexter.

that he and three others "presently after evening Prayers on Thursday last put on their Hats and run and Hallooed in the College Yard in contempt of the Law of College." For these offences he was fined one shilling. The second case arose the next year, and the charge was that Ellsworth was present "at Bulkley 2d's," at "a general treat or compotation of wine both common and spiced in and by the sophomore class," and the punishment was a fine of four shillings. There were degrees of guilt, for two ringleaders were fined five shillings, and Ellsworth and two others four shillings, while the majority of the offenders were let off at two shillings. These performances do not strike one as very damning. They do, however, seem to prove that Ellsworth was once a boy, and that the boys of colonial New England were not entirely unlike their descendants — at least, when they went to college. Perhaps we may also infer that Ellsworth was already out of sympathy with his father's ambition that he should be a minister.

Why he left Yale is not entirely clear. President Clap entered in his official journal, under the date July 27, 1764, that "Oliver Ellsworth and Waightstill Avery, at the desire of their respective parents, were dismissed from being members of this College."[1] But among the descendants of Ellsworth at least two other stories are told to account for his departure from New Haven. One is, that at midnight in midwinter he inverted the college bell and filled it with water, which promptly froze.[2] But this explanation hardly

[1] Entry copied by Professor Dexter.
[2] H. C. Lodge, oration on Ellsworth, in "A Fighting Frigate and Other Essays," 70, note.

consists with the date of his dismissal. Unfortunately for the other story, it has been told of more than one celebrity, and of other colleges than Yale. It is that Ellsworth was caught by a college officer giving in his room what in his day was called a "treat" but in the college nomenclature of the present day would be called a "spread"; and that the officer, about to enter and disperse the company, was stopped by hearing Ellsworth's voice uplifted in prayer — for there was a college law that no student should be interrupted at his devotions.[1] Of this story there is a second version which, even if it were never told of any one but Ellsworth, sounds too modern for belief. It is that the officer was making a round of the dormitory in search of signs which the students had stolen from New Haven tradesmen, and that the words of the prayer he heard were the words of Matthew xii. 39.[2]

For Ellsworth's career at Princeton, tradition is almost the only source; the written records of the immediate government of the College of New Jersey in colonial times are not preserved.[3] Younger than either Yale or Harvard, Princeton was also smaller. There can hardly have been a hundred students when Ellsworth entered. Age and size apart, it differed from the other two mainly by a stronger infusion of Calvinism in its theology and of Scotch and Scotch-Irish blood in its membership. John Witherspoon

---

[1] Letter from Mrs. Alice L. Wyckoff, of Buffalo, N.Y.

[2] Letter from Mrs. Geneve (Ellsworth) Stuart, a great-granddaughter of Ellsworth.

[3] For Princeton at this time see MacLean's "College of New Jersey"; De Witt and Williams, in "Universities and their Sons"; De Witt and Wilson, in "Memorial Book of the Sesquicentennial Celebration of Princeton University"; Gaillard Hunt's "Madison," I, Chap. II, etc.

had not yet consented to come over from Scotland and head the institution, but President Samuel Finley (1761–1766) was a Scotch-Irish Presbyterian minister, with a great reputation in the middle colonies and Virginia.

In respect of the curriculum and the number of teachers, Princeton offered to young Ellsworth no more than Yale had offered; but it was, apparently, rather more fortunate in its tutors, and in the spirit that informed both the teachers and the taught. The arts of speaking and writing, in particular, appear to have been taught uncommonly well and studied with extraordinary enthusiasm. It is certain that of all the colonial colleges, Harvard and William and Mary not excepted, no other was at this time training so many debaters for the Continental Congress and the still un-dreamed-of Constitutional Convention.[1] Waightstill Avery, Ellsworth's companion in migration, had before him a good career in public life in North Carolina. In the class which they joined, numbering but thirty-one, and a large class for Princeton, were Luther Martin of Maryland and at least three others with parts to play in the coming political changes. William Paterson, graduated the year before, was living in the village and in constant association with his younger mates. Benjamin Rush, John Henry, Tapping Reeve, Hugh Henry Brackenridge, Philip Freneau, Henry Lee, Pierpont Edwards, Gunning Bedford, James Madison, and Aaron Burr were all in classes close before or after Ellsworth's class of 1766. Of those students who were not, as the event proved, in training for statesmanship,

[1] Woodrow Wilson, in "Memorial Book of Princeton Sesquicentennial Celebration," 110–114.

fully half were preparing for the ministry. It is no wonder that courses in oratory and composition were popular, or that the Stamp Act controversy aroused at Princeton even more discussion than at Yale.[1]

Tradition and reminiscence indicate that Ellsworth entered with zest into the somewhat fervid life of his new academic home. A respectable scholar, he was, we are told, remarkably successful in college politics, displaying an uncommon shrewdness, a gift of management, and a talent for debate.[2] The best-known story of his Princeton days is of how he circumvented a rule forbidding students to wear their hats in the college yard. Arraigned for breaking the rule, he pointed out that a hat, to *be* a hat, must consist of a crown and a brim, and proved that the head-piece he had worn in the yard was without a brim — as he had in fact torn off that essential portion of it.[3] A better-authenticated and more important tradition indicates clearly enough what the young fellow's tastes and powers were. There seems to be little doubt that he was one of the founders of the Well Meaning Club, a debating club, which was suppressed in 1768, but later revived and reorganized as the Cliosophic Society. Another club, formed about the same time, first called the Plain Speaking Club, and likewise suppressed in 1768, was reorganized by Madison, John Henry, and Samuel Stanhope Smith, and named the American Whig Society.[4] Among the college debating clubs

---

[1] " Twenty-two commence this fall, all of them in American Cloth." Madison to his father, Gaillard Hunt's " Madison's Writings," I, 7.

[2] Wood and Jackson Mss.

[3] *Ibid.* ; *University Magazine*, November, 1891.

[4] Hunt's " Madison," 15; De Witt and Williams, in "Universities and their Sons," I, 482–484 ; McLean, " College of New Jersey," I, 364.

throughout the country, these two Princeton societies
hold at present the first rank for age, for celebrity, and
for the names on their rolls of membership. It seems
most likely that Paterson, who was fond of such
activities, and precisely the sort of man to lead in
them, was the moving spirit when Clio was founded ;
but with his name tradition has firmly associated
Ellsworth's, Luther Martin's, and Tapping Reeve's.[1]
There is scarcely to be found even in the records of
the Oxford Union a coincidence more curiously prophetic. We are told, also, that both these clubs were
mightily concerned about the Stamp Act and the
relations of the colonies to the mother country. It is
true that New Jersey and the other central colonies
contributed less leadership to the American movement
than New England or Virginia ; but Princeton already
drew her students from surprising distances. The
acquaintances Ellsworth made there, and the outlook
he gained, were doubtless a better introduction to the
whole field of colonial politics than he could have
got at any other college. He seems to have formed
there the habit of caution and to have developed the
instinct for compromise which were later conspicuous
characteristics. At any rate, he had got what few but
the wealthiest young colonials could have — an education a long way from home.

When he went back to Connecticut, however, his
father had not relinquished the plan of making him

[1] De Witt and Williams, in "Universities and their Sons"; J. A.
Porter, in *Century Magazine*, September, 1888. For Paterson, W. Jay Mills,
"Glimpses of Colonial Society and the Life at Princeton College" (made
up chiefly of Paterson's letters). The corresponding secretary of the
Cliosophic Society states that there is no record of Ellsworth's connection
with the society now in its possession.

a minister. He accordingly spent the next year in the study of theology under Dr. John Smalley of New Britain, a young clergyman of parts, who rose to influence and distinction.[1] But Ellsworth had by this time a clear and strong bent towards the law. When Dr. Smalley directed him to prepare his first sermon, the first ten sheets of his manuscript were given over to careful definition of his terms.[2] His teacher and his father were at length persuaded that his mind and tastes were better suited to the bar than to the pulpit.

It was four years, however, before he was admitted to the bar; and for those four years, from 1767 to 1771, the record of his life is very scant. He studied law under the first Governor Griswold and under Jesse Root of Coventry, a young attorney with whom he was later associated in the Continental Congress, and whose name appears many times in the public records of Connecticut. But Ellsworth can hardly have given the whole of the four years to his studies. In one account of his life, it is stated that he taught school for a little while[3] — an experience curiously common in the lives of eminent Americans. When he began practice as a lawyer, he was in debt, and a rational inference is that after he abandoned theology his father made no further expenditures for his education.

In any case, however, his education in the law could

[1] J. Hammond Trumbull, "Memorial History of Hartford County," II, 309–310.

[2] "Centennial Papers of the General Conference of Connecticut" (1876), 107–108.

[3] Longacre and Herring, "National Portrait Gallery" (1839), IV, article on Ellsworth.

not have been elaborate. There were no law schools
in the colonies. The people of Connecticut were
thought to be peculiarly and perversely litigious, but
the Commentaries of Blackstone were still unknown
among them. The first American edition of the work
was printed in 1771 or 1772, and a copy with Ellsworth's name and the date 1774 on the fly-leaf is still
in existence;[1] one conjectures that he never possessed
the book, probably never even saw it, until he had been
several years in practice. His text-books were Ba-
con's "Abridgment" and Jacob's "Law Dictionary."[2]
In fact, there were no text-books, properly so-called.
It may be added that until very near the time when
he began to practise there was considerable opposition
to the common law in Connecticut.[3] The colony
had begun its legislative history with what looks like
a complete disavowal and rejection of the system. It
was never adopted by statute, but came in gradually
by a change of usage on the bench and at the bar,
as professionally trained practitioners became more
numerous. Even when the decisions of the English
judges were familiarly cited in the Connecticut courts,
the means of studying them were scant and crude.
Good law libraries were extremely rare, and the labors
of the colonial lawyer were not made easy by treatises
and digests. It is altogether improbable that Ellsworth possessed, at the outset of his professional
career, any such store of facts or principles as would
now be required of him in an examination for admis-

---

[1] William Bliss, in *New York Evening Post*, April 9, 1875.

[2] Wood Ms.

[3] *Analectic Magazine*, III, 382; "Judicial and Civil History of Connecticut," by Loomis and Calhoun, pp. 176–177; Preface to Kirby's Connecticut Reports; Wood Ms., etc.

sion to the bar of any New England state. Yet the way he did learn the law was not unlike the method of studying and teaching it which has come of late into a very wide acceptance. He mastered it only by searching out and storing in his mind the principles at the heart of particular cases. In that process is involved the essence of the modern case-system. It is doubtful if a better training for the reason has ever been devised.

But even the opportunity to learn law in this way was for a time withheld. Cases to study and to try were not immediately forthcoming. Ellsworth had first to undergo a discipline in patience and frugality which seems to have been severe enough to make his professional career in all respects representative. Somebody has said that poverty and an early marriage make the best beginning of a lawyer's life; and both were in his portion. To pay the debts incurred while he was preparing for the bar, he had but one resource — a tract of woodland on the Connecticut which had come to him by inheritance or gift.[1] He tried in vain to sell the land, and then, shouldering an axe, attacked the timber, for which there was a market at Hartford. In this way he cleared himself of debt. But for three years after his admission to the bar his professional earnings, by his own account, were but three pounds, Connecticut currency. And yet, in 1772, a year after his admission, he was married.

His bride was Abigail, the second daughter of Mr. William Wolcott of East Windsor, a gentleman of substance and distinction, and a member of that same

[1] Wood Ms.; Henry Flanders, " Lives and Times of the Chief Justices of the Supreme Court," 2d series, 59–60.

Wolcott family which had held so high a place in the community from the very beginning. A story is told, that when Ellsworth made his first visit to the Wolcott house he called for an elder sister, but that the black eyes of Abigail, who sat demurely carding tow in the chimney corner, made him change his mind, and the next time he went there he called for her. She was only sixteen at her marriage.[1] A portrait that we have of her, painted when she was in middle life, suggests rather the good and cheerful housewife than the sort of colonial beauty whom colonial dames are now so fond of celebrating. But the tradition is that she was a beauty, and one or two anecdotes present her to posterity as an uncommonly loving and lovable woman. Unrelaxing in industry, she was given to charity, and had an unfailing kindness for all about her. That a briefless young lawyer should win, apparently without objection from her family, the daughter of so respectable a house, is evidence of the wholesome democracy in which they lived. It is evidence, too, of the sincerity of their affection for each other. That, happily, was strong enough to last through all their lives. The biographer of Ellsworth is often tempted to complain of the scarcity of purely personal details; but he is happily spared the temptation to stimulate the interest of his readers with any parade of family skeletons. In all that pertained to his family and his home, Ellsworth was both wise and fortunate.

The two began life on a farm which belonged to Ellsworth's father, and which the son now took over

[1] Jabez H. Hayden, in "Memorial History of Hartford County," II, 565.

to cultivate, either, it seems, on shares, or on a lease for rent.[1] It lay in the northwest part of old Windsor, which was then called Wintonbury, and is now called Bloomfield. The land was unfenced, and Ellsworth with his own hands cut and split the rails and built a fence about it. Too poor to hire a servant, he did himself all the heavier household chores, and twice a day when court was in session he walked the ten miles between his farm and his office in Hartford. Once, when a wealthier neighbor passed him in a carriage and told him that a man in his position ought to be riding and not walking, Ellsworth cheerfully replied that everybody must walk some time or other in his life, and that he for his part preferred to do his walking while he was young and strong. Of course we are also told, for a climax to the story, that a time came later when Ellsworth kept a carriage and his neighbor had to walk.[2]

The farm, rather than the pound a year he earned at his profession, must have been the young man's main support during the year or two longer that he had to wait for his first important case. He became an intelligent and zealous farmer; that is more than conjecture. But neither this nor his study of the law can be reckoned his principal achievement between his college days and that success which was soon to be his portion. Scanty as the record of those years is, we know that they covered a very fine and admirable study and development of his powers, for when Ellsworth first came fully into the light his character was rounded and hardened into the best type of colonial New England manhood. In later life, he himself,

[1] Wood Ms.   [2] *Ibid.*

being asked for the secret of his effectiveness, told modestly and convincingly the story of his growth. Early in his career, he said, he made the discouraging discovery that ♦he had no imagination, nor any other brilliant quality of mind. Determined, however, to make the most of such powers as he had, he resolved to study but one subject at a time, and to stick to it until he mastered it. In the practice of his profession, his rule was to go at once to the main points of a case and to give them his entire attention.[1]

In this candid self-examination, this honest acceptance of his limitations, this manly and courageous decision, one finds enough to command one's hearty respect. But it is not to be supposed that by this self-study and this plan of life alone the reasonably mischievous and reckless youngster of Yale and Princeton was at once transformed into a cautious and hardheaded but uncommonly upright lawyer and statesman. None of Ellsworth's New England contemporaries was more thoroughly representative of New England civilization at its best; and colonial New England was already — Switzerland, perhaps, excepted — the soundest democracy in the world. Nowhere else was liberty restrained by such strong reverences, or safeguarded by so practical an instinct, or fortified by a morality so

---

[1] Flanders, 64–65, following Wood Ms. Jackson's version is perhaps better: " To a young lawyer who asked him for the secret of his success in life, his reply was: ' Sir, after I left college I took a deliberate survey of my understanding. I felt that it was weak — that I had no imagination and but little knowledge or culture. I then resolved on this course of study : to take up but a single subject at a time, and to cling to that with an attention so undivided that if a cannon were fired in my ears I should still cling to my subject. That, sir, is all my secret.' " Jackson had the story from John Allyn, who told it on the authority of his nephew, Professor Goodrich of Yale.

widespread and so thoroughgoing. New England society, even in its unspoiled colonial state, had its faults, and some of its faults were hateful. The bit of talk about himself which I have just given is, for instance, almost the only frank and ingenuous revelation of his nature we shall find in all that Ellsworth ever wrote and spoke. When he became a man of substance, it was said that he took the utmost pains to conceal from his own household the extent of his wealth. Secretiveness and unresponsiveness were bound to be common among a people who cultivated, almost to excess, the fine qualities of self-reliance and forethought. We shall never be acquainted with Ellsworth or any other colonial New Englander as we are with famous Americans from other quarters, and with famous Englishmen as well. Wanting, as a rule, in amiability and ready sympathy, the colonial Yankees had also more positive faults. Pecksniffs as well as Dombeys there were no doubt among them. Where all were so free to live their individual lives according to their own ideals, some were surely selfish as well as self-contained. Where so large a number were religious, some were doubtless sanctimonious and hypocritical.

But if we judge them in the mass it is hard to match them for competency in the management of their own affairs, whether as individuals or in bodies politic, or for fidelity to their difficult ideals. By Ellsworth's time, the puritan theology was already relaxed into a fairly livable creed. Before he died, the famous unitarian movement had begun in Massachusetts. A general broadening of ideas and sympathies accompanied the religious change. Sloughing off the worst defects of its quality, New England society displayed during the first half of the nineteenth century a spectacle of intelligence, of energy, and of general healthfulness and soundness, which has probably never been surpassed.

Ellsworth, whatever vagaries he had indulged in his boyhood, took into his nature and kept throughout his life the best characteristics of his kind. He came to his fine opportunities a completely grown-up man, his character hardened into permanent lines; a quiet but ready man, thoughtful and deeply religious, but also ardent, industrious, practical, and shrewd. For the rest, he had got from his ancestors and his healthful country life a superb endowment of physical strength and hardiness. According to the family tradition, his height was six feet two, and he was broad-shouldered and robust. His countenance was not positively handsome; if we may judge from his portraits, until age and suffering had softened it, there was neither sweetness nor distinction in his face; but he had the strong jaws, the long chin, the firm lips, the steady eyes, which always indicate the man of purpose and persistency. To an unimaginative man like Ellsworth, however, with little of the artist or the actor in his nature, such a figure and presence was of far less advantage before the public than it might have been had his temperament been different. He used and valued his bodily endowment for hard work rather than display. The interest of his life is not to be found in dramatic exhibitions of his powers. It lies, rather, in the tasks which his hand found to do — tasks whose value and importance we cannot even yet feel sure that we have measured. He brought to his work parts which cannot be called extraordinary in themselves; but he plied them with an abundant energy, he ruled them with strong will, he devoted them always to high purposes, and he made them serve.

CHAPTER II

THE BAR AND THE ASSEMBLY

THE beginning of Ellsworth's rise to eminence was professional success; and this, when it did come, seems to have come both swiftly and abundantly. According to his early biographers, a single case, involving an important legal principle, proved to be the sort of opportunity that leads to countless others. The young lawyer managed it so skilfully that he not only secured a verdict for his client but won for himself the respect of his neighbors.[1] Perhaps it was on this occasion that he heard from the lips of a stranger what he afterward declared were the first words of encouragement that ever heartened him in his ambition. " Who is that young man ? " the stranger was saying; " he speaks well." [2]

At any rate, from about the third year of his membership of the bar, his practice grew very fast, and he rose quite as fast in the esteem of his fellows. At the autumn session of the General Assembly in 1773, he took his seat as one of the two deputies from Windsor, and his name appears in every list of the deputies thereafter until May of the year 1775.[3] That year,

[1] Wood and Jackson Mss.; George Van Santvoord, "Sketches of the Lives and Judicial Services of the Chief Justices of the Supreme Court of the United States," 196.

[2] Mrs. Sigourney, in "National Portrait Gallery," IV, Article on Ellsworth.

[3] Roll of State Officers and General Assembly of Connecticut; Colonial Records of Connecticut, XIV, 159, 214, 252, 325, 388, 413. All the biogra-

the year of his thirtieth birthday, was doubtless to him, as to many another young colonial, the *annus mirabilis* of his whole career. Tradition has fixed upon it as the date of his removal to Hartford from the Wintonbury farm. It also saw him engaged in the first of those Revolutionary tasks which were to claim him continually until the end of the struggle for independence should summon him to a still more conspicuous part in the constructive work that followed. From that year to his death, in fact, he was scarcely for an instant free from important public responsibilities. But he did not relinquish his profession. Throughout the Revolution, and until the new national government was organized under the Constitution, he was always either actively in practice or else on the bench. It was by the law that he laid the foundations both of his fortune and his fame. It will be best, therefore, before we follow him into the service of his countrymen, to seek some notion of the kind of man he was in the common, daily struggle, and more particularly to learn what we can of his character and figure at the bar.

For this inquiry, few records are available, and those are of little use. In the courts where Ellsworth practised, the stenographer was of course unknown; nor did any daily paper ever spread before its readers a

phers of Ellsworth have been extremely loose in their statements concerning the offices he held in the earlier part of his career. Where dates are given, they are nearly always incorrect. Perhaps the official records were not accessible when these accounts were written. It is hardly worth while to specify their inaccuracies. Not one of them gives the impression that he was in the Assembly as early as 1773. In May, 1774, his name first appears in the list of Justices of the Peace for Hartford County. Ibid., XV, 8.

detailed narrative of a single cause in which he was engaged. Compared with our present usage, the reporting of that day, both official and unofficial, was bafflingly meagre. Moreover, Ellsworth himself, though by no means slow of speech, was curiously averse to the pen. There can scarcely be another man of comparable importance in our history who has left behind him so few papers of any sort in his own handwriting. Not one of his court speeches is preserved to us. It is quite probable that none was ever written out. Even his briefs are said to have been exceptionally condensed, setting forth only the principal headings of his arguments.

Fortunately, however, a number of his contemporaries have left us their impressions of him as an advocate; and several of these contemporaries were themselves of an eminence to give their judgments weight. One, at least, is better known to-day than Ellsworth is; his name indeed is quite probably familiar to more English-speaking people than any other American name but Washington's. In 1779, young Noah Webster was a student in Ellsworth's office and an inmate of his home.[1] Many years later, one of Ellsworth's sons was married to Webster's eldest daughter. This personal connection may perhaps have heightened the lexicographer's opinion of the statesman's importance, for Webster was given to dilating on all things in any way related to his own career. But he was also trained to state facts carefully, and to Joseph Wood, Ellsworth's son-in-law and biographer, he once declared that Ellsworth, even at the time when

---

[1] H. E. Scudder's " Noah Webster," in American Men of Letters series; Goodrich, in " Revised Webster's Dictionary," XV, XXII.

Webster was in his office, had usually on his docket from a thousand to fifteen hundred cases. In fact, Webster added, there was scarcely a case tried in which Ellsworth was not of counsel on one side or the other, and his mind was under a constant strain throughout the sessions. Sometimes, from sheer physical weariness, he would gird his loins with a handkerchief as he rose for an argument in some new case. Perhaps the number of his cases is partly explained by the statement that he excelled in *nisi prius* trials. Webster habitually spoke of him as one of the " three mighties " of the Connecticut bar — the other two being William Samuel Johnson and Titus Hosmer.[1]

However this testimony may need to be qualified, it is clear that Ellsworth's professional career was extraordinary. It is doubtful if in the entire history of the Connecticut bar any other lawyer has ever in so short a time accumulated so great a practice. It probably reached its height in the years immediately after the war, for the great change gave rise to much litigation, and by that time his reputation was established and his powers at the full. Measured either by the amount of his business or by his earnings, it was unrivalled in his own day, and unexampled in the history of the colony. Naturally shrewd, and with nothing of the spendthrift in his nature, he quickly earned a competence, and by good management he increased it to a fortune which for the times and the country was quite uncommonly large. From a few documents still in existence, it is clear that he became something of a capitalist and investor. He bought land and houses, and loaned out money at

[1] Wood Ms. ; "Memorial History of Hartford County," I, 121.

interest. He was a stockholder in the Hartford Bank and one of the original subscribers to the stock of the old Hartford Broadcloth Mill (1788).[1] But if there were no documents to prove that he was a man of substance, the residence in Windsor which he appears to have either bought or built long before he reached the age of retirement, and where he made his home in the years of his highest public services, would be evidence enough.

Were this substantial progress and worldly prosperity alone to be considered, we should still be sure that Ellsworth was a man among men, surpassing the great majority of his contemporaries in sense and energy, a good representative of the strong and sturdy stock he came of. He was not of those who, though fitted for exceptional services or charged with uncommon talents, are yet unequal to the world's incessant and more commonplace demands. But the fact of his getting on so well and fast has its full value to the biographer only when it is added that not one word has come down to us to intimate that there was ever brought against him the slightest charge of trickery or overreaching, or any intimation that as a lawyer he was ever accused of any practice at all out of keeping either with his own personal dignity or the standards of the bar. On the contrary, the praise of his contemporaries emphasizes his integrity quite as often as his ability.

As to the kind and quality of his excellence as a

---

[1] Inventory of his estate, made, doubtless, very soon after his death. A copy of this document was brought to light after the present work had been begun. Ellsworth papers in the Public Library of the city of New York; "Memorial History of Hartford County," I, 331, 564.

lawyer, these attempts at portraiture agree fairly well
among themselves. They seem also to confirm his
own conclusion that he lacked imagination ; but in
other respects they by no means sustain his extremely
modest estimate of his gifts. Dr. John Trumbull, the
author of " McFingal," who was doubtless the best wit in
the colony, if not in all the colonies, and hardly therefore the sort of man to grow enthusiastic over a display of mere unillumined energy in oratory, and who
was himself a lawyer and a judge, has left a good
comparison between the two foremost advocates of the
Hartford bar. " When Dr. Johnson rose to address
a jury," he writes, " the polish and beauty of his style, his
smooth and easy flow of words, the sweet, melodious
voice, accompanied with a grace and elegance of person
and manners, delighted and charmed his hearers. But
when Judge Ellsworth rose, the Jury soon began to
drop their heads, and winking, looked up through
their eyebrows, while the thunders of his eloquence
seemed to drive every idea into their skulls in spite
of them." [1] Johnson, though now but little known,
was no mean figure to be thus put forward first in
order to a climacteric contrast. The son of the first
president of King's College, and himself the holder
of degrees from Yale, Harvard, and Oxford, he had
enjoyed and profited by still another opportunity for
acquiring culture ; for he had represented Connecticut
several years at court. It is said that while he lived
in London he was admitted to that remarkable circle
which gathered round another and more famous Dr.
Samuel Johnson, and won for himself the great man's
distinguished approval. Active in the Stamp Act

[1] Flanders, 67.

Congress, and throughout that phase of the colonies' resistance, he was perhaps the foremost man in Connecticut until his unwillingness to go the lengths of an attempt at complete independence left him a few years in retirement. His work in the constructive period after the war was second only to Roger Sherman's and Ellsworth's.[1]

To the less restrained of his and Ellsworth's eulogists, he appeared always as the Cicero to the other's Demosthenes. It is more important to be sure of the real sources of the strength of a public character than to point out his limitations. Stilted, therefore, as this praise of the two colonial lawyers may be, we need not reject the reasonable inference that Johnson was a remarkably pleasing and accomplished public speaker, and that Ellsworth excelled in a style of oratory that was unadorned, headlong, and compelling. Dr. Timothy Dwight, sometime president of Yale, who tells us that Ellsworth was his "particular friend," described his oratory in these words: " His eloquence, and indeed almost every other part of his character, was peculiar. Always possessed of his own scheme of thought concerning every subject which he discussed, ardent, bold, intense, and masterly, his conceptions were just and great; his reasonings invincible; his images glowing; his sentiments noble; his phraseology remarkable for its clearness and precision ; his style concise and strong; and his utterance vehement and overwhelming. Universally, his eloquence strongly resembled that of Demosthenes; grave, forcible, and inclined to severity." Elsewhere, the same authority describes him as

[1] "William Samuel Johnson and the Making of the Constitution," by W. G. Andrews; E. E. Beardsley's " Life and Times of Johnson."

in his addresses to the jury "frequently pouring out floods of eloquence which were irresistible and overwhelming."[1] To this, quoted by Wood, an unknown marginal commentator on Wood's Ms. makes answer, " Dwight must have drawn on his imagination, for Ellsworth was by no means an eloquent speaker." But Wood rejoins, " Dwight was not mistaken, as can be abundantly shown."

Fortunately, however, there is at least one characterization of the man and the advocate, drawn from contemporary sources, which is convincingly discriminating and restrained. A few years after the death of Ellsworth, there was published in the *Analectic Magazine*[2] an appreciation which is probably still the best portrayal of his intellectual character and methods.

" He had not," according to this intelligent eulogist, "laid a very deep foundation either of general or professional learning; but the native vigor of his mind supplied every deficiency; the rapidity of his conceptions made up for the want of previous knowledge; the diligent study of the cases which arose in actual business stored his mind with principles; whatever was thus acquired was firmly rooted in his memory; and thus, as he became eminent, he grew learned.

" The whole powers of his mind were applied with unremitted attention to the business of his profession, and those public duties in which he was occasionally engaged. Capable of great application, and constitutionally full of ardor, he pursued every subject to

---

[1] Dwight's " Travels in New England," I, 301, 303.

[2] May, 1814, Vol. III, pp. 382–403. The author is supposed to have been Gulian C. Verplanck of New York, a grandson of William Samuel Johnson.

which he applied himself with a strong and constant interest which never suffered his mind to flag or grow torpid with listless indolence. But his ardor was always under the guidance of sober reason. His cold and colorless imagination never led him astray from the realities of life to wanton in the gay visions of fancy; and his attention was seldom distracted by that general literary curiosity which so often beguiles the man of genius away from his destined pursuit, to waste his powers in studies of no immediate utility. At the same time, his unblemished character, his uniform prudence and regularity of conduct, acquired him the general confidence and respect of his fellow-citizens — a people in a remarkable degree attentive to all the decorum and decencies of civilized life."

It is the old story, perhaps, of the will's supremacy. It is useless to recur to the contrast and controversy between the men who succeed and accomplish by reason chiefly of what is commonly called character and the men who, with finer instincts and keener susceptibilities and rarer talents, too often end in failure, leaving the world no better for their lives. To most readers, Ellsworth's life would doubtless be a more alluring study if, instead of exhibiting such a steady growth in tasks and competence, he and his career were found irregularly brilliant, appealing, with a series of ups and downs, of faults and atonements, to the whole wide range of our human sympathies. It is only in a sober mood, with daylight senses, that one can follow with interest and with understanding the course of such a life. The guiding genius of it all was an English constancy, quickened with a New England keenness, an American readiness and capacity for change. It is impossible to read those descriptions which his contemporaries have made of him without reflecting that nearly all they say of him would apply, with but slight abatements, to hundreds of other New England men, unknown or famous. His distinction consists chiefly in the enlargement of powers and merits which are not uncommon in themselves.

Yet I think we should be mistaken if we were led to believe that Ellsworth was commonplace either in his parts or his personality. Were we to search out the one human characteristic or endowment that has achieved the most, for good and evil, in the whole history of mankind, we should doubtless fix on that one central gift of ardor, energy, purpose, which was surely his. Nothing else will so invariably, so finally, command our homage. It stands, better than all the other gifts and powers put together, the test of actual results. Unlike the others, it is most impressive, not in first encounters, but through long acquaintance and the fullest trial. Men of many or of brilliant gifts may quickly stir our admiration, or, if we are rivals, afflict us with immediate discomfitures. The man with this gift, particularly if in his case it is not advertised or indexed by more obvious superiorities, has always, in his conflicts and rivalries, the advantage of a strength concealed. One does not guess the lengths of effort he will go to, the perfect use that he will make of all his forces. In all his engagements he will present to his more brilliant adversaries a front like that the sober infantry of Sparta showed so often to the varied and imposing line of the Athenians — an opposition more daunting than war-songs and banners. Like the Spartans at Mantinea, such men do not need to hearten themselves with telling over the reasons why they ought to win their battles; they need only remember, what all brave spirits know, that battles are not won till they are fought, that tasks are not accomplished by merely proving one's ability to do them.[1]

But Ellsworth had also a quickness of perception, a swiftness in the use of all his mental powers, which may well be accounted as of itself a talent — and a talent of the highest value. Without it, for instance, he could hardly have handled at all the great mass of his professional work, interrupted as it was with public demands upon his time. His rule, to go at once to the main points of his cases, or of whatever matter he had in hand, seems, and doubtless was, as he formed it, a counsel of modesty; but is it not a rule which we should all most gladly follow if we could? He excelled particularly in exposition. His argument was frequently convincing when he had done no more than merely state the case. More than one observer of his life told Wood of this peculiar excellence of his oratory. " Mr. Ellsworth's clear and vivid apprehension and lucid statement of the facts involved in a case would frequently," they declared, " throw out a blaze of light that instantly dispelled all doubts and difficulties, to the surprise and admiration of every attendant." If he was systematic and cautious, he was no mere plodder in his work.

Nor was he in fact wanting in the power of commanding respect and attention for his own sake, apart from his work.

For that effect, also, in the immediate contact with one's fellows, the central gift is probably the

[1] See Thucydides, " Peloponnesian War," V, 69.

best of all, particularly as the possessor of it advances in achievement and in self-confidence. Aided as it was in Ellsworth's case by an uncommon physical endowment, it was enough to make him, according to one perhaps too glowing eulogist, a person of extraordinary presence. It is Dr. Dwight who on this point is again the loudest in his praise. " Mr. Ellsworth," he writes, " was formed to be a great man. His presence was tall, dignified, and commanding; and his manners, though wholly destitute of haughtiness and arrogance, were such as irresistibly to excite in others, wherever he was present, the sense of inferiority. His very attitude inspired awe." Dwight adds that " in every assembly, public and private, in which he appeared, after he had fairly entered public life, there was probably no man, when Washington was not present, who would be more readily acknowledged to hold the first character."[1] Dwight, no doubt, was partial to Ellsworth both as a Connecticut worthy, and as his personal friend; but the tribute is sustained by other men's descriptions. Hollister, for instance, who in writing his " History of Connecticut " seems to have drawn freely on the recollections of his elders, makes a very similar portrait.

" Ellsworth," he says, " was logical and argumentative in his mode of illustration, and possessed a peculiar style of condensed statement, through which there ran, like a magnetic current, the most delicate train of analytical reasoning. His eloquence was wonderfully persuasive, too, and his manner solemn and impressive. His style was decidedly of the patrician school, and yet so simple that a child could follow without

[1] Dwight's " Travels in New England," I, 302.

difficulty the steps by which he arrived at his conclusions. That he also had the best judicial powers that were known in that elder age of our republic will not be disputed. Add to these qualities an eye that seemed to look an adversary through, a forehead and features so bold and marked as to promise all that his rich, deep voice, expressive gestures and *moral fearlessness* made good, add above all that reserved force of scornful satire, so seldom employed, but so like the destructive movements of a corps of flying artillery, and the reader has an outline of the strength and majesty of Ellsworth."[1]

All alike bear testimony that Ellsworth's impressiveness was never marred by haughtiness or an overbearing way with lesser personages. His manners, though perfectly dignified, were also perfectly simple and democratic.

To attempt in this fashion a character of the man while he is still at the threshold of his career is doubtless a somewhat unusual proceeding. It is better, as a rule, to disclose a personality with deeds and incidents, to let the man's life make plain his quality. But that preferred biographic method is peculiarly hard to apply to Ellsworth, partly for reasons that have already been suggested. In his activities, as well as in his meagre writings and his all-too-few recorded utterances, there is too little of self-revelation, too little of what we can be sure was characteristic. It is necessary, if we would keep in mind any distinct and personal vision of him, to use at once the help we have at hand from men who saw him in the flesh. Moreover, his tasks were often so momentous, those

---

[1] G. H. Hollister, "History of Connecticut" (1855), II, 441–442.

which were constructive in their nature have proved so lastingly, so increasingly important, that we are moved to use what knowledge we can get of his character as a means to explain his achievements and to judge how great his part was in his collaborations with other statesmen, instead of treating his work as material to interpret him. There are few lives in which what may be called the public values so outweigh the personal.

It was doubtless his growing reputation as a lawyer and his membership in the Assembly that caused him to be drawn at once into the stirring activities of the great year 1775, and determined what his part in them should be. Of his part in the patriot movement up to this time little is recorded. It is stated that he was for a while a member of the militia or of some other volunteer force, and that he was once or twice called into the field, though never engaged in any action.[1] But when or where he served is no better known than when or where he was earlier engaged in school-teaching. Wood says merely that his service was in the militia during the Revolutionary War, when the state was threatened with invasion. It does appear, however, that he was from the first thoroughly in sympathy with the popular feeling and early committed to the movement of resistance. When the crisis came, he would have been cold indeed if for any reason but Tory convictions he had stood apart from his kindred and his neighbors.

The whole story, if one reviews it afresh from the point of view of manhood, which is so very different from the childish acceptance of heroism and virtue and

[1] Flanders, 68.

devotion as matters of course with which one heard it first, remains, surely, one of the most inspiring and astounding ever told. The Revolutionary movement, with all that has ever been unearthed of a nature to belittle its motives and its men, was singularly noble and singularly wise. Much of what is most highly vaunted in our more recent past seems, by comparison, in spite of its bigness, vapid, showy, and half-hearted. Save only in the nobler passages of the fight over slavery, we find nowhere else in our history such wonderful sincerity and simplicity, such recklessness of all but high considerations, such courage of convictions, so childlike and magnificent a confidence in principle. The best virtue that has yet appeared in our national life and character was all encompassed in the flame of that first enthusiasm. No civic or citizenly quality we now possess surpasses, or could surpass, the spirit of nationality that leaped alive in all the little towns and cities and plantations from New Hampshire to Georgia when the obstinate king and the vain ministry, instead of thanking their stars that they were safely past the trouble over the Stamp Act, blundered on to the tea tax and the Boston Port Bill.

None of the colonies caught fire more quickly than Connecticut. The little province proved a veritable tinder-box. Ten years before, her government had responded to the first announcement of the Stamp Act programme with the promptest and strongest of remonstrances. Jared Ingersoll, who was at once commissioned a special agent at London, probably accomplished more than any other of the agents there by way of inducing the ministry to soften the intended blow. Yet when he himself returned as the

Stamp Master of the colony, an uprising of the people, bigger and more determined than he or any other had foreseen, forced him, in the most spectacular manner, to resign this office. The Sons of Liberty, headed by Israel Putnam, were strong in all the towns of the colony; it has even been claimed that the order originated there. In Connecticut's earlier controversies with the home government, her course, though resolute, had been singularly cautious and respectful. But from this time not even Massachusetts was more openly courageous. Roger Sherman, a lawyer-merchant of New Haven, " between fifty and sixty, a solid, sensible man," took stronger ground than even Otis or John Adams on the right of Great Britain to control the trade of the colonies.[1] Sherman had been more or less engaged with public affairs for twenty years; but now, retired from business, he gave his whole time to the service of his colony and the cause of the colonies in general. In all the general measures of protest and resistance against those acts of the home government which were deemed oppressive, the government, the towns, and the people of Connecticut were eager and enthusiastic. Watching with intense concern the course of events in Massachusetts, they expressed by words and acts that were anything but uncertain their sympathy and anger. When Townshend's act to tax the colonies was passed, Connecticut merchants entered generally into the non-importation agreement, and seem to have kept it better than their neighbors of New York. In 1770, after many indignant town

[1] John Adams's Diary, II, 343. See also Boutell's " Sherman," 63, 64. Perhaps the best account of Connecticut in the Revolution is still the old-fashioned but readable narrative of Hollister, in his " History of Connecticut."

meetings,— that perfect means of popular agitation,— delegates from all the towns met at New Haven to concert a programme of non-importation and the building up of home manufactures. The sentiment against the use of articles imported from Great Britain rose to violent heights and expressed itself in fairly comical ways. In 1770 also, Jonathan Trumbull entered upon the office of governor, which by successive annual elections he continued to hold for fourteen years. Men like Jefferson and Henry and Rutledge held the same office in other colonies at different times in the Revolutionary era, but Trumbull, for his conduct of the office itself, doubtless outranks them all. He was not merely in sympathy with the popular movement; he was a bold and devoted leader of it. Not even Putnam went beyond him in courage, and he exhibited, moreover, a statesmanlike wisdom and shrewdness that was equal to his enthusiasm. He came in time to enjoy in an extraordinary degree the confidence and affection of Washington, and felt, as few men did, the chieftain's strong arm lean upon him for support. It was Washington who gave him his sobriquet of " Brother Jonathan."

Save that the actual collision came first at Boston, there was nothing to distinguish the resistance of Connecticut from that of Massachusetts. If possible, the towns of Connecticut were in even greater haste than those of Massachusetts to proclaim that Boston's fight was their fight. When the ministry, abandoning all the duties except those on tea, made its attempt to force tea into the colonial ports, Connecticut people had no opportunity for a tea party of their own; but when General Gage arrived at Boston to carry out the

Port Bill and the other force bills of 1774, the Connecticut towns came to Boston's rescue with generous contributions and the most open sympathy, and the Connecticut Assembly, being then in session, took the lead in calling for a continental congress. The excitement rose to fever heat as one after another the fateful moves were made by Gage on the one hand and Adams and Hancock and Warren on the other. At last came the runners with the tidings of bloodshed at Lexington and Concord, and Putnam, dropping his historic plough in its historically unfinished furrow, was for a moment in consultation with Trumbull at Lebanon, and then away on his ride of a hundred miles and more in eighteen hours to Concord, the militia following him, first in little squads, then in companies, and then in regiments. Arnold, the New Haven storekeeper, seizing without authority the powder he needed for his company, was gone, too, on his way to Cambridge and Ticonderoga and Quebec, and immortality and infamy. The plan of the attack on Ticonderoga and Crown Point was instantly conceived at Hartford. The means to furnish the expedition were subscribed by Connecticut men. When it reached the Green Mountains, it was joined there by Ethan Allen and others who were themselves Connecticut men by birth. It was finally paid for by the Connecticut Assembly.

That body was in session by the 26th of April, nine days after the fighting in Massachusetts; and the deputy from Windsor was at once engaged with his fellows upon measures from which there could be no retreat. They passed an embargo on food-stuffs; sent a committee to wait on Gage with a powerful remonstrance from Governor Trumbull, and another committee to look after supplies for those citizens who were gone already to the relief of Massachusetts; commissioned runners to keep them informed of all the new and startling happenings; organized one-fourth of the militia into six full regiments, officered them, and looked about for arms and powder to equip them; imposed new taxes to cover these preparations; and called on all the ministers, with their congregations, to "cry mightily to God."[1] To supervise the expenditures for all these warlike activities, they constituted a commission called the Committee of the Pay Table, and one of the five members was Oliver Ellsworth.[2] It was perhaps because of this, his first Revolutionary task, that his name does not thereafter appear in the rolls of the Assembly until 1779. At the May session of that year he was again a deputy, this time for Hartford; but at the same session he was chosen a member of the Council of Safety, a board of advisers which shared with the governor the responsibility for all war measures, and at the October session he did not attend.[3]

The work of the Pay Table seems to have steadily increased from the beginning. It was then empowered to audit and discharge all accounts incurred in the defence of the colony, and ordered to proceed according to such directions and rules as the Assembly should pass from time to time; and from time to time the Assembly did pass votes of a nature to enlarge its duties and responsibilities. It became a sort of fiscal

[1] Colonial Records of Connecticut, XIV, 413–441.
[2] *Ibid.*, 431, for resolution.
[3] State Records of Connecticut, II, 249, 287.

war board, in constant correspondence with all commissaries and other persons who had to do with paying or supplying Connecticut troops and militia. Perhaps the earliest letters of Ellsworth now extant are notes to Governor Trumbull about particular claims — dry, business communications which doubtless fairly reflect the tedious and prosaic nature of the work.[1] There is no sign, however, that he ever complained of it; and there is evidence that he did it faithfully and well, for it was he who was chosen for certain important missions that were necessary parts of it. In February, 1776, the Council of Safety having voted that one of the committee be sent to the Commander-in-Chief of the Continental Army to request repayment of moneys advanced by Connecticut to her contingent in his command, it was Ellsworth who went,[2] and thus, perhaps, he got his first sight of Washington, who was still at Cambridge, laying siege to Boston. Ten days later, according to the minutes of the Council, "Mr. Ellsworth, having been to Genl. Washington by order etc., to obtain the money lately paid by our committee to the soldiers etc., and not able to get it, is returned and present and conversed with about it etc.," — and it is voted that he or some other apply to Congress.[3] It does not appear that he went to Philadelphia, but in May he was sent to General Schuyler to seek recovery of the sums already paid by Connecticut to troops employed in Canada.[4] Again, in the following December, while the first campaign in the Jerseys

---

[1] Sept. 18, 1776; Dec. 1, Dec. 6, 1777; Trumbull Papers in Library of Massachusetts Historical Society.

[2] Colonial Records of Connecticut, XV, 235.

[3] Ibid., 238.   [4] Ibid., 314–315.

was in progress, he went with several others into the
Western counties to raise reënforcements for General
Lee — one of the many extraordinary exertions of
Trumbull and the people of Connecticut in the common cause.[1] Ten years later, when debate arose in
a very great company over the ways in which the
colonies had borne their several shares of the common burden, Ellsworth's full knowledge of the facts
enabled him to point out, with quiet assurance, that
Connecticut had done more and paid more, according
to her numbers and her wealth, than any of the states
whose representatives dared to criticise her. It is
also to be remembered that this first work of his, petty
and local though it seemed, was yet of a kind that
was quite as vital to the success of the cause as any of
the stirring and heroic things Arnold and Putnam
were doing in the field. If it had only been as well
done everywhere as it was by Connecticut and her Pay
Table, the victory might have come sooner, and the
struggle would have left behind it fewer unpaid bills
and less derangement of the currency. Such devotion as Ellsworth showed in this employment was
rarer than the soldiers' skill and bravery. But it was
also, no doubt, a better preparation for his later tasks
in statesmanship than soldiering could possibly have
been.

In 1779, he became a member of the Council of
Safety, and there his duties were much like those
assigned to the Board of War, the chief executive arm

[1] State Records of Connecticut, I, 109. See also, for his services on the
Pay Table, *ibid.*, 183. In the Trumbull collection there is a letter from
Ellsworth and Payne to Governor Trumbull, dated at Windsor, July 10,
1779, urging him to procure artillery for the militia, to resist an impending
invasion of the state.

of the Continental Congress. This may perhaps have been a promotion; but two years earlier he had taken another office, which probably demanded more of him in time and energy than it paid for in either money or distinction. In 1777, he was chosen state's attorney for Hartford County.[1] The office of king's attorney, instituted in 1704, had not during the colonial period been eagerly sought after, though it does seem to have been held by men of very good standing, and with the change of name there came no lessening of the requirements and no increase of pay. The fees were small, the cases uninviting.

Yet Ellsworth continued to hold it until 1785, and all we know of him is of a nature to make us feel sure that he did not slight its duties on account of his own private practice or his various other public offices. To these, that same year, another and a higher was added. At the October session, the Assembly resolved, " That Roger Sherman, Eliphalet Dyer, Samuel Huntington, Oliver Wolcott, Titus Hosmer, Oliver Ellsworth, and Andrew Adams, Esq[rs], be and they are hereby appointed delegates to represent this State at the General Congress of the United States in America for the year ensuing and until men be chosen and arrive in Congress if sitting; any one or more of them who shall be present in said Congress are hereby fully authorized and impowered to represent this State in said Congress." [2] The next year, when Ellsworth was again in the list, this peculiar commission was altered so as to require

---

[1] None of his biographers gives the date correctly. Several sketches would lead one to think that it was 1775. For the office, and Ellsworth's incumbency, see "Judicial and Civil History of Connecticut," 157–162.

[2] State Records, I, 417.

that not less than two nor more than four of the seven delegates should be always in attendance.[1] After 1779, the practice was for each town to nominate to the Assembly twelve candidates. As the Assembly listed the candidates in 1780 according to the number of nominations each had received, the order of the names may perhaps indicate the relative popularity of the men. Ellsworth's was the first, and among those that followed it were Roger Sherman's, Samuel and Benjamin Huntington's, and others scarcely less distinguished.[2] He was reëlected every year until, in the autumn of 1783, he declined to serve any longer.

[1] State Records, II, 134-135.   [2] *Ibid.*, II, 264, 462.

CHAPTER III

THE CONTINENTAL CONGRESS

Oct. 8, 1778, " Mr. Ellsworth, a delegate from Connecticut, attended and took his seat in Congress." [1]

Occupied at home with so many other duties, Ellsworth had suffered nearly a year to elapse from the time of his first election before he took his place among the civil rulers of the loosely joined Confederacy of States. It may be as well to give at once the terms of his actual attendance. Six years a delegate, he went to Philadelphia but five times in all. His first service, lasting a little over four months, ended Feb. 18, 1779, when leave of absence was granted him. Beginning again in the middle of December, 1779, his name appeared on the roll-calls until the latter part of June, 1780; on July 3, another member was appointed to his place on a standing committee. Absent nearly a year, he reappeared at Philadelphia at the beginning of June, 1781, and sat until September. Returning on Dec. 20, 1782, he sat until near the close of January. His final attendance was from April 1 until midsummer, 1783.[2]

---

[1] Journal of Continental Congress, IV, 583.

[2] Roll of State Officers and General Assembly of Connecticut, pp. 459–460; Journals of Continental Congress, V, 65, 451; VI, 103; VII, 118, 171, 177, 192–193; VIII, 45, 111, 124, 170, 291. Letters of Ellsworth, in the Trumbull collection and elsewhere, confirm certain of these dates. A letter written from Philadelphia to his brother David is dated Jan. 9, 1778; but it seems clear that this was a slip, Ellsworth forgetting that a new year

Unfortunately, this sort of spasmodic membership was not exceptional. None of the states kept its full quota in constant attendance. Even the great standing committees, whose work was largely executive in character, were subject to incessant changes in their membership. It is no wonder that Washington, after pointing out that short enlistments were the cause of the worst embarrassments in the military line, promptly added, "*A great part of the embarrassments in the civil* flow from the same source." So far as Congress alone was concerned, the practice is partly attributable to economy; but it is also partly attributable to the plain fact that the colonies, though they had united in declaring and in striving to achieve their independence, were as yet scarcely started on the road to a real union, to nationality. The members of Congress were delegates, hardly representatives. They were responsible collectively to their several states, rather than individually to their constituents. They were held, in fact, to a regular accounting with the governments of their states. Ellsworth's letters from Philadelphia to Governor Trumbull might almost be despatches from an ambassador to a secretary of state.[1] Ordinarily, he and

was begun. Another letter to the same brother, written from Philadelphia on Nov. 10, 1779, — more than a month before the Journal record of Ellsworth's second appearance in Congress, — is harder to explain. That he was there and did not take his seat is scarcely credible. He speaks in the letter of the ill health of his father, and the only conjecture I can offer is that this or something else suddenly recalled him to Connecticut.

[1] Most of these letters are among the Trumbull papers in the library of the Massachusetts Historical Society, and have been printed in the Society's "Collections," fifth series, IX, X, seventh series, II, III. By the kindness of the Society's librarian, Dr. Samuel A. Green, I have been permitted to use the originals.

his colleagues for the time being collaborated in joint epistles. All votes in the chamber were taken by states, and a delegation evenly divided on any question lost its vote altogether.

Nevertheless, Ellsworth's work in the Continental Congress is not negligible, either from the point of view of a biographer or in a broader study of the times. It began before he went to Philadelphia. Dec. 11, 1777, Congress appointed a committee to investigate the causes of the failure of an expedition to Rhode Island, naming him one of the members,[1] and Van Santvoord adds that he and two associates took a mass of testimony and presented a report.[2] But the report led to no further action. Congress was doubtless far too busy with other expeditions to carry out its announced purpose to account for all the expeditions that had failed.

In the autumn of 1778, when Ellsworth went at last to Philadelphia, the first fine ardors of the Revolution were long since spent. Both sides had come to see clearly the nature of the struggle, and that it was bound to be long and difficult, whichever side might win. For the leaders of the patriot cause there had been many bitter disappointments: from the loss of battles, from the falling away of the weaker-hearted in their own party, from convincing proofs of the enemy's superior strength in wealth and discipline and numbers. But at least, on the other hand, the cause they fought and worked for was now, by the Declaration of Independence, and by many acts equally significant and irrevocable, completely blazoned to the world.

[1] Journals, III, 425–426, 444–445. There were five members.
[2] Van Santvoord, 199.

They were no longer fighting for a mere redress of grievances; they were trying to keep alive a new member of the family of nations. France had already recognized them, and was aiding them with money, with ships, with soldiers. Nor had success in arms been wholly wanting. Save the desperate counter-strokes at Trenton and Princeton, Washington's army, it is true, had never won a decided victory in a pitched battle; but Burgoyne and his army were captives, and the grand strategy of the enemy for the year 1777 had undeniably failed. Emerging the next spring from his supreme ordeal at Valley Forge, Washington had been cheered by the news of the treaty with France, and then by Sir Henry Clinton's evacuation of Philadelphia. In June, he had fought at Monmouth a pitched battle which was at worst indecisive, and which, but for the misconduct of Charles Lee, might well have been a victory. That he and his little armies could do no more was the fault — so far as it was a fault at all — of the states, which did not adequately recruit or supply them, and of a central government which was still but little more than a government by consent. The Articles of Confederation, which would at least, so soon as they should be ratified, give the authority of a written agreement to such concessions of power as they made to Congress, had been laid before the legislatures of the states; but these were slow to ratify. Meanwhile, through its standing committees, Congress was discharging as best it could the various functions of a proper government; and by requisitions on the states and borrowing abroad it was doing what it could to procure the means to keep the armies in the field.

The Continental Congress, which had been, at its first session, the ablest group of men ever gathered under one roof in America, had by this time lost to the state governments and to foreign courts a number of its most illustrious members. Franklin and John Adams were in Europe. Jay and Jefferson and Henry and John Rutledge were occupied with high services to their several states. Washington, of course, was in the field. At the first roll-call after Ellsworth took his seat, only thirty-two delegates answered to their names. But some of the names that were answered to would have shone in any list. To that particular roll-call Samuel Adams and Gerry, Roger Sherman, Dr. Witherspoon, Richard Henry Lee, Laurens, and Drayton responded. Gouverneur Morris was a member, though not then present, and, for a little while longer, Robert Morris also. In a few weeks, John Jay took his seat from New York.

It is doubtful, however, if any of these men surpassed in wisdom, or in experience and influence, the colleague whom Ellsworth found awaiting him, and whose name is signed with his to several letters which were despatched to Governor Trumbull in the next few weeks. Roger Sherman was by this time a veteran in the Continental politics, and we know that Ellsworth profited to the full by the older statesman's counsel and friendship. He once declared that he had taken the character of Sherman for his model; and on this remark John Adams, it is said, made comment that it was praise enough for both. They worked together on many occasions for the interest of Connecticut and the good of the whole country, and though they frequently differed, and their names appeared on opposite sides on various questions, no jealousy or personal antagonism of any kind between them ever came to light.

The dry and meagre Journals of the Congress reveal but little of the human quality of the debates, which were always secret. To read them seems a tiresome and not a particularly profitable sort of historical delving, until, dismissing the notion that our American political system was "struck off at a given time by the brain and purpose of man,"[1] the student comes to understand that he is groping among the roots of institutions which are now grown to a colossal power and reach. Ellsworth, for instance, soon received assignments to three standing committees, which may be regarded as the rudimentary forms of three great departments of our present government. One was the Marine Committee, which a little later became the Board of Admiralty; by another change, its duties were soon devolved upon a department of naval affairs, headed by a secretary or manager, whose counterpart under the Constitution is the Secretary of the Navy. The second, already styled the Board of Treasury, attained, through much the same succession of changes, a like ancestral relationship to the present Department of the Treasury. The third was the Committee of Appeals; and that, it is now quite clear, was the first forerunner of the present Supreme Court of the United States; its work was the begin-

---

[1] Gladstone, in "Kin beyond Sea." Yet Gladstone's famous sentence is not deserving of the ridicule and the downright contradiction which it has occasionally drawn forth. It is only by contrast with the British Constitution, "the most subtle organism which has proceeded from the womb and the long gestation of progressive history," that he attributes to the American Constitution such an instantaneous birth.

ning of all our federal jurisprudence. In view of what came after, Ellsworth's membership in it has been singled out as the most significant fact of his first term of service.

And the Journals, indeed, supply us with no great mass of facts to choose from. They inform us that he voted *aye* on two sets of resolutions, of a distinctly New England flavor, and opposed mainly by delegates from the South, proclaiming the necessity of a very strict morality among a people fallen on such evil times, and condemning in most pointed terms the evil amusements of play-going, gaming, and horse-racing.[1] They also tell us how he voted on a few other questions, none, however, of a nature to indicate very clearly his general views. With R. H. Lee and Samuel Adams, he served on a special committee to attend to a memorial from Governor Trumbull, calling attention to the unrewarded services and sacrifices of his son, Colonel Joseph Trumbull, who had been the commissary-general of the army.[2] He was on another special committee to look into certain seizures of property at the time when Philadelphia was evacuated by the British;[3] and he was also on the committee which, after investigating fully Robert Morris's management, through the firm of Morris and Willing, of certain large purchases for the army, not merely exonerated Morris from all the charges against his integrity, but praised him highly for ability and patriotism.[4] This report may very well have opened the way for the later determination of Congress to put Morris in control of the Continental finances. *Per*

[1] Journals, IV, 590, 602–603.
[2] *Ibid.*, 597.
[3] *Ibid.*, 614.
[4] *Ibid.*, V, 28, 49–51.

contra, when charges were brought against Benedict
Arnold, who was at this time in command at Philadelphia, living beyond his means, consorting most
with an aristocratic and decidedly Tory set in the
society of the gayest of all colonial cities, and about
to be married to the beautiful daughter of a prominent
Tory family, Ellsworth voted against the motion to
postpone investigation.[1] Another important assignment was to a committee of all the states, charged to
investigate the disputes among our agents abroad and
to consider the whole subject of our foreign relations.
When it reported, Congress voted to recall several of
our representatives at European courts and adopted
rules intended to prevent such disagreements and conflicts of authority as that which had arisen between
Messrs. Silas Deane and Arthur Lee.[2] His last
assignment was to a committee which conferred with
Washington about the office of inspector general.

Unfortunately, too, his letters do not greatly increase our knowledge of the clearly active and varied
part which he was already playing at Philadelphia.
The letters to Trumbull for this term of service are
all joint epistles; the first two signed by Sherman and
Ellsworth, the remainder, written after Sherman had
gone home, by Eliphalet Dyer, Ellsworth, and Jesse
Root. Like most joint letters, they are dry and matter-
of-fact; but if they had been written by Ellsworth
alone they would not, in all probability, have been
much more readable. Three or four letters which he
did write at this time to his younger brother, David,
have been preserved.[3] The first of them begins with

---

[1] Journals, V, 55. [2] Secret Journals of Congress (ed. of 1820), II, 517, 525.
[3] For copies I am indebted to Mr. G. E. Taintor of Hartford.

a " Dear Sir," and another " Sir," with a comma, pre-
cedes, "your affectionate brother " at the end.

" Neither the business of Congress," it runs, " nor
amusements of this gay City have been able to make
me forget my friends at Windsor. Among others of
them you in particular have my most constant remembrance and continued good wishes. If in anything at this distance I can serve you, you will oblige
me by letting me know it. Do you want any (thing)
that I could purchase for you here? Almost everything is to be bo't here tho' at exorbitant prices. A
principal object under consideration of Congress at
present is if possible to establish the credit of the
currency, and so to reduce prices. The best time to
have done this is indeed past. I do not, however,
despair of its being affected yet. My little family I
suppose are now at Windsor and doubt not they have
your particular care to make them comfortable in my
absence, and the rather as you have none of your own
yet to be concerned for. I desire a suitable remembrance to all our family."

It is not a particularly unfavorable specimen of
Ellsworth's epistolary style during these years of ab-
sorbing work. As he grew older, more signs of culture began to appear in his rare letters, and also — for
in this, too, he was a New England type — a bit more
of himself and his human interests and affections, and
even, here and there, mild displays of humor. But the
Revolutionary statesmen were not, as a rule, amusing
correspondents. They strike one as an uncommonly
serious-minded and self-contained group of men.
Such high spirits as Gouverneur Morris sometimes
displayed were rare among them. Ellsworth's allusion

to his brother's lack of any family of his own may
have been meant for a sly hint of a suspicion that the
other was soon to be married. A little later, the fact
of an engagement being announced, he wrote his congratulations. But the nearest he came to a joke on
an occasion which might be considered somewhat
favorable for a bit of teasing was to wish that Goshen,
the town in which the young woman lived, might
prove to be flowing in milk and honey. " Everybody,"
he again breaks off from his brother's affair to say, " is
now thinking and talking about the paper currency."
No doubt, the pleasure-loving set in Philadelphia,
which Arnold preferred to his more sober Whig
acquaintance, found Ellsworth and his fellows less to
their liking than André and the other young English
officers whom these busy patriots had displaced.

The letters to Trumbull also are largely devoted
to the currency. That subject, and the almost equally
discouraging delay of the states in ratifying the articles, were at this time causing the greatest anxiety
among all thoughtful Whigs. The Continental issues
of paper money had depreciated to such a point that
it was seen clearly something radical must be done to
give them higher value, or else some other medium
must be contrived. Meanwhile, certain states which
had no claims to Western lands, led by Maryland, were
insisting that the states which did have such claims
ought to surrender them to the general government,
and were making that concession a condition of their
acceptance of the articles.

" The affair of finance," wrote Sherman and Ellsworth in October,[1] " is yet unfinished; the arrange-

---

[1] Oct. 15, 1778, Trumbull Papers.

ment of the Board of Treasury is determined on, but the officers are not yet appointed — to-morrow is assigned for their nomination. The members of Congress are united in the great object of securing the liberties and independence of the states, but are sometimes divided in opinion about particular measures.

" The Assembly of New Jersey in their late session did not ratify the confederation, nor has it been done by Maryland and Delaware States. These and some other of the states are dissatisfied that the Western ungranted lands should be claimed by particular states, which they think ought to be the common interest of the United States; they being defended at the common expense. They further say that if some provision is not now made for securing lands for the troops who serve during the war, they shall have to pay large sums to the states who claim the vacant lands to supply their quotas of the troops.

" Perhaps if the Assembly of Connecticut should resolve to make grants to their own troops, and those raised by the States of Rhode Island, New Jersey, Delaware and Maryland, in the lands south of Lake Erie, and west of the lands in controversy with Pennsylvania,[1] free of any purchase or quitrents to the government of Connecticut, it might be satisfactory to those states, and be no damage to the State of Connecticut. A tract of thirty miles east and west across the state would be sufficient for the purpose, and that being settled under good regulations would enhance

---

[1] Meaning the Susquehanna lands, claimed by both Connecticut and Pennsylvania; the dispute was now pending before a tribunal established by Congress. " The lands south of Lake Erie " included, of course, the region later known as the Connecticut Western Reserve.

the value of the rest. These could not be claimed as crown lands, both the fee and jurisdiction having been granted to the Governor and Company of Connecticut."

This was doubtless one of the first suggestions looking to that qualified cession of her Western claims which Connecticut made a few years later. It was also with gifts of Western lands that the state finally made compensation to her soldiers and to citizens who had suffered losses during the war.

In January, Trumbull having made inquiries about the progress of confederation, Ellsworth, Dyer, and Root replied:[1] "We have only to answer that the States of Maryland and Delaware have not yet acceded, and we are waiting with impatience for their union, and as the articles drawn comprehend the thirteen states jointly, it is at least a doubt whether the assent already obtained from eleven states is not founded on the joint consent of the whole thirteen, and unless the remaining two join, the whole is void, and it will make it necessary to send back to each state for their approbation, if no more than eleven states unite in the confederation, which would take up much time, besides the inconvenience which might attend, therefore are still waiting in hopes of the compliance of the other two."

Early in February, they wrote to the governor that only Maryland now held out; but the little state, as the event proved, was courageous and resolved enough to hold out two years longer and until, by extorting from the claimant states the cessions she demanded, she had accomplished for them all a long step toward the real union they were all so sadly in need of.

[1] Jan. 4, 1779, Trumbull Papers.

As to the finances, the Connecticut delegates had the pleasure to inform the governor, early in November, that his son had been unanimously chosen to the head of the new arrangement of the treasury; and at the beginning of the new year they transmitted the measures adopted by Congress "to relieve its sinking credit, and possibly, gradually to appreciate its value. A portion of each day," they added, "was set apart for that purpose, and was not closed till Saturday night last. We thought it prudent to retain Brown[1] till he could transmit to you the proceedings of Congress on that subject, lest his return, without any intelligence, might fix the impression on the minds of the people that Congress was only amusing them with bare pretences, while in fact they meant to have the bills die in the possessors' hands." Detaining the messenger another day, they sent on the apportionment of a tax of fifteen million dollars which Congress had voted to request the states to raise. Connecticut's quota was one million seven hundred thousand dollars, and her delegates pointed out that it could be paid more easily at once, while the Continental bills were sunk so low, than later, when, as it was hoped, they would rise in value. Of other not unimportant matters they also wrote, and always both with ardent patriotism and good common sense; and from time to time they communicated tidings, from various quarters, of moment to the great cause.

But there is nothing of the Committee of Appeals. It is quite probable that Ellsworth himself did not at first divine that of all his duties in Congress

[1] A messenger who was constantly travelling backward and forward between Philadelphia and Hartford.

this was the most distinguished. It may well have taken him years to perceive how truly constructive was the work which he and his fellow-committeemen soon had the chance to do. He does not seem to have moved very fast in the direction of federalism and the advocacy of a strong central government. Perhaps the zeal of his own state, up to this time, in all that pertained to the cause, kept him from seeing how inadequate to the management of Continental affairs the independent action of thirteen states must in the long run prove.

As to the necessity for a federal court or courts to sit upon cases which it would be obviously unfair to submit, for final decision, to the courts of any one state, only the actual coming up of such cases, and not the forethought of any state or statesman, first made it plain. One such controversy was that which arose between Connecticut and Pennsylvania over the ownership of the Susquehanna country. But cases of the class to which this belonged were not numerous enough to create of themselves a clear necessity for a permanent tribunal. The system of privateering which Congress early authorized, and the beginning of a navy which it accomplished, soon, however, led to disagreements that were numerous, and clearly of a nature to demand adjudication by some Continental court.

It was Washington himself who first brought the subject before the Congress. Writing from Cambridge in November, 1775, he called attention to a number of prize cases that had already been brought before him, and to an act of the Provincial Assembly of Massachusetts establishing a Court of Admiralty.[1] "Should

[1] Sparks, "Writings of Washington," III, 154-155.

not a court," he asked, "be established by authority of Congress, to take cognizance of prizes made by the *Continental* vessels?" Congress at once referred the suggestion to a very strong committee, and in accordance with its report advised all the colonies to establish courts for cases of capture. It was also resolved "That in all cases an appeal shall be allowed to the Congress, or such person or persons as they shall appoint for the tryal of appeals."

Here was a clear assumption of a distinctly national judicial authority. But when the resolutions were sent to Washington he remarked, naturally enough, that to make them complete a court must actually be established. Within a short time, all the colonies but New York had followed the example of Massachusetts. But when, in August, 1776, the first appeal came in, Congress hesitated and postponed, and ended by merely referring it to a special committee to decide. Seven cases were handled in this fashion. Finally, on Jan. 30, 1777, a standing committee of six was appointed "to hear and determine upon appeals against sentences passed on libels in courts of admiralty in the several states, agreeable to the resolutions of Congress." One of the six was Sherman. In May following, this committee was discharged, and a new committee of five appointed in its place. By the time Ellsworth became a member, thirty-eight appeals had been disposed of, and there had been no resistance to the authority of Congress.[1] The committee sat

---

[1] J. Franklin Jameson, The Predecessor of the Supreme Court, in his "Essays on the Constitutional History of the United States"; J. C. Bancroft Davis, 131 U. S. Reports, Appendix; Sparks, "Writings of Washington," III, 197; Journals of Congress, III, 43, 174.

in the State House at Philadelphia, and appeals were coming in regularly. But when he had been about a month a member one was received which led very quickly to a questioning of the authority of the committee and of Congress. The cause is therefore deservedly celebrated, and Ellsworth's sitting on the somewhat anomalous tribunal which tried it may well be accounted one of the accidents which help to shape even the least haphazard of careers.

Gideon Olmstead and others, Connecticut men, being captured by the enemy, had been put on board the British sloop *Active*, bound from Jamaica to New York. During the voyage, they rose against the master and crew, overpowered them, confined them in the cabin, and steered for Egg Harbor, in New Jersey. When they were in sight of port, the brig *Convention*, belonging to Pennsylvania, Captain Houston commander, took possession of the *Active* and brought her to Philadelphia, where Houston libelled her before the Pennsylvania Court of Admiralty as lawful prize to the *Convention*. Olmstead, for himself and his fellows, interposed a claim to cargo and vessel. The cause was tried before a jury, and it was decided that Olmstead and his party were entitled to one-fourth of the value of the prize, and that the other claimants were entitled to the remaining three-fourths. The Connecticut men appealed to Congress, the case was referred to the committee, and the appeal was heard on December 15. After a full discussion, the judgment of the state court was reversed. The *Active* was adjudged to be the lawful prize of Olmstead and his companions, and the case remanded to the state court, which was directed to execute the decree. The Pennsylvania judge acknowledged the committee's authority, but was unwilling to disregard the jury's award. Instead, he ordered the marshal to sell the sloop and cargo, and bring the proceeds into court. The Connecticut claimants thereupon moved the committee for an order to the marshal to execute its decree. This motion was pending when the committee, receiving a warning from Benedict Arnold that it must act quickly if it would assert its authority, and urged also by the claimants, assembled one morning at eight o'clock and granted an injunction to restrain the marshal from paying into the judge's hands the sum obtained by the sale. The injunction was, however, disregarded. In this way there arose the first clear conflict between the judicial authority of a state and of the United States.

The committee found itself as powerless to enforce its decree as Congress was to enforce its requisitions. Fearing to endanger the public peace by prolonging the controversy, it merely entered in its minutes that it would take no further action in the matter "until the authority of the court be so settled as to give full efficacy to their decrees and process."

But this was not the end of the case. Nearly thirty years later it came in another form before John Marshall and his associate justices of the Supreme Court of the United States, and there was another collision with the authorities of Pennsylvania before the decision which they rendered, sustaining the committee, was finally carried into effect.[1] The prize money had been given into the keeping of Rittenhouse, the Philadelphia banker, and at his death it passed into the

[1] United States *vs.* Peters, 5 Cranch's Reports, 115.

keeping of his executrix. In 1802, Olmstead and others brought suit against the executrix in the United States Circuit Court for Pennsylvania. The judge, Peters, decided in their favor; but the Pennsylvania legislature ordered a counter suit to be brought in a state court and charged the governor to protect the executrix. The plaintiffs thereupon applied to the Supreme Court for a mandamus, and a United States marshal, evading the guard of militia set about the house of the executrix, which the populace had nicknamed " Castle Rittenhouse," succeeded in enforcing it.

Nor was this the end of the committee. When it rendered its report, Congress referred the matter first to a special committee and then to a committee of the whole house. It was debated for two entire days, and a series of resolves were passed, over the opposition of the Pennsylvania delegates, insisting that Congress and the committee were within their powers in all that they had done. A committee was also appointed to confer with a committee of the Pennsylvania Assembly, and the resolves were later transmitted to the legislatures of all the states, that they might " take effectual measures for conforming therewith." [1]   Several states did make formal concession of the right of appeal to Congress in cases of capture.

Ellsworth had left before these steps were taken, but he was back in his seat and again a member of the committee when the next stage of this institutional development was reached. That was in January, 1780, when Congress, finally taking the advice of Washington, resolved " That a court be established

[1] Journals, V, 43, 86–90, 217–222.

for the trial of all appeals from the courts of admiralty in these United States, in cases of capture, to consist of three judges, appointed and commissioned by Congress." A week later, three able lawyers were named for this first federal court, one of them Ellsworth's colleague, Titus Hosmer.[1] Their salaries were ultimately fixed at two thousand two hundred and fifty dollars each, and the court was styled "The Court of Appeals in Cases of Capture."[2] Meanwhile, the committee went on with its duties until the new tribunal was organized, when all cases still pending were transferred to the court. Once or twice thereafter, Congress had occasion to defend the course it had taken on the question of prizes, but the Articles of Confederation conceded the authority it had already exercised, and the court remained in existence until 1786, when it ceased to sit merely because there were no more cases on its docket.[3] By his share in creating it, Ellsworth — no doubt unwittingly — had been training his hand for the noblest task it ever found to do; and in his membership of the committee which preceded it he had had an experience which must have proved of value in the highest office he was ever to hold. Characteristically, however, he has left no record of these things in any of his letters.

---

[1] Journals, VI, 17. [2] Ibid., 75, 182.

[3] The history of the Committee of Appeals and the Court of Appeals is carefully given in J. F. Jameson's "The Predecessor of the Supreme Court," in his "Essays on the Constitutional History of the United States in the Formative Period," and by J. C. B. Davis, in the "Centennial Appendix" to 131 U. S. Reports. These two writers have left little to be discovered on the subject. See also H. L. Carson, "History of the Supreme Court of the United States," I, 33–64, 213–215.

But it is no great wonder that he neglected in his letters even so big a question as this, when other needs of the struggling young government were so much more imperative than the need of a judiciary. In the winter and spring of 1779–1780, it was again the finances that absorbed the attention and activity of Congress; and Ellsworth, even before he returned to Philadelphia, had been occupied with a scheme of betterment — albeit a bad one. The Eastern states were trying to unite on a plan to remedy the evil of a depreciating currency, and they hit upon the hopeless and vicious plan of a limitation of prices by law. Massachusetts taking the lead, a convention for that purpose was held at Hartford in October, 1779, and Ellsworth was one of the four Connecticut delegates. It was agreed that Connecticut and New York should pass laws to limit prices similar to those already passed by the three states to the eastward; and resolutions were adopted favoring the raising of more money by taxation and the repeal of certain state embargoes, and calling on all the states as far west as Virginia to send representatives to a larger convention for limiting prices, to be held at Philadelphia in January. To this, also, Ellsworth was a delegate. When it met, however, four of the invited states failed to appear by delegates. There were adjournments from day to day, an adjournment without day, a reassembling on the arrival of the delegates from Massachusetts and Rhode Island, more adjournments from day to day, a call on New York and Virginia, which had not yet acted, and then an adjournment to April, in hope that they would act. But they never acted, and the convention never reassembled. Congress had been brought to favor the plan, but it could not bring the states into agreement.[1]

It was as well that they never did agree. No such expedient as this would have done any good of itself, and it might have delayed more hopeful measures. The Continental currency could not be saved by anything short of peace and the lodging of the power to tax in the government which had issued it. It had sunk so low by this time that those who held supplies would hardly exchange them for the notes at any price. In January, Ellsworth wrote to Governor Trumbull that in the neighborhood of the army meal was selling at eight dollars the quart, and corn at half a dollar the ear.[2] Congress had, in fact, already decided to abandon the old method of obtaining supplies, to issue no more bills of credit, and to make no more money requisitions on the states. It was trying, instead, a plan of requisitions for specific commodities. Washington had led the way by calling on the state of New Jersey for food for his army, and naming the kind and quantity of provisions which he expected from each of the several counties. His demand was met with an unexpected promptness, and about the same time Connecticut also sent on to the half-starved troops a supply of beef. To superintend the new method, Congress — as was its wont when there was executive work to do — appointed a committee; and to this committee Ellsworth was assigned the day after he took his seat. The service was doubtless as laborious

---

[1] For both conventions, Connecticut State Records, II, 474–475, 572–579; letters from Ellsworth, and from Sherman and Ellsworth, to Trumbull, in the Trumbull Papers.

[2] Jan. 14, 1780, Trumbull Papers.

as it was obscure. It brought him neither fame nor any other compensation. Indeed, the time when distinction could be won in the Congress seemed to be past. The famous names on the roll of members were fewer than they had ever been. In March, Madison took his seat as a delegate from Virginia, but the young man was as yet scarcely known beyond the boundaries of his native state. Ellsworth, it is clear, had no desire to linger at Philadelphia. The following, from a letter to his brother David, shows how little ambition had to do with his being there, and in what spirit he consented to remain:[1] —

" When I came away I expected to have returned home before this time, but nobody is yet arrived to take my place, tho' I have encouragement that there will be soon. It would be both more pleasing and more profitable to me to return home to my own family and business than to remain here any longer at this time, but you know when a soldier goes forth in publick service he must stay until he is discharged, and though the weather be stormy and his allowance small yet still he must stand to his post. All this you understand well by experience. I am much less concerned, however, about my family than I should be if I had not left the care of them with so faithful a hand as Mr. Lyman and furnished him with the means of procuring them what they may stand in need of. You will soon know when I am got home by seeing me at your house."

Yet this was the longest of all his attendances. Just historians can only deplore their inability to paint in glowing and attractive colors the sober,

[1] March 24, 1780.

silent, uninviting labors for great causes which deserve, but cannot win, the highest celebrity and praise. A single brilliant exploit in the field, a single eloquent sentence on some dramatic occasion, would doubtless have done more to keep alive the memory of a man like Ellsworth or his colleague, Sherman, than all the patience, judgment, energy, and devotion, with which, through many weary weeks and months, they gave themselves to the things which no one wished to do, yet which must be done, and could only be done by men of first-rate ability.

The new plan for supplies seemed for a while to be working fairly well. Late in January, Sherman and Ellsworth wrote to Trumbull, telling of the failure of the scheme to limit prices, but ended cheerfully, " It is with pleasure however we can add that there appears to be in the states generally a good forwardness to furnish their quotas of taxes and other supplies, which, aided by measures now under consideration, it is hoped may produce effects equally salutary."[1] A few days later, Ellsworth wrote again :[2] " The supplies and prospects of the army are more comfortable. The general was reduced to the necessity of demanding from the several counties in New Jersey specific supplies, with which they complied, even beyond the requisitions, with much spirit. Maryland is said to have fully complied with the requisition of Congress to that State, for 1500 barrels of flour. Delaware has also exerted herself much in the same way." But the business affairs of the Confederacy could never be kept in a good train until the currency should be reformed. About the same time, Ellsworth

[1] January 26, Trumbull Papers.   [2] January 30, *ibid*.

was writing to his brother David, " I cannot tell you when we shall have peace or good money." The outcome of the long and anxious debating of Congress over the problem of the currency was a determination to abandon the Continental paper already in circulation, and try to substitute another issue based on the credit of the states, which had, what Congress had not, the power to tax. Sherman and Ellsworth promptly communicated the plan to Governor Trumbull.[1] Hastily written as their letter doubtless was, dry and matter-of-fact though it is, one might search long without finding another contemporary document, unless it should be some letter of Robert Morris himself, setting forth more correctly the state of the finances at this time and the actual working of that side of the new government. Taken with a letter of Trumbull, then on its way to the delegates, telling what Connecticut had done of her own motion — that is to say, no doubt, of Trumbull's motion — to establish the credit of the state by " *the efficacy of honest truth* " in dealing with the public creditor, it well exhibits the kind of patriotism in civil office that alone made possible the final victory of the armies.[2] The crisis weighed so heavily on Ellsworth's mind that three days later he wrote again to the governor, and in a style that was, for him, uncommonly moved and personal.[3]

" Permit me," this letter runs, " as a private citizen to express my wishes, that the late Resolution of Congress on the subject of finance may meet your Excel-

[1] See Appendix A.
[2] For a somewhat gloomier view of the situation, see a letter from Madison to Jefferson, written one week later. Hunt's " Madison's Writings," I, 59–61.
[3] March 23, 1780, Trumbull Papers.

lency's approbation and support. Your Excellency must have long seen with alarming apprehensions the crisis to which a continued depreciation of the paper currency would one day reduce our affairs. It is now, Sir, just at hand. Without more stability in the medium and far more ample supplies in the Treasury than for months past, it will be impossible for our military operations to proceed, and the army must disband.

" The present moment is indeed critical, and if let slip, the confusion and distress will be infinite.

" This, Sir, is precisely the point of time for the several Legislatures to act decidedly, and in a manner that the world will forever call wise. It is now in their power by a single operation to give a sure establishment for public credit, to realize the public debt at its just value, and without adding to the burthens of the people to supply the Treasury. To furnish one common ground to unite their exertions upon, for the accomplishment of these great purposes, your Excellency will perceive to be the spirit and design of the Resolutions referred to. They speak a language too plain to need any comment. I will only add concerning them that (they) have been the product of much labor and discussion ; and tho' some states may have reason for thinking they are not the best possible, yet they are the best Congress would agree upon.

" And should they be rejected, I confess I do not well see on what ground the common exertions of the several states are to be united and continued hereafter."

Never eloquent on paper, Ellsworth here reveals, more fully than in any earlier writing that has come down to us, how deeply his reserved, cautious, but constant nature was moved by whatever affected the cause for which he was toiling in such unshowy ways. Washington might have written very much in this fashion; indeed, there are letters of his to governors and to Congress that are not dissimilar in tone.

That same day, Messenger Brown came in with Trumbull's letter and copies of the Assembly's acts, and Sherman and Ellsworth wrote again, together, urging the proposals of Congress. A plan to reduce the battalions already in the field, simply for economy, was, they said, actually favored. Another plan of economy was to leave unfilled the vacancies in the several Continental lines. They also praised the governor and the Assembly for their efforts to sustain the credit of the state and for taking the lead of all the states with measures to carry out the new proposals. Ellsworth was deeply gratified.

"I thought it my duty," he wrote to the governor a little later,[1] "to read in Congress the account I had received from Connecticut, and was kept in countenance by their just approbation. And it is devoutly to be wished that the well-timed and animated example of so respectable a state may have its due influence with the rest.

"A number of their Assemblies, as New York, New Jersey, Pennsylvania, Maryland and Virginia are, it is said, now convened or convening, and will be informed through the channel of the Philadelphia papers, if not otherwise, what Connecticut has done."[2]

[1] May 5, Trumbull Papers.

[2] The next day, May 6, Madison wrote to Jefferson: "Congress have the satisfaction . . . to be informed that the legislature of Connecticut has taken the most vigorous steps for supplying their quota both of money and

Throughout the spring, and well into the summer, he was still occupied with the baffling task of Congress — to secure money without taxation. Biographers of Washington are not wrong in praising his incessant wrestling with Congress and the states for the means to carry out his plans; but they sometimes, one feels, fail to remember that Congress could not do more than it was doing. At last, in June, Ellsworth, as a member of another committee, helped to carry through a plan which proved to be the beginning of better things. It was Robert Morris's scheme to secure supplies for the army by a subscription, with the guaranty of Congress that the subscribers should be repaid; and the machinery of the subscription took a form which made it, if not precisely a bank itself, the predecessor of the first of the national banks. Ellsworth's committee having reported in favor of the proposal, it was hastily indorsed, the guaranty was given, and a standing committee, with Ellsworth at its head, was appointed to coöperate with the officers. The relief this measure gave to Washington can scarcely be overestimated.

Meanwhile, Ellsworth's letters, taking a wider and wider range, had been keeping the governor informed of many things which he might otherwise have been slow to learn. For the enemy was now transferring his activities to the South, and the wiser heads were also looking, more and more hopefully, to Europe,

commodities; and that a body of their principal merchants have associated for supporting the new paper. . . . A similar vigor throughout the Union may perhaps produce effects as far exceeding our present hopes, as they have hitherto fallen short of our wishes." Hunt's "Madison's Writings," I, 62–63.

[1] Journals of Congress, VI, 95.

where diplomacy was much engaged with American affairs. Late in January, Ellsworth wrote:[1]

" Congress have recent assurances that France and Spain on the one hand as well as Great Britain on the other are sparing no possible measures and preparation for the ensuing season, and by taking early advantage thereof to render it decisive on the great question of American independence. And that these states might not be unfurnished for the necessary exertions on their part, his most Christian Majesty has, in addition to timely communications, issued an order to his ministers ample to supply them with arms and ammunition."

He continued to watch the movements of our allies and the general European situation with a clear understanding that the outcome of our struggle did not depend on our own exertions alone. He was also not unmindful of the work of the Spaniards along the coast of the Mexican Gulf, — an episode of the conflict which historians have somewhat neglected, — but followed, with an interest justified by the outcome, the expedition of Galvez against the British province of West Florida. In a letter written in May, he discussed, with what was for him unusual fulness and freedom, the state of England as it affected the prospect of peace:[2]

" No official information has been received very lately from Europe, but from the current of publications on that side of the water, and especially the English papers, it does not appear that any power has yet been found sufficiently uninformed to join Great Britain in the wicked and Romantic attempts at re-

[1] January 26, Trumbull Papers.   [2] May 9, *ibid.*

ducing to obedience what she yet styles her rebellious Colonies. And as she cannot obtain assistance, she seems willing to have it believed that she stands in need of none, and accordingly goes on with a show and pretension of being sufficient for all things of herself; much, perhaps, as a merchant on the eve of Bankruptcy makes an uncommon parade of wealth and business in order to keep up the delusion until chance may have had time to achieve something in his favor. The comparison, however, fails in this respect, that it is no secret to the world that the circumstances of Great Britain are bad, and that her wisest men are filled with consternation. She is ready to be crushed with the weight of her own debt, which is accumulating upon her by the whole expense of the war, and for which she is already mortgaged to pay forever an annual interest of seven millions sterling. Her revenues being fully charged with the interest, it is impossible for her ever to reduce the principal but by a sponge or revolution, and as impossible for her to go on much further in borrowing. She is also embarrassed with the claims of oppressed Ireland, which may perhaps advance upon her, and she is less able to contest them. Scotland, also, tho' habitually servile to the Throne (speaks ?) with determinate insolence, and will be heard. Add to which, county conventions, in spite of the Ministry, are now forming in various parts of England, under the first characters of the nation, for reducing within due bounds the influence of the Crown, and the public expenditures; or, which is the same thing, oversetting the present venal and Utopian system of administration.

" From these marks of the weakness and dissolution, she bears within herself, it is reasonable to expect that Great Britain will ere long cease from troubling us; and unless she can speedily regain the sovereignty of the seas, she may be reduced from her Insular situation, to hold her own existence at the mercy of her enemies.

" The use good men in America will derive from these considerations, will be of encouragement to persevere in the present contest, and continue working with the Lord until, by his good pleasure, the great business of our political Salvation shall be fully accomplished."

Ellsworth was here deceiving himself, as were others also, concerning the imminence of a collapse of England's credit. Her marvellous powers of endurance and recovery, and the soundness of her financial system, were soon to bear the test of wars far longer and more costly than the war in America. But he was wise to draw encouragement, even at a time when all the news from the southward was bad news, from England's international isolation and from the temper of the English people themselves. An admirable English historian of the period[1] is making it clearer than ever that from first to last a great part of the people of England, possibly the greater part, opposed the policy of the king and his ministers with the colonies, and that it did indeed fill with consternation the wisest of her statesmen. Ellsworth had soon to announce to the governor that Charleston had fallen early in May, and before he returned to Con-

[1] Sir George Otto Trevelyan, whose " American Revolution " is still (1905) unfinished.

necticut the enemy were overrunning the Carolinas. Gates's defeat at Camden and Arnold's treason at West Point were still to follow. Yet the chances are that during the long period which elapsed before he came again to Congress he remained hopeful of a final victory.

Perhaps his entering on the duties of yet another office was one of the reasons why he stayed so long away from Philadelphia. He was this year chosen a member of the governor's council, and the governor's council in Connecticut, besides its merely advisory function, was the upper house of the legislature; and the legislature was still the Supreme Court of Errors. Membership in the council, therefore, was not a sinecure, but imposed activities that were now executive, now legislative, and now judicial. As Ellsworth remained a member until 1785,[1] he held, from this time until the end of the war, apart from whatever share he still had in the work of the Pay Table, three public offices. Few Continental Congressmen can have had such good excuses for their absences.

When he did go back, in June, 1781, it was for the least important, as well as the briefest, of his terms of service. Ill health was his reason for cutting it so short. As early as the first of August he wrote to Trumbull that he found himself too unwell for a constant attendance in Congress, and that his family and business also needed his attention. He urged, therefore, that some other member of the delegation be sent on by the first of September.

Meanwhile, Sherman was again his colleague, and

[1] Roll of State Officers and Members of the General Assembly of Connecticut.

they wrote somewhat more cheerfully than the year before concerning the state of the finances and the outlook for the cause.[1] For one thing, the Articles of Confederation were now in force. Though the new Continental and state bills were no better than five for one in specie, Robert Morris had lately taken the office of superintendent of the finances and much was expected of him. Hopes were entertained that the emperor of Prussia and the empress of Russia would soon offer to mediate. The military situation in the South was more encouraging.

Still, there was work enough to do, and Ellsworth had his share of it. Morris's management of the finances had doubtless convinced Congress by this time that all the departments ought to have single heads, and Ellsworth served on the committee to apply this principle to the marine.[2] Other subjects with which he dealt as a member of various committees were General Greene's conduct of the Southern campaign, the pay of delegates from several Southern states too poor to sustain their representatives, the traitorous commerce of New Yorkers with the enemy, and a proposed convention with France concerning the interchange of consuls, vice-consuls, and agents.[3] On several of these committees, Madison, now by long continuous attendance risen to much influence, was his colleague. Van Santvoord, studying closely the motions and the roll-calls on questions of a sectional nature, finds that on all such issues Ellsworth stood with his New England colleagues, sometimes clearly op-

[1] July 12, 1781, Trumbull Papers.
[2] Journals, VII, 141, 152.
[3] Ibid., 157, 158, 165, 168, 177; Secret Journals, III, 20.

posing the interests of South Carolina and other Southern states, which were now championed in Congress by John Rutledge. It is true that on a motion to send some arms into South Carolina for the use of the militia Ellsworth moved to amend by leaving the disposition of the arms to General Greene.[1] He also wished to postpone, perhaps to kill, a motion to relieve certain inhabitants of South Carolina who had been recently released by a cartel from a cruel imprisonment.[2] Georgia and the Carolinas having furnished supplies to the armies in that quarter, it was proposed to credit them with a proportionate allowance on their quotas of taxation, and this, too, he opposed. Unquestionably, there was in Congress plenty of sectional feeling and a lively bickering among the states. But these facts are not enough to prove that Ellsworth was governed by merely sectional devotions and antipathies. He did support the motion to provide for the unpaid Southern delegates.[3] Slow as he was to follow Madison and Hamilton on the road to nationalism, he was in truth exceptionally broad in his patriotism, keeping always first in his desires the objects that were common to men of the patriot party everywhere.

Before he came again to Philadelphia the greatest of those objects was substantially secured. Peace had not been declared, but the fighting was over. Commissioners at Paris were negotiating with the envoys of England and of France treaties which, whatever else they might contain, would, it was now quite certain, concede the independence of America. Strangely enough, one of Ellsworth's tasks at home had been to vindicate from a charge of gross disloyalty to the now

[1] Journals, VII, 142.   [2] *Ibid.*, 152.   [3] *Ibid.*, 158.

victorious cause no less a patriot than Jonathan Trumbull. Charged with conniving at the trade with the enemy, and even with engaging in it, the governor had asked the Assembly to make an investigation. A committee was promptly appointed, and Ellsworth rendered the report.[1] It completely exonerated Trumbull, declaring that the slander had probably been started by some unknown emissary of the British.[2] The incident may serve to indicate the place which Ellsworth himself held at this time in Connecticut.

In Congress, also, notwithstanding it was fifteen months from his last appearance there, it is clear that he took at once a place among the leaders. Madison and Rutledge were still members, and in November, 1782, Alexander Hamilton had joined them; and the journal, meagre as it is, affords material for the inference that these three, with Ellsworth and James Wilson of Pennsylvania, were the foremost men in the chamber during the following winter and spring. Their names appear again and again whenever really important subjects are dealt with. Fortunately, however, we are no longer dependent entirely on the Journals for our knowledge of the proceedings. In the autumn of 1782, Madison, an admirable reporter, began to take down the substance of the speeches. Some months later, the house voted down a motion of Hamilton to open its doors to the public whenever the finances should be up;[3] but Madison's notes went far to open them for later generations.

---

[1] Feb. 13, 1782, Trumbull Papers.   [2] *Ibid.*
[3] Ellsworth voted against this motion when it was renewed in April. Journals, VIII, 252.

There was at this time a distinct revival of energy in Congress. The end of the fighting, which had released some able men from military service to share in the debates, had also, of course, brought new questions to decide; and there were other questions, equally pressing, which had been held back until the peace should be achieved. Foremost of them all, however, was still the old and unsolved problem of how the general government was going to sustain itself and meet its obligations without the power to raise money either by customs duties or direct taxation. Morris had exhausted all his skill in borrowing; to pay the loans he had contracted, to redeem the still outstanding paper currency, to devise a sure and steady inflow of revenue — these things were beyond his power, unless the states as well as Congress should hold up his hands. The Articles had left the right of laying taxes with the states; and these, now that the crisis was past, were sunk into a stolid inactivity worse than that of two years earlier. Morris had to report that on the requisition of 1782 only South Carolina had paid her quota in full, and that was in supplies to troops within her borders. The proportions of their several quotas paid in by the other states ranged from one-fourth by Rhode Island down to one-one-hundred-and-twenty-first by New Hampshire. From three states, nothing whatever had been received.[1] "Imagine," Morris wrote to Franklin in January, 1783, "the situation of a man who is to direct the finances of a country almost without means (for such you will perceive this to be), surrounded by creditors whose

[1] W. G. Sumner, "Financier and Finances of the Revolution," II, 55.

distresses, while they increase their clamor, render
it more difficult to appease them; an army ready to
disband; a government whose sole authority consists in the power of framing recommendations." It
is no wonder that a fortnight later he wrote to Congress, " If before the end of May effectual measures
to make permanent provision for the public debts of
every kind are not taken, Congress will be pleased
to appoint some other man to be superintendent of
their finances."[1]   Nor is it any wonder that Congress
did not accept his resignation.   He yielded, and
kept his office, perhaps in the hope that through a
change in the system something might be done to relieve both him and the country from their humiliating
plight.

That was the pressing business of the hour.   A
few saw also beyond the hour, and strove to turn the
situation to such account that the system might be
fitted for the permanent and constant duties of a real
government in time of peace.   Of these, Hamilton
was the ardent leader.   Fresh from the office of
Continental receiver for New York, he knew at first
hand the utter inefficiency of requisitions as a means
of revenue.   During the summer he had drafted for
the New York legislature some resolutions which
were sent to Congress, urging a general convention
to amend the Articles.   He had come himself to
Congress mainly to see if it were possible to build
up, on the basis of the Articles, a government strong
enough to live.   Restless under makeshifts and impatient with incompetence, he went at his purpose
with an energy that sometimes frightened where it

Diplomatic Correspondence of the Revolution, XII, 310, 326.

did not overcome. Madison, who had long been gravitating to the same general desire, pursued it much more cautiously and tactfully. Wilson of Pennsylvania made an able third. Rutledge was the stoutest champion of the states. Ellsworth occupied the middle ground and took, for the time, a course that was moderate to the point of hesitation. In this he doubtless correctly represented his section. In the movement for a stronger government, New England had as yet taken but little part. Moreover, the delegates from Massachusetts had fallen below Connecticut's in point of ability and influence, and neither Rhode Island nor New Hampshire had a commanding voice. Unsustained by any clearly national impulse in the people behind him, and without support from any New England colleague of more than ordinary force, Ellsworth, not unnaturally, was slow to accept a leadership so radical and fiery as Hamilton's. He and Rutledge were soon again in controversy over plans to relieve the state of South Carolina;[1] but on the bigger issues he found himself at first quite as close to the South Carolinian as to Hamilton and Madison and Wilson.

He had been but a few days in his seat when the whole subject of finance was again, in a most unpleasant fashion, forced to the front. Another scheme of revenue had come to failure. Nearly two years earlier, Congress had asked the states for authority to lay a duty of five per cent on all imports, and with this request all but two states had in some sort made compliance. Georgia had failed to act at all, but only Rhode Island, which derived a considerable revenue

[1] Journals, VIII, 48; Hunt's "Madison's Writings," I, 316.

from imports intended for Connecticut, had positively
refused.   A committee was appointed to visit the
little state and urge the scheme upon her governors.
But when the emissaries were about to take their
departure, word came that Virginia also, having once
consented to the impost, had now reversed her
action.

This was at the end of 1782.   Before a week of the
new year had passed, a committee of officers from the
army at Newburgh, N.Y., arrived in Philadelphia with
the solemnest and sternest of appeals for payment
of the troops.   Not even the constantly recurring
rumors of peace with independence could long divert
the members of Congress from what, in a letter home,
Madison described as the cloud that was lowering on
the North River.   The one stubborn fact that over-
hung and darkened all things was the fact of bankruptcy.   From this time until the middle of April,
save for certain necessary interruptions to attend to
the peace treaty, Congress, now by special committees, now by a general committee of the states,
now in committee of the whole, was searching for
a path to solvency and honor.

The debate took a wide range, for in the general
problem there were many specific perplexities.   The
army demanded not merely present pay, but security
for arrears, compensation for deficiencies in rations
and clothing, and commutation of the half-pay for life,
which Congress had already voted, into an equivalent
in gross.   There was the foreign debt, and Morris's
inability to negotiate new loans until the old were
somehow secured and interest provided.   There were
the various forms of the domestic debt, with the claims

of different classes of creditors and the frequently conflicting interests of the various states. But it all came
back to the main question, How could money be
obtained? Hamilton, Madison, and Wilson at once
declared that nothing would serve but general or Continental taxes, whether by impost or excise. The
states must grant this power to Congress, or the Confederacy, now that it had won its independence, would
fail from sheer and ignominious weakness. But a
group of lesser men, led by Rutledge, and including
Madison's own colleagues from Virginia, opposed this
policy at every turn. They would adhere to the Articles; they feared and distrusted tyranny at home quite
as much as they had feared and distrusted it in the
Parliament and the King across the water; they
would never consent to give into the same hands
"the purse and the sword." This last was a favorite
catch phrase.

Ellsworth's first reported speech came on a day of
general debate,[1] and Hamilton's reply, followed by
Madison's cooler and more cautious argument, marks
the high tide of the whole discussion. The question
was on Wilson's motion, modified by an amendment
of Madison, " That it is the opinion of Congress that
the establishment of permanent and adequate funds
to operate generally throughout the United States is
indispensably necessary for doing complete justice to
the creditors of the United States, for restoring public
credit, and for providing for the future exigencies of
the war." When the two opposing views were set
before the house, " Mr. Ellsworth acknowledged himself to be undecided in his opinion; that on one side

[1] Jan. 28, 1783.

he felt the necessity of continental funds for making good the continental engagements, but on the other desponded of a unanimous concurrence of the States in such an establishment. He observed that it was a question of great importance, how far the federal Gov^t. can or ought to exert coercion against delinquent members of the confederacy; and that without such coercion no certainty could attend the constitutional mode which referred everything to the unanimous punctuality of thirteen different councils. Considering, therefore, a continental revenue as unattainable, and periodical requisitions from Congress as inadequate, he was inclined to make trial of the middle mode of permanent state funds, to be provided at the recommendation of Cong^s., and appropriated to the discharge of the common debt." [1]

Hamilton's quick reply disclosed the defect of his admirable quality.[2] Too strenuous in his statesmanship to yield to merely politic considerations, and neglecting the one ground on which Ellsworth had criticised his policy, viz. that it was unattainable, he dwelt at length on the sure inadequacy of the other's proposal and then, utterly disregarding the suspicions of the state-rights party, boldly avowed that one reason why he wished Congress to have the power in question was because the energy of the central government was, in general, far too slight. It was not strong enough, he said, to pervade the states and draw them into a union. He considered, therefore, that it was expedient " to introduce the influence of officers deriving their emoluments from and consequently interested in supporting the power of Congress."

[1] Hunt's " Madison's Writings," I, 334.   [2] *Ibid.*, 335.

Madison saw the blunder, and jotted down in his notes, perhaps on the very instant: " This remark was imprudent and injurious to the cause which it was meant to serve. This influence was the very source of jealousy which rendered the states averse to a revenue under collection as well as appropriation of Congress. All the members of Congress who concurred in any degree with the states in this jealousy, smiled at the disclosure. Mr. B(land) and still more Mr. L(ee), who were of this number, took notice in private conversation, that Mr. Hamilton had let out the secret." [1] A moment later, when Madison himself rose to speak for the resolution, he showed how indispensable to such a leadership as Hamilton's was his own perfect poise, his tact and courtesy, his patient fairness with all points of view. These two, wittingly or not, had already entered on the task of building for the young confederacy a true constitution of government. They were trying now to set in place the only corner-stone from which that edifice could possibly arise. It is doubtful if in the long struggle with public opinion which was thus beginning the quick and darting genius of Hamilton would ever have prevailed had there been no Madison to smooth the way, to placate opposition, to do, in fine, whatever genius leaves to talents, industry, and judgment, — if, indeed, these gifts in Madison do not also deserve the name of genius. Stating first, with masterly clearness, the problem of the hour, he took up, one by one, the various plans suggested, and showed conclusively that none of them would work in practice without that great concession of the power to tax which state-rights men revolted at.[2]

[1] Hunt's " Madison's Writings," I, 336.   [2] *Ibid.*, 336–340.

It is hard to see how any open mind could long hold
out against his reasoning; and Ellsworth, clearly, was
one of those whose minds were open. The next day,
when Wilson proposed an elaborate scheme of taxation,
and Rutledge responded with a plan to ask the states
to levy a duty of five per cent on imports to pay the
foreign debt, each state to be credited, on its quota of
the debt, with such amounts as might be gathered
at its ports, he criticised both proposals.

" Mr. Elseworth thought it wrong," Madison reports,[1]
" to couple any other objects with the impost; that the
states would give this if anything; and that if a land
tax or an excise were combined with it, the whole
scheme would fail. He thought, however, that some
modification of the plan recommended by Cong[s].
would be necessary. He supposed when the benefits
of this Contin[l]. revenue should be experienced it would
incline the states to concur in making additions to it.
He abetted the opposition of Mr. Woolcot [2] to the
motion of Mr. Rutledge, which proposed that each
State should be credited for the duties collected
within its ports; dwelt on the injustice of it, said
Connecticut, before the revolution did not import one-
fiftieth, perhaps not one-one-hundredth part of the
merchandise consumed within it, and pronounced that
such a plan w[d]. never be agreed to. He concurred in
the expediency of new-modelling the scheme of the
impost by defining the period of its existence;[3] by
leaving to the States the nomination, and to Congress

[1] Hunt's " Madison's Writings," I, 348–349.

[2] Oliver Wolcott, Sr., his colleague. Madison seems to have had a hard
time with New England proper names. Gorham of Massachusetts, *e.g.*,
constantly appears as Ghoram, and Ellsworth as Elseworth.

[3] The period proposed was twenty-five years.

the appointment of Collectors, or *vice versa ;* and by a
more determinate appropriation of the revenue. The
first object to which it ought to be applied was, he
thought, the foreign debt. This object claimed a
preference as well from the hope of facilitating further
aids from that quarter, as from the disputes into w^{ch}.
a failure may embroil the U.S. The prejudices agst
making a provision for foreign debts which s^{d}. not
include the domestic ones was, he thought, unjust and
might be satisfied by immediately requiring a tax in
discharge of which loan-office certificates should be
receivable. State funds for the domestic debts would
be proper for subsequent consideration. He added, as
a further objection against crediting the States for the
duties on trade respectively collected by them, that a
mutual jealousy of injuring their trade by being foremost in imposing such a duty would prevent anyone
from making a beginning."

He was still inclined to a compromise position, but
the movement of his mind was plainly toward the
policy of a stronger central government. Leaving
Philadelphia about this time, he was gone till April,
but very soon after his return it appeared that common sense, and perhaps also a broadening sense of his
own duty, were fast overcoming his state-rights scruples.
During his absence, the party in favor of giving to the
government strength enough to meet its obligations
had had the better of it in debate. Events outside
had been constantly supplying them with telling arguments and instances. Morris's letter, for a while kept
secret, had been given to the country. France, the
leading foreign creditor, had sharply demanded that
Congress take some action on her claims and Hol-

land's. The army's discontent had seemed for a time to
be fast turning into mutiny, and Washington, although
he quelled the disposition toward violence, plainly
declared that in his opinion his soldiers' wrath was
just. By the middle of April, Congress was brought
to favor a general scheme which included both a
federal impost of five per cent and specific duties on
certain articles of general use. Future requisitions on
the states were to be based on population, instead of
land, which was the basis fixed by the Articles; and it
was agreed that in estimating population five negro
slaves should count as three white freemen. These
proposals passed on April 18, and Ellsworth voted for
them. He had doubtless, by this time, quite abandoned
his preference for permanent state funds. The proposals, however, were themselves a compromise. They
fell so far short of Hamilton's desire, and he had so
little hope in them, that he would not vote for them.
Nevertheless, he and Madison and Ellsworth were
appointed a committee to commend them to the states.
The moderate but strong address they sent out to the
legislatures was the work of Madison, but Ellsworth
gave it his approval. A fortnight later, he wrote to
Trumbull:[1]

" A plan of revenue for funding the public debt
which has taken up much time in Congress will be
immediately forwarded for consideration of the State,
accompanied with the documents necessary to give information on the subject. As might naturally be
expected at the close of so long a war, we find a considerable debt on our hands, which all will agree it
much concerns our national character and prosperity

[1] May 13, Trumbull Papers.

to provide for, however various may be the opinions as to the mode of doing it."

It is significant, too, that Ellsworth should have been set at the head of a committee of nine, now at last appointed to consider the New York resolutions, which had been before Congress more than a year. It was a strong committee, names like Hamilton's and Wilson's coming after Ellsworth's; but there is no record of any action taken on the subject of a convention while Ellsworth remained chairman.[1] This, however, does not prove there was none taken: for after the passage of the revenue measure Madison's notes grow scanter, and he is constantly referring us to the keyhole glimpses which are all the journals afford. We know that in June, backed by Hamilton, Ellsworth was urging Congress to take a step essential to a stronger union by completing the transfer of Virginia's Western claims to the Confederacy.[2]

Meanwhile, in foreign affairs also, and particularly in the business occasioned by the peace, he had been conspicuously employed. Early in the winter, when a Rhode Island delegate had wished permission to send to the governor of his state certain extracts from letters from Europe, Ellsworth and Hamilton served on a committee which reported against the proposal.[3] A few days later, with Hamilton and Madison, he reported in favor of a treaty of amity and commerce with the Netherlands. In this report, one of the longest ever made to the Congress, there was enclosed

[1] Bancroft's "United States," VI, 80, 99.

[2] Hunt's "Madison's Writings," I, 474.

[3] Journals, VIII, 88–89. He was also on the committee which reported against a claim of certain Rhode Island officers based on the depreciation of the money they were paid in.

the treaty itself and a series of forms and blanks for the various interchanges of officials and of courtesies which it called for. " Both the Committee and Congress," Madison remarks, " were exceedingly chagrined at the extreme incorrectness of these national acts." The debate that followed led to a motion for the purchase of a few books of reference for the use of Congress in such cases, and that motion was, no doubt, the beginning of the history of the libraries of Congress and the department of state. But it was not the actual beginning of those libraries. Not even "a few hundred pounds" could be spared for such a purpose.[1]

The first of May, while Congress still had nothing of the peace treaty but the preliminaries, Ellsworth, Hamilton, and Rutledge reported, in response to a letter from John Adams, instructions favorable to a treaty of amity and commerce with Great Britain.[2] Again with Hamilton and Madison, and with Wilson also, Ellsworth concurred in a report directing Washington to occupy the frontier forts so soon as the British should give them up.[3] When the provisions of the treaty were fully known, he and Hamilton advocated a call on the states to carry out the recommendation concerning the Tories,[4] and they were both on a committee which drew up an address to the states, urging them to conform in all good faith to such provisions as had to do with confiscations and with debts due from

[1] Journals, 91, 109; Secret Journals, III, 289-318; Hunt's "Madison's Writings," I, 318-319.
[2] Secret Journals, III, 340. Madison ridicules this letter of Adams for its palpable self-seeking and self-praise.
[3] May 12, Journals, VIII, 259.
[4] Hunt's "Madison's Writings," I, 463.

Americans to Britons.[1] Clearly, he was one of those in whom the war had left but little rancor. He was also one of those who felt, even at this time, that the United States had little to gain from the lowering of England's rank among the nations. Writing to Trumbull,[2] he argued that England's debt and the great expense of her peace establishment, which in his judgment had forced her to treat with America, would also probably insure her good behavior for a long time yet to come; and he added:

" Neither the safety of this country or the balance of power of Europe requires that Great Britain should be at all more reduced than in fact she is; and it is (only) by avoiding that distraction of councils and corruption of manners that have brought her down, that America can hope to rise or long enjoy the blessings of a revolution, which, under the auspices of Heaven, she has gloriously accomplished."

Here was a temper prophetic of the federalist to be; the revolutionist as well as the state-rights man was moving with the current of events, open-eyed to new conditions. No sentimentalist, he would let the dead past bury its dead.

On the question of ratifying the provisional articles without waiting for the definitive treaty, " Mr. Ellsworth," Madison reports,[3] " was strenuous on the obligation and policy of going into an immediate execution of the treaty. He supposed that a generous and ready execution on our part w^d accelerate the like on the other part." For some reason, when a treaty

---

[1] Journals, VIII, 266–268 ; Secret Journals, III, 355.
[2] May 13, Trumbull Papers.
[3] April 14, Hunt's " Madison's Writings," I, 450.

of amity and commerce with Russia was up, he made and carried, Madison opposing, a motion to limit it to twenty-five years.[1] But his views on foreign affairs seem to have been, as a rule, sane and unprovincial, and not without enlightenment and insight. Early in May, he wrote to his colleague, Wolcott, who had gone home:[2]

" Nothing yet appears to induce a suspicion that the treaty will fail of being carried into effect, on both sides, as fast as the nature of the case will admit. Certainly, we cannot wish to see it violated or annulled ; nor has Great Britain so much reason to be dissatisfied, under all circumstances, as North, Fox, and their partisans pretend, — for their object probably is to hunt down the present minister, and to transfer the popular odium from the criminal to the executioner. If Great Britain, induced thereto by the folly of a former administration, must make us independent of herself, it is wise in her to do so with grace, and *in a manner that shall also keep us independent of France.* This principle was, no doubt, well explained and enforced by Messrs. Adams and Jay. But it would have been a weakness in a British minister not to have adopted it, and in as large an extent as in the present treaty seems to have been done, even as to the Loyalists, who are said to have been sacrificed for nothing."

He was no such violent Anglophobe as Rutledge and others were plainly showing themselves to be, and had not in him the making of a partisan of France; but neither was he, like Hamilton, enamored of the British system. When news came of the famous

[1] Secret Journals, III, 350–354.   [2] May 6, Wood Ms.

coalition of Lord North with the Whigs, he wrote to Trumbull: [1]

" A packet just arrived at New York from Falmouth, it is represented, brings information that the Definitive Treaty was signed, and that the British were to leave this coast, at farthest, by the first of August. The packet also brings a list of the new British ministry, established the second of April, which I take the liberty to enclose. From the strange coalition of which it is formed, there is little reason to doubt but that another change of a partial nature will follow, as soon as the present convulsive state of that nation shall have subsided. Lord North, who is the fixed favorite of his Sovereign, and a man of the most system, business, and address, will early find means to lay aside Mr. Fox and his coadjutors when he can well do without them, as he has already done with one set of opponents, whom he let come forward to perish in the odium of exciting measures which he had rendered necessary."

He served, again with Hamilton and Madison for colleagues, on the committee which had in charge the general subject of neutrality agreements.[2] But the most distinguished conjunction of the three names was on still another committee, appointed early in April, " to provide a system for foreign affairs, for military and naval establishments, and also to carry into execution the regulation of weights and measures, and other articles of the Confederation not attended to during the war." [3] The task was nothing less than the devising of a complete permanent system of administration.

He continued to be called on for such high services

[1] June 4, Trumbull Papers.   [2] Secret Journals, III, 366–368.
[3] Hunt's " Madison's Writings," I, 441.

throughout the spring, and until the busy session
came to its humiliating close. He himself does not
seem to have foreseen or dreaded any such *émeute* as
that which drove the delegates away from Philadelphia.
His letters contain no such gloomy forebodings of the
conduct of the unpaid troops as Madison's are filled
with. He had written to Wolcott, early in May,[1] that
three months' pay would probably be made to the army
on disbandment, one-third in cash, the rest in Mr.
Morris's notes; and that Morris would remain in office
until all his engagements should be fulfilled. When
the question arose, whether to discharge the troops
or merely give them furloughs, he was for discharging them at once.[2] Even so late as June 18, 1783,
he was writing to Trumbull, apparently without uneasiness:[3]

"The furloughed part of the army are on their way
home. Some have arrived here from the southward.
They receive three months' pay, but all in Mr. Morris's
notes, which run six months." Yet it was but three
days later that a band of about five hundred mutinous
soldiers of the Pennsylvania line surrounded the State
House, where Congress was sitting, and with arms in
their hands demanded a settlement of their accounts.
Sitting under the same roof was the executive council
of Pennsylvania; and to this body Congress sent at
once a committee — Hamilton, Ellsworth, and Peters
— to take order for the calling out of the state militia.
But the Council would not act. Congress finally adjourning, the troops permitted the members to disperse.

[1] May 6, Wood Ms.
[2] May 20, Hunt's "Madison's Writings," I, 468.
[3] Trumbull Papers.

Reassembling that evening, they voted that in case no means should be found to put down the rioting the President should summon them to meet at Princeton or at Trenton. Hamilton and Ellsworth, serving as a committee of conference with the Pennsylvania authorities, failed to bring them to any determined action, and the President issued his summons. At the end of June, therefore, Congress reassembled at Princeton. Hamilton, for the committee, made a report which seemed to reflect severely on the Pennsylvania authorities, and when the council complained of it Ellsworth merely moved a resolve which exonerated them from any active part in the insult to Congress. Another committee — Hamilton, Ellsworth, and Bland — reported an order to General Howe to march on Philadelphia.[1] But Washington, deeply mortified at what had happened, was already taking measures to put down the mutiny. Congress was not further molested, and Ellsworth remained at Princeton about a fortnight longer. Late in July, Benjamin and Samuel Huntington arrived, and Samuel Huntington took his place on the committee to consider the proposal of a general convention.[2]

This was the end of his service in Congress. Writing to Trumbull on July 10,[3] he gave, in his usual matter-of-fact way, a moderate version of what had happened, and added:

" How long Congress will remain here is uncertain.

[1] Journals, VIII, 279–287, 292; Hunt's "Madison's Writings," I, 482, 484; Bancroft's "United States," VI, 97; Diplomatic Correspondence, 1783–1789, I, passim.
[2] For other services of Ellsworth in Congress in this period, see Journals, VIII, 91, 124–125, 176–177, 261.
[3] Trumbull Papers.

They will hardly return to Philadelphia, without some assurance of protection, or even then with the intention to stay longer than till accommodations shall be elsewhere prepared for a fixed residence.[1] But, Sir, it will soon be of very little consequence where Congress go, if they are not made respectable, as well as responsible, which can never be done without giving them a power to perform engagements, as well as to make them. It was, indeed, intended to have given them this power in the Confederation, by declaring their contracts and requisitions for the common defence sacredly binding on the States; but in practice it amounts to nothing. Most of the States recognize these contracts and comply with the requisitions so far only as suits their particular opinion and convenience. And they are the more disposed, at present, to go on in this way, from the irregularities it has already introduced, and a mistaken idea that the danger is over, — not duly reflecting on the calamities of a disunion and anarchy, or their rapid approach to such a state. There *must*, Sir, be a revenue somehow established, that can be relied on, and applied for national purposes, as the exigencies arise, independent of the will or views of a single State, or it will be impossible to support national faith or national existence. The power of Congress must be adequate to the purposes of their constitution. It is possible, there may be abuses and misapplication, still it is better to hazard *something*, than to hazard all."

---

[1] Ellsworth had been on the committee to consider the question of permanent residence, but the subject was postponed until autumn. Journals, VIII, 271.

It is not surprising that he was unwilling to come back to Congress;[1] or that, the next year, he also declined an election to the Board of Treasury, a commission set up for the management of the finances in place of Robert Morris, who had finally withdrawn, or, as he himself probably considered, escaped.[2] The choice of Ellsworth to this office by his former associates was a tribute to his capacity, but not to his shrewdness. His severe judgment of the Confederacy is even more convincing than Hamilton's, who went home in complete despair of it; for Ellsworth, never given to crossing bridges until he got to them, had come to his conclusions slowly. Always accepting dutifully the tasks assigned him, he had done his part well in the civil business of the struggle for independence; but holding, doubtless, that to each day its own evil was sufficient, he had not pressed forward in time of war to grapple with the problems of the hoped-for peace. Now, however, that peace was come, even his unhasting and conservative intelligence saw clearly the necessity of changes the most radical. Perhaps his gift of shrewd and practical analysis enabled him to see also that the time was not yet quite at hand; or perhaps, on the other hand, we must conclude that he was lacking in that rare, militant ardor of reform which Hamilton was so abundantly endowed with. At any rate, until the time was fully come, and through the tireless labors

[1] In May, 1783, he was elected for the year beginning Nov. 30, 1783. He resigned, however, and another was elected in his place. Roll of State Officers and Members of General Assembly of Connecticut, 460.

[2] The Board was instituted May 28, 1784, and six days later Daniel of St. Thomas Jenifer, Ellsworth, and William Denning were elected members. Journals, IX, 255–256, 309.

of Madison and Hamilton and Washington and a half-dozen other kindred spirits a great occasion was prepared, Ellsworth had no conspicuous part in the movements for a stronger constitution.   Instead, he passed quietly back into the labors of his profession and the service of his state.

CHAPTER IV

THE GREAT CONVENTION

His state was by no means disposed to part with his services. It is a question whether, in any representative government anywhere, the terms of public servants have ever been shorter, or their actual tenure more protracted, than in the colony of Connecticut. Officials both of the towns and of the colony were elected every year; but a good man, once elected, was, as a rule, reëlected until he died or resigned or moved up higher.[1] This democracy was not fickle. The usage continued for some time after the Revolution, and until, by the increase of population, the coming in of foreign elements, the growth of cities, the rise of parties, and perhaps by other causes, the political life of Connecticut and of all New England was gradually altered. If Ellsworth had never again entered the service of the United States, the chances are that his own people would have continued to choose him to higher and higher places in their state government so long as he was willing to accept them.

At the time of his retirement from Congress he held, it will be remembered, two not unimportant offices at home. He was still a member of the governor's council and state's attorney for Hartford County. In 1785, however, he accepted a judicial office of such a character that he could not continue

[1] See Sherman in Constitutional Convention, "Documentary History of the Constitution," III, 216–217.

to hold the other two. For a good many years, the
General Assembly had been from time to time devolv-
ing some of its judicial functions upon separate tribunals.[1] To that end, a "Particular Court" had been
set up as far back as 1638. It was succeeded in 1666
by a "Court of Assistants," made up from the council,
and this in turn gave way, in 1711, to a Superior Court.
Meanwhile, town and county courts had also been
established. In 1784, a law was passed which constituted the council, with the lieutenant-governor, a
Supreme Court of Errors, and it was in this tribunal
that Ellsworth's first judicial services were rendered.
Soon afterward, however, he was chosen also to the
Superior Court, and then, a law being passed to prevent
the same person from sitting in both the court and
the council, he retired from the council.[2] About the
same time, Jesse Root, who had taught him law, succeeded him as state's attorney for Hartford County.
For the next four years, his only office, apart from one
which for a few months took him back again to Philadelphia, was his place on the bench of the Superior
Court. The court consisted at this time of a chief
judge and four associate judges; and Roger Sherman
was one of the associates.

It is to be feared that only lawyers would find much

---

[1] In October, 1783, as chairman of a special committee of the General
Assembly, — presumably a joint committee of both houses, — Ellsworth
reported adversely on a proposal to relieve the legislature of a part of its
business by referring various petitions and memorials to some other tribunal. Trumbull Papers.

[2] Loomis and Calhoun, " Judicial and Civil History of Connecticut " ;
Johnston's " Connecticut," 189–190. From a letter of Ellsworth to Trumbull, written from Philadelphia, and now in the library of the Connecticut
Historical Society at Hartford, it appears that in March, 1780, he declined
an appointment to the Superior Court on the ground of ill health.

matter of interest in Ellsworth's career as a member
of his state's judiciary. A few great judges and famous
causes apart, the judicial side even of our national history fails to arouse in laymen the interest it deserves.
The development of our state courts is a chapter of
our institutional life that is not yet written; and if it
were written, it would probably be but little read. To
say that the Superior Court was a busy tribunal, with
a wide and various jurisdiction, both appellate and
original, that this was a formative period in the jurisprudence of Connecticut, and that Ellsworth's opinions,
so far as they were recorded, sustain his reputation as
a good lawyer and a just and able judge — this, perhaps, is to set down all that any but a very few readers
would care to learn. There were, however, at least two
classes of cases that came before him and his brother
judges concerning which a word more should be said;
for they presented to the court important opportunities
to choose between the old and the new. It could
either adhere to the provincial and archaic in the law
and usage of the commonwealth, or it could by its
decisions bring Connecticut's procedure in line with
modern tendencies. There were criminal causes involving punishments which would now seem barbarous
and cruel; and there were causes, both criminal and
civil, which brought out clearly the question of Connecticut's attitude toward the common law.

Alexander Johnston contends, with an uncharac-
teristic warmth, that the Blue Laws of Connecticut
ought never to have been made the standard illustration of puritanic narrowness and tyranny which to
most Americans they still remain.[1] Perhaps he is so

[1] Johnston's "Connecticut," 105–106.

far right that they ought not to be invidiously distinguished from the criminal and sumptuary laws of the
other New England colonies, and of other countries,
which belong to the same period of hard and fast ideas
in law, morals, and religion.   But to the present age
they do seem, nevertheless, absurdly inquisitorial and
excessively severe.   There were too many capital
offences; lesser crimes were punished in ways that
strike us now as harsh, unreasonable, absurd; and
laxities now entirely disregarded were treated as
crimes.   By the end of the Revolution, the code was
somewhat moderated by statute, and also, no doubt,
tempered with mercy and discretion in the courts.   As
in old England, some archaic laws, reflecting past conditions, were probably left unenforced, or even forgotten.
Nevertheless, while Ellsworth was on the bench in
Connecticut, some severe and curious sentences were
handed down.   At a session of the Supreme Court in
January, 1785, for instance, one Moses Parker, convicted of horse-stealing, was condemned " to sit on the
wooden horse half an hour; to receive fifteen stripes,
pay a fine of £10; be confined in the gaol and the
work house three months; and every Monday morning, for the first month, to receive ten stripes, and sit
on the wooden horse as aforesaid." [1]   The ride on the
wooden horse was probably the least severe of this
choice assortment of penalties; for the instrument of
torture was nothing worse than a log of wood, supported by four legs.   The criminal took his ride in
public, booted and spurred, usually before a large crowd
of amused spectators.   At the same session, Moses
Lusk, for counterfeiting, was also sentenced to be

[1] Van Santvoord, 222, and note.

whipped, fined, and imprisoned, and Judah Benjamin, a polygamist, received a sentence even harsher than Hester Prynne's in Hawthorne's "Scarlet Letter." Ten stripes were laid upon his back; the shameful "A" was branded on his forehead; and he was ordered to wear a halter about his neck so long as he should tarry in Connecticut, on penalty of thirty stripes if he were ever found without it.

Save that the tendency of the times was away from such severity, it is hardly possible to define the general attitude of Ellsworth and his fellows toward these rigorous laws. In at least one case, however, the court declined to be governed by the old puritanic usage. In a civil suit brought on a promissory note,[1] the defence set up was that the instrument had been executed at two o'clock in the morning of the Sabbath day. As no statute was clearly violated, and as it appeared that the note was given to release from prison a brother of the defendant, the court held it valid.

But for such advances as Connecticut was at this time making in the administration of justice she was more indebted to a young lawyer struggling into practice than to any of her judges. Beginning with two or three cases tried in 1785, Ephraim Kirby was making for the Superior Court the first fairly thoroughgoing reports of judicial decisions ever published in this country. His first volume,[2] covering substantially Ellsworth's term of service, closed with 1788, and there was no second; but he had, of course, his successors. He was greatly aided in his pioneer enterprise by a law passed in 1785, which required the judges to write out their decisions whenever they

[1] Carpenter *vs.* Crane, 1 Root's Reports, 98.   [2] Published 1789.

turned on a point of law. No one in the least familiar
with the use now made of many series of printed reports needs to be told the value of the practice which
was thus introduced; but Kirby himself has described
in his preface a troublesome confusion, somewhat
peculiar to Connecticut, which reporting doubtless
helped the judges to be rid of. "Our courts," he
writes, "were still in a state of embarrassment, sensible that the common law of England, though a highly
improved system, was not fully applicable to our situation; but no provision being made to preserve and
publish proper histories of their adjudications, every
attempt of the judges to run the line of distinction
between what was applicable and what was not,
proved abortive. For the principles of the decisions
were soon forgot or misunderstood, or erroneously
reported from memory. Hence arose confusion in the
determination of our courts, the rules of property
became uncertain, and litigation proportionately
increased."[1]

One doctrine was, that the law of Connecticut
was "derived from the law of nature and revelation ";[2]
and there were certain decisions rendered directly
contrary to common law principles. In several of
these cases, Ellsworth was the spokesman of the court.
But other decisions not only recognized the common
law but applied it "with strict and technical precision."[3] The best example is the case of Hart *vs.*
Smith,[4] in which the court held that *assumpsit* would
not lie to recover money paid by mistake in settling
an account. In this particular case, Ellsworth dis-

---

[1] For Kirby, see Van Santvoord, 218–219.   [3] Van Santvoord, 216.
[2] Root's Reports, Preface.   [4] Kirby, 127.

sented, and took a broader view, now generally accepted. His opinion on the question of what authority the common law of England had in Connecticut does not anywhere clearly appear.

In one account of the state's judicial history, he is eulogized as probably the ablest of all her judges.[1] But for this high estimate the single volume of Kirby and a few memoranda by Judge Root, who also essayed reporting, can hardly have constituted the sole material; it was based also, no doubt, on Ellsworth's services in a greater tribunal, and perhaps on a survey of his whole career.

Two biographers[2] have chosen the same decision to display his quality as a state-court judge. The case[3] involved the question of a married woman's right to devise her real estate to her husband, and Ellsworth took at the outset the ground that the right to devise is a municipal and not a natural right. He then proceeded:

" Admitting, however, that a right of devising estate was a natural right, it would not follow that a *feme-covert* has it, though there be no statute to take it away. Many natural rights are controlled by long use and custom, which may be evincive of common consent, and acquire, to every purpose, the force of law. Others are controlled by the reason of the case, arising out of some special relation or condition. We have no statute to divest a *feme-covert* of her personal estate; and yet nobody doubts but, by the act or condition of coverture, it becomes the husband's;

[1] Loomis and Calhoun, 176–177.
[2] Flanders and Van Santvoord.
[3] Adams *vs*. Kellogg, Kirby, 195, 438.

nor have we any that she shall not contract and bind her person and estate, as a *feme-sole* may; yet she cannot do it. It cannot, then, be inferred that a *feme-covert* has power to devise an estate, from the score of natural right. As to her supposed common law right to devise her estate, there has not been a custom or any adjudications to found it upon, either in this country or that from which we emigrated." And he went on to show, by briefly tracing the history of devises by women, that neither the common nor the statute law conceded to *feme-coverts* the right in question. The usage among the ancient Romans he attributes to their general notions of marriage; the tie was lighter than in Christian countries, and the woman freer in all her relations with her husband and society. His ending deals very broadly with the considerations of policy and of justice involved in the controversy.

"With regard to the policy of extending such a power to *feme-coverts*, it may be remarked, that there is not the same reason for it as there was for the statute empowering a husband to sell his wife's lands with her consent. From a sale of them she might have comfort and necessary support, but not from a devise. Besides, the freedom of her consent in that case is to be evinced, as fully as it may, by examination before a magistrate; which circumstance also, as well as that of recording, gives immediate notoriety to the transaction, that all concerned may scrutinize it while it can be done to advantage. Nor do the general reasons urged for the institution of wills extend to a *feme-covert*. That of their use in family government does not, because the government is not placed in her hands. Nor does that of their utility in stimulating to industry and economy; for her exertion adds nothing to the stock she is to dispose of. The crumbling down of overgrown estates need not be mentioned here. The possession of this power must be as inconvenient for *feme-coverts* as it is unnecessary. It must subject them to endless teasing and family discord, as well as frequently their heirs, and sometimes their children, to the loss of property, which the law has been studious to preserve for them. Add to which, exposed as they are to coercions imperceptible to others, and dangerous for them to disclose; placed in the power of a husband, whose solicitations they cannot resist, and whose commands, in all things lawful, it is their duty to obey. Their wills, taken in a corner, and concealed from the world till they have left it, can afford but very uncertain evidence of the real wishes of their hearts. Political considerations, therefore, so far as they can be of weight, serve to confirm the opinion, that a *feme-covert* has not power to dispose of her estate by will."

This is cogent reasoning, and the language terse and trenchant. Ellsworth, one feels, was not only a judge of more than ordinary wisdom but the kind of man who pondered on human relationships to practical conclusions — a man that could be trusted with the ordering of society and the safeguarding of interests and rights. His power of reasoning from policy was, no doubt, well tested when he and his associates dealt with certain unexampled cases which the war gave rise to. In these, the court's decisions were both wise and liberal. In one, an action brought against a deputy commissary for army purchases, it found for the defendant, holding that he was not liable, since he was acting merely as the agent of the public. In another, they decided that a negro slave had become a freeman when his master permitted him to serve in the Continental army.[1]

But in view of the greater things that Ellsworth was so soon to have a share in, it is difficult to combat our comparative indifference to the kind of work to which at this time he was giving himself.

The country, drifting though it seemed toward a division into separate confederacies or a disintegration into its unit states, was in reality soon to display in constructive politics an energy and virtue more remarkable than any it had shown in war; and with the coming of that period in his country's history there came also an end of the little things in Ellsworth's public career. From the year 1787 until the close of his active life there was scarcely anything he did or helped to do that will not demand to be remembered so long as the republic shall endure and keep its form.

Yet there does not survive a single speech or even a letter to show that during the interval following his retirement into the service of Connecticut he took any part whatever in the movement for a better system for the whole country. Neither did Connecticut have much part in it. Of all her public men, only Ellsworth's former protégé, Noah Webster, appeared conspicuously among the advocates of a stronger Union.

---

[1] Root's Reports, 93, 98. In this brief account of Ellsworth as a Superior Court Judge, I have drawn freely on Van Santvoord, whose treatment of the subject, though also brief, is careful, intelligent, and well informed.

When Virginia and Maryland took the lead and brought about a convention at Annapolis, Connecticut sent no delegates. The General Assembly had accepted the scheme of revenue commended to the states by Congress in the spring of 1783, but not without a long delay and a protest against one feature of it; for in Connecticut and other parts of New England the commutation of the army's half-pay was disrelished, and the right of Congress to grant the half-pay itself was questioned.[1] As New York would not accede to the scheme, it failed, and from that time Connecticut's responses to the requisitions of the helpless Congress were, like those of other states, absurdly slight. When a call was issued for a second convention of all the states, to meet at Philadelphia in May of 1787, she was almost the last to choose her delegates. Yet she was suffering very seriously from one of those glaring defects of the existing confederation which Madison and Washington and a few other broadly patriotic men were trying now to remedy. Of the products of other countries which her people consumed, only a very small proportion were brought into her own ports. The rest came chiefly through the ports of her neighbors, New York and Rhode Island, to whom in this way Connecticut paid tribute. That was one reason why New York and Rhode

[1] Oct. 24, 1783, Ellsworth wrote to Samuel Holton of Massachusetts: "I congratulate you also on another piece of intelligence that your wise and patriotic state has granted the impost — fully — by a unanimous vote of the Governor and Senate, and a majority of 16 in the House, — which I hope will have a good influence on our Assembly now sitting, the lower house of which have been too much disposed to risk everything rather than grant a revenue which might apply to commutation." Ellsworth Papers in the New York Public Library.

Island lagged behind in the movement to strengthen
the central government; why New York, though she
commissioned Hamilton one of her delegates to the
convention, sent along with him Yates and Lansing,
state-rights extremists, so that he should find himself a minority of one in his own delegation, and why
Rhode Island never would elect any delegates at all.

Connecticut elected hers on May 12,—only two days
before the date on which the convention was to have
assembled. The first choice of the Assembly was
Ellsworth, William Samuel Johnson, and Erastus
Wolcott of East Windsor.[1] But Wolcott declined
to serve, and Roger Sherman was chosen in his
place. Ellsworth must have set off very promptly,
for on May 28 he was in his seat in Independence
Hall in Philadelphia. That was the second sitting
of the convention, for many other members had been
late, and it was not called to order until the 25th.
Sherman appeared two days after Ellsworth, and
Johnson on the second day of June. Fortunately, a
member from a very different quarter of the Union,
Major William Pierce of Georgia, has left on record
the impression which these three Connecticut statesmen made upon him at the time.[2]

To Dr. Johnson this contemporary conceded " a
strong and enlightened understanding," but could not
find in the learned gentleman's speeches anything to
warrant his reputation for oratory. His discourse
was, indeed, eloquent, clear, and highly instructive,
but something in his voice displeased the ear. His

[1] Stiles's " Ancient Windsor," I, 905.
[2] *American Historical Review*, III, 310–334; given also in the notes to
Vol. III of Hunt's " Madison's Writings," *passim*.

manners, however, were distinguished, and he won the liking of his fellows by the sweetness of his temper and the affectionate way he had of addressing them. This was very different from his elder colleague's style. "Mr. Sherman," Pierce wrote, "exhibits the oddest shaped character I ever remember to have met with. He is awkward, unmeaning, and unaccountably strange in his manner. But in his train of thinking there is something regular, deep, and comprehensive, yet the oddity of his address, the vulgarisms that accompany his public speaking, and that strange New England cant which runs through his public as well as his private speaking make everything that is connected with him grotesque and laughable: — and yet he deserves infinite praise, — no man has a better heart or clearer head. . . . He is an able politician, and extremely artful in accomplishing any particular object; — it is remarked that he seldom fails. . . ." The youngest of the trio is described more briefly: " Mr. Ellsworth is a Judge of the Supreme Court in Connecticut; — he is a gentleman of a clear, deep, and copious understanding; eloquent, and connected in public debate; and always attentive to his duty. He is very happy in reply, and choice in selecting such parts of his adversary's arguments as he finds make the strongest impressions, — in order to take off the force of them, so as to admit the power of his own. Mr. Ellsworth is about thirty-seven years of age,[1] a man much respected for his integrity, and venerated for his abilities."

There was scarcely another delegate whom Pierce could praise with so little abatement. Yet his char-

---

[1] He was forty-two, in fact.

acter of Ellsworth consists with other portraits, and Pierce can scarcely have had any partiality for a New England man whom he probably saw now for the first time in his life. Beyond question, Connecticut's delegation was one of the strongest on the floor. Each of the three was a man of force, likely to hold his own in any representative assembly, and they labored together in exemplary friendliness, with an uncommon unanimity of purpose and opinion. No other Eastern state had chosen so happily.

Many writers have sought about for words to praise the great convention, but none, I think, has hit upon a better phrase than Major Pierce's; he calls it "the wisest council in the world." Sherman, who had sat in Congress with many of the older and more famous of the delegates, — himself the next in age to Franklin, — did not find himself abashed in such a presence, but began at once to take a full share in the discussions. Ellsworth, however, less known, and younger than Sherman by nearly a quarter of a century, sat for a fortnight in silence, forming, no doubt, his own deliberate judgment of the situation and the schemes proposed, and his own shrewd estimate of all these strong and independent men about him. Apart from the rollcalls, his name does not appear in any record of the proceedings under an earlier date than June 11, when he merely seconded a motion of Sherman's.[1]

Meanwhile, the convention, plunging at once into its work, had covered much important ground. With-

---

[1] "Documentary History of the Constitution," published by the Department of State, Washington, III, 108. This collection of documents is my authority for all specific statements about the convention for which no other authorities are given.

out some knowledge of its general plan of procedure, it will not be easy to see clearly what was the share of Ellsworth or of any other single member in the final outcome of its labors and debates.

Edmund Randolph, governor of Virginia, had led the way into the great field of statesmanship open to the Assembly by proposing, in an elaborate speech, a series of resolutions agreed upon by several of the Virginia delegates, and based on a plan of Madison's. They set forth the general scheme of a strong central government, to be made up of a distinctly national legislature of two houses, the first to be elected by the people, the second by the first, and of a national executive and judiciary, to be chosen by the legislature. The troubles which the old confederation had encountered from its lack of authority over individuals were squarely met by granting to the central legislature the right to make laws in all cases to which the several states were incompetent, or in which, through their uncontrolled activity, " the harmony of the United States " might be interrupted. There was even conferred a power to negative state laws which should seem to contravene the new articles of union, and to coerce any state that would not meet its obligations. Here was much more than a mere improvement of the articles. By giving to the government an immediate operation upon individual citizens, its whole character would be radically changed. It would be self-supporting and supreme. In making laws, in enforcing them by its executive, in administering justice through its courts, it would act always of its own authority and force, neither waiting for the states to approve its measures nor depending on them to pay the bills.

The Virginia resolutions, introduced the day after Ellsworth's arrival, were at once referred to a committee of the whole house, where they were under consideration until June 13, when the committee rose and reported them back to the convention with changes and additions. Throughout this early period of the debates, national men and the national motive had the ascendency. Hamilton, it is true, would have gone much farther than even Randolph proposed. He wished to overthrow completely the power and sovereignty of the states, and he wished also to abandon democracy and make the government distinctly aristocratic. But Read of Delaware was apparently the only other delegate who fully shared these views. Gouverneur Morris, though contemptuous of democracy and bent on anchoring all to property, fell somewhat behind the thoroughgoing Hamilton. Madison and his Virginian colleagues, whose prestige was, no doubt, controlling at the outset, were not committed either against democracy or against a reasonable authority in the states. As the debate proceeded, the representatives of New Jersey, Delaware, and Maryland gradually gained the confidence to speak out strongly against those parts of the Virginia plan which threatened the sovereignty and the equality of the several states, and they were abetted by Hamilton's New York colleagues. By the time the committee rose, there was a clear confrontment of national men and state-rights men, with the delegates from the larger states, as a rule, on one side, and the delegates from the smaller states on the other. The controversy ranged over various specific questions, but it centred about the question of how the central legislature should be chosen and composed.

The three delegates from Connecticut had come to Philadelphia with no other design than the general purpose to amend the old articles in those respects in which they had proved defective. After Sherman's death, there was found among his papers a series of nine proposals, which exhibit his view of what was needed in order to a better general government.[1] He desired merely to give Congress, constituted as it was, certain additional powers, among them the control of foreign and interstate commerce, and the power to levy and collect duties on imposts. He would have made its laws binding on the states and the people in everything pertaining to the common interest, he favored setting up a supreme central tribunal, and he would also have denied to the states certain powers which they had misused, like the power to emit bills of credit. But the scheme did not contemplate any radical change in the form or the basis of the government. Ellsworth, whether or not he helped to frame these proposals, showed, when he began to play a part in the convention, that they expressed substantially his own view also. He had, however, before Johnson came, differed with Sherman frequently, for on a number of questions the vote of Connecticut was " divided " and lost. The inference to be drawn from these early roll-calls is that of the two Sherman was somewhat the more rigid state-rights man. But they stood together, and Johnson with them, when the

---

[1] Evarts's "Sherman," in Sanderson's "Biographies of the Signers," 42–44; L. H. Boutell's "Sherman," 132–134. Bancroft ("History of the United States," VI, 231, note) thinks that this paper was probably written after Sherman's arrival in Philadelphia, and favors the notion that Ellsworth had a hand in framing it. Boutell, however, assigns it to "the latter part of Sherman's service in the Continental Congress."

issue between the small states and the large was clearly drawn. That was the issue before the convention when they made their motion of June 11.

The day before, William Paterson of New Jersey had with fire and bitterness assailed the whole plan before the house for its clear purpose and tendency to destroy the equality of the states in their common government by basing directly on population the apportionment of representatives in the legislature. Wilson, who seems from the first to have been the special champion of proportional representation in both houses, had answered him without making any concessions. Paterson and his following denied the convention's right, under the guise of amending the old articles, to accomplish such a revolutionary change, accused the great states of planning to reduce their lesser associates to utter impotence and insignificance, and began now to declare defiantly that the small states never would federate on any such terms. On the other hand, Wilson and others, pointing out that an equality of states in Congress meant in practice the government of an overwhelming majority of the people by a ridiculously small minority, declared that the great states would not submit to such injustice. The issue between the national and the federal or confederate principle was made quite as plain as that between the interests of the greater states — particularly Massachusetts, Pennsylvania, and Virginia — and the interests of the little states like New Jersey and Delaware. It seems now, in fact, much plainer; for there has never come about any such division between the big and the little states as was so often foreboded. Nevertheless, that apprehension was the source of the angriest of all the conflicts in the convention.

On the 11th, the whole subject of the ratio of representation in both houses was still under discussion. Various proposals had been made, and among them one by Sherman that contained the essence of a plan of compromise which the convention, after many times rejecting it, came at last to accept as the only way out of the controversy. The motion was that in the second branch of the legislature each state should have one vote. Shortly afterward, a motion for an "equitable ratio" in the first branch being carried (Connecticut voting ay), Rutledge's plan of a ratio based on contributions to the revenue was set aside for Wilson's simple rule of population. At this point, Sherman called for a question on the second branch, and Ellsworth, rising for the first time, seconded him.

They were voted down by Massachusetts, Pennsylvania, and all the states south of Maryland. Georgia and the Carolinas, expecting a rapid growth in wealth and numbers, felt that their interest lay with the great states. Of the little states, both New Hampshire and Rhode Island were still unrepresented. Wilson and Hamilton, promptly seizing the opportunity, pushed the national principle as far as it ever was advanced at any time in the convention. They moved the same ratio for the second branch as for the first, and the motion was carried by the same majority of six states to five. For weeks, this clause was stubbornly retained in the resolutions, which were now, to use a favorite phrase of Madison, "on the anvil," and gradually being hammered into the shape of a constitution.

The next day, Ellsworth and Sherman joined in a motion for annual elections to the first branch of Congress. Whenever this subject was up, Connecticut stood for brief terms of service. Her experience of annual elections had been peculiarly fortunate, and doubtless accounts in part for the strong faith in democracy which her delegates now exhibited at every opportunity. They stood alone against the whole clause on the term and pay of representatives, objecting both to the length of the term and to payment from the national treasury instead of by the states.

In the bigger contest between the two groups of states over the question of the national or federal character of the system to be established, the rising of the committee was the signal for an open show of force by the partisans of the little states. The convention adjourned for two days, to give them time to formulate their plan, and on the 15th Paterson reported it. There is no authentic list of those who helped him to frame it, but Madison states that it " had been concerted among the deputations, or members thereof, from Cont., N.Y., N.J., Del., and perhaps Mr. Martin of Maryland,"[1] explaining, however, that they consorted from different principles. Connecticut and New York were opposed to a departure from the principles of the old confederation ; they were willing to give a few new powers to Congress, but not to set up a national government. Delaware and New Jersey were chiefly concerned for an equality of representation. Madison adds that the attitude of the whole conservative party began now to produce serious anxi-

[1] "Documentary History of the Constitution," III, 124. See also Luther Martin's account in Elliot's "Debates," I, 344–389.

ety for the outcome of the convention. Howsoever the new plan was put together, it followed in its main lines the nine proposals which were afterward found among Sherman's papers, and which one historian has styled "the plan of Connecticut."[1] In place of the first resolution of the Virginia plan as it now stood, calling for a distinctly national government of three departments, Paterson proposed merely to amend and extend the old articles so as to meet the actual exigencies of the government and preserve the Union. His specific proposals were all in keeping with this general definition of the object to be sought. Not merely was Wilson's plan for electing the second branch of the legislature rejected; the second branch itself was rejected, and the old Congress left as it was, save that its powers were increased.

The consideration of the new plan, apart from general comparisons with its rival, never went beyond its opening resolution. Referred, along with the amended Virginia plan, to a committee of the whole house, it was scathingly criticised by Wilson and hotly defended by Paterson. The question being between the first resolutions of the two antagonistic programmes, Ellsworth offered, as a better means to take the sense of the committee, a resolution "that the legislative power of the United States should remain in Congress." Madison agreed that Ellsworth's motion was the better form for a division, but it was not seconded. This was on Saturday, the 16th. On Monday, Hamilton occupied the entire sitting of the committee with a long speech, condemning both plans as too weak and too democratic, and presented in rough outline a plan of

[1] Bancroft, VI, Table of Contents, and pp. 231-232.

his own. On Tuesday, the 19th, after a strong and patient argument from Madison, the Paterson scheme was definitely rejected, and the plan based on the Virginia resolutions again reported to the convention. Only New York, New Jersey, and Delaware voted no. Apparently, the Connecticut men were either somewhat moved by the strength of the national arguments and the national spirit, or else they had acted with the extreme state-rights men only to prevent the national men from going too far, not in the wish to keep the government entirely federal. The very next day, Sherman let fall something which may perhaps be taken to mean that there was already in the air the project of a compromise between the two warring theories. Speaking on the general form of the legislature, he declared that he was for one chamber rather than two; but he added that if the difficult question of representation could not be otherwise got over he would consent to two, provided each state were allowed an equal voice in the second.

If, however, the idea of compromise was in the air, this was for a while the only sign of it in the debates. The convention was now a second time going over the whole ground, examining in detail the report of the committee, minutely discussing it from many points of view, striking out, expanding, and amending. The majority was still with the large states and the national principle. At the outset of the second revision, however, Ellsworth secured a conspicuous amendment. For the phrase "a national government" in the opening resolution he moved to substitute "the government of the United States." The motion passed without dissent, and the title was never changed again. Perhaps, therefore, he ought to be credited with the naming of the government. He also began now to speak much more frequently, though seldom at great length; and there are signs that when he did speak the strongest men in the convention paid attention.

But it is misleading to try to estimate his or any other delegate's influence solely on the basis of what he did and said in the convention and in the committee of the whole. Robert Morris, for instance, never made a single speech; but it is hard to believe that he had nothing whatever to do with the outcome. Statesmanlike as this great body was, extraordinary as it was for nobleness and singleness of purpose, many of the members were veterans in politics; and they certainly did not on this occasion forbear to seek their ends by other methods than debate in the full assembly. We know from Madison and others that proceedings on the floor were on several important occasions governed by agreements elsewhere and otherwise arrived at. And of Ellsworth in particular we know that from his boyhood days at Princeton he had shown an uncommon skill in this kind of work. He was, in fact, an excellent politician, and he had even more than his share of Yankee shrewdness and of Yankee fondness for a bargain. The chances are that if, as early as Sherman's speech of the 19th of June, there was an understanding of any sort about the final composition of the houses, his younger colleague knew of it and was a party to it. And if, in abetting Paterson and Martin and other state-rights extremists, the men of a somewhat less uncompromisingly particularistic bent were merely trying to frighten the national men into certain concessions, Ellsworth doubtless fully understood that also.

Whether or not that was their object, they undoubtedly did inspire the gravest apprehensions in the leaders of the majority. When Paterson proposed his plan, Madison recorded that the opposition to a national government "began now to produce serious anxiety for the result of the convention." Mixed with the fear that the extreme state-rights men might withdraw altogether, there was the apprehension that New Hampshire might soon come in and bring about a deadlock, and there was also, perhaps, some uneasiness about the course of Georgia, which was still the least populous of all the states, and must look well into the future for any reason for voting with the great-states party. Moreover, Delaware had expressly instructed her delegates against any change of that provision in the articles which gave to each state one vote in Congress. The opponents of proportional representation were not without resources for resistance or for compromise.

Meanwhile, as the revision proceeded in convention, Ellsworth sustained with speeches some of the opinions which he had indicated already by his votes in committee. He spoke for annual elections to the first branch of the legislature,[1] urging that the people were fond of frequent elections and might in one branch safely be indulged; and when the clause providing that representatives should be paid from the national treasury again came up, he moved to strike it out in order to substitute payment by the states. He pointed out[2] that under the proportional plan

[1] June 20.   [2] June 22, Yates, in Elliot's "Debates," I, 434.

this would mean no hardship to the smaller states; that the standard of living differed in different states; and that therefore uniformity would work unequally and might arouse opposition.   Hamilton, who was one of his opponents on this point, prophesied that the state governments would be the rivals of the general government, and ought not, therefore, to be its paymasters.   Ellsworth promptly retorted: " If we are so exceedingly jealous of state legislatures, will they not have reason to be equally jealous of us ?   If I return to my state, and tell them, ' We made such and such regulations for a general government because we dared not trust you with any extensive powers,' — will they be satisfied ?   Nay, will they adopt your government ?   And let it ever be remembered that, without their approbation, your government is nothing more than a rope of sand." [1]   But on both these points he was beaten.

By the 25th of June, the revision had come again to the constitution of the second branch of the legislature.   As the resolution stood, the legislatures of the states were to choose this branch.   Wilson moving to strike the clause out in order to a choice by electors, Ellsworth replied in his first speech of any considerable length. [2]   " Whoever chooses the member," he contended, " he will be a citizen of the

[1] "Documentary History of the Constitution," III, 190.
[2] *Ibid.*, 209–210; Yates, in Elliot's "Debates," I, 446–447; King, in "Life and Correspondence of Rufus King," by C. R. King, I. 607. With Ellsworth's speeches in the convention I have followed Bancroft's method, collating all the reports to be found. It is, I think, a legitimate method to obtain a notion of what he actually said, and particularly to make his reasoning clear.   None of the reports is perfect.

state he is to represent and will feel the same spirit and act the same part whether he be appointed by the people or the legislature. Every state has its particular views and prejudices, which will find their way into the general councils, through whatever channel they may flow." The forecast was right, for even to the present day the entire delegation of a particular state, senators and representatives, will usually stand together when its interests are in issue or its desires need to be expressed. He was also of opinion that if wisdom were the object in the second branch the legislatures and not the people ought to elect it. Turning then to the mooted question of what part the states should have in the new system, he said:

"We must build our general government on the strength and vigor of the state governments. Without their coöperation it would be impossible to support a Republican government over so great an extent of country. An army would scarcely render it practicable. The largest states are the worst governed. Virginia is obliged to acknowledge her incapacity to extend her government to Kentucky. Massachusetts cannot keep the peace one hundred miles from her capital, and is now forming a standing army for its support. How long Pennsylvania may be free from a like situation cannot be foreseen. If the principles and materials of our government are not adequate to the extent of these single states, how can it be imagined that they can support a single government throughout the United States? We know that the people of the states are strongly attached to their own constitutions. If you hold up a system of general government destructive of their constitutional rights, they will oppose it. Some are of opinion that, if we cannot form a general government so as to destroy the state governments, we ought at least to balance the one against the other. On the contrary, the only chance we have to support a general government is, to graft it on the state governments. I want to proceed on this ground, as the safest, and I believe no other plan is practicable."

It really seems as if at this time Ellsworth had felt his way nearer than any other member not merely to a practical adjustment but to that conception of a partly national, partly federal system which this assembly contributed to the art of government. It was a new conception, and to ordinary thinking far from easy. Neither Ellsworth nor the convention can be said to have created or invented it, but only to have discovered it. The delegates were gradually led to it by the demands of the actual situation which they had in hand.

Madison and others were for going on at once to the question of the ratio in the Senate, but for a little while the convention continued to consider the method of election, the stipend, and the term of service. Wilson was defeated, and the choice of the second branch by legislatures was not again seriously attacked. But when Sherman spoke for a short term of service, Hamilton took the other side, and in a brief but very remarkable speech his intellect played upon the happy working of democracy in Connecticut in a way that fully explains why this young statesman of thirty was *felt* by his associates in the convention as scarcely any other man of his time was when

strong men came together. He showed, in fact, a
clearer comprehension of Connecticut's still simple
civilization than Sherman had, who had known it all
his life. Hamilton had divined it, as, according to
Talleyrand's famous encomium, he divined Europe.
Ellsworth, for his part, moved again for payment by
the states, and encountered for his particular opponent
Madison, who pointed out that if the motion passed
the states would really have a power of recall, and
fix the term of service to suit themselves. It was
voted down, and then, adopting without debate the
resolution empowering each house to originate measures of all kinds, the convention took up, out of their
order, the two resolutions that dealt with the ratio of
representation. When Luther Martin had finished
a speech, delivered " with great diffuseness and considerable vehemence," and so long that it ran over
well into the second day, Lansing of New York
brought forward the extreme state-rights proposal to
leave the suffrage in the new legislature precisely as
it was in the old Congress, and the controversy was
soon as warm as it had ever been. Franklin, whose
greatest services in the convention were rendered less
by statesmanship than by knowledge of human nature,
and particularly by the tact and wisdom he displayed
in dealing with the men about him, rose and moved,
with a short and serious speech, that thenceforth,
every day, the help of Heaven be implored. The
sitting ended without a formal adjournment.

It was clear to all that the convention had come
to the turning point in its history; its success or
failure would depend on its course with the question
of the suffrage in the two houses. It is true that

the antagonism of interest between the large states and the small was fanciful; the apprehension of it is a striking instance of the fallibility of the strongest minds. But the issue between the national and federal principles was both real and vital. If the new system was to be, in any respect whatever, truly federal, then the states, as states, must continue to be somehow represented in the government. Apparently, while many saw that this was so, the delegates from Connecticut saw somewhat sooner and more clearly than the others that the two principles could be harmonized and correlated, and they also saw a way to do it. Perhaps they were impelled by an immediate desire to win from the convention as much of what they had originally demanded as it could possibly be brought to concede; but for being, in that respect, no more than human, they ought not to be greatly blamed. With the best and wisest of their fellows, they were also, no doubt, quickened in their contriving by an earnest wish to bring about such an agreement as would keep the convention from breaking up in anger and despair.

The next day, the 29th, Johnson opened the debate, speaking for a compromise, the people to be represented in the first branch, the states in the second. It should have been plain to the state-rights extremists that their fight for the old arrangement — a single house, with an equal vote for every state — was lost. Hamilton and Madison assailed them with powerful reasoning and moving appeals. Gorham spoke so despairingly of the prospect if they should remain obdurate, that Ellsworth remarked, " He did not despair; he still trusted that some good plan of government would be devised and adopted." Lansing's motion was then voted down, and proportional representation in the first branch was adopted. Johnson and Ellsworth immediately moved to take up the resolution on the suffrage in the second branch. That motion carrying, Ellsworth moved to substitute the rule of the old Congress for the second branch, and spoke at greater length than ever before.[1]

" He was not sorry, on the whole, that the vote just passed had determined against this rule in the first branch.[2] He hoped it would become a ground of compromise. He confessed that the effect of his motion was to make the general government partly federal and partly national. This would secure tranquillity, and still make it efficient; and it would meet the objections of the larger states. The proportional representation in the first branch was conformable to the national principle and would secure the large states against the small. In taxes they would have a proportional weight. An equality of voices was conformable to the federal principle, and was necessary to secure the small states against the large. He trusted that on this middle ground a compromise would take place. He did not see that it could on any other. And if no compromise should take place, our meeting would be in vain, and worse than in vain. If the large states refused this plan, we should be forever separated. If the Southern states agreed to a popular instead of a state representation, we should produce a separation. To the Eastward, he was sure that Massachusetts was the only

[1] Madison, Yates, and King, as above.
[2] Connecticut had voted for Lansing's motion.

State that would listen to a proposition for excluding the states, as equal political societies, from an equal voice in both branches.[1] The others would risk every consequence rather than part with so dear a right. An attempt to deprive them of it was at once cutting the body of America in two, and, as he supposed would be the case, somewhere about this part of it. The Union must be cut in two at the Delaware. The large States, he conceived, would, notwithstanding the equality of votes, have an influence that would maintain their superiority. Even in the executive, the larger states had ever had influence. Holland, as had been admitted (by Mr. Madison), had, notwithstanding a like equality in the Dutch Confederacy, a prevailing influence in the public measures. Small communities, when associating with greater, could only be supported by an equality of votes. The power of self-defence was essential to the small States. Nature had given it to the smallest insect of creation. He could never admit that there was no danger of combinations among the large states. They will, like individuals, find out and avail themselves of the advantage to be gained by it. It was true the danger would be greater if they were contiguous and had a more immediate common interest. Yet they might be partially attached to each other for mutual support and advancement. They would be able to combine, and therefore there was no danger. A defensive combination of the small states was rendered more difficult by their greater number. Three or four could more easily enter into combination than nine or ten.

---

[1] No doubt he meant (and probably said) " excluding the states, etc., in both branches, from an equal voice."

"He would mention another consideration of great weight. The existing confederation was founded on the equality of the states in the article of suffrage; was it meant to pay no regard to this antecedent plighted faith? It was not yet obvious to him that the states would depart from this ground. When in the hour of our common danger we united as equals, should it now be urged by some that we must depart from this principle when the danger is over? Would the world say that this is just? We then associated as free and independent states, and were well satisfied. Let a strong executive, judiciary, and legislative power be created; but let not too much be attempted, by which all may be lost. Nor would he be surprised (though we made the general government the most perfect, in our opinion,) that it should hereafter require amendment. But at present this was as far as he could possibly go. If this convention only chalked out lines of good government, we should do well. He was not in general a half-way man; yet he preferred doing half the good he could, rather than do nothing at all. The other half might be added when the necessity should be more fully experienced."

Time has dispelled the fear of the larger states' combining, and the event has justified the convention in departing from the letter of its commission and supplanting with a better the system it was authorized only to amend; but this was, nevertheless, a remarkable speech. None that preceded it had grasped the entire problem of an adjustment so fully and so firmly. Of all Ellsworth's speeches that have been preserved in any form, only two or three can be compared with it. For two days the leaders of the national group

were trying in vain to break the force of it; and until
the vote was taken on his motion — probably the most
momentous of all the divisions, for the fate of the convention seemed to depend on it — he was the leader of
his side. Up to this time, whenever the second branch
was under discussion, Sherman had seemed to take the
lead; but now Ellsworth's figure was much the more
distinct. The state-rights extremists had been thrust
aside, and he, with the plan of a compromise, stepped
into the forefront of the opposition.

Before the next day's debate began, Brearly of New
Jersey moved that a message be sent to New Hampshire to urge the immediate attendance of her delegates; it was presumed, of course, that they would
side with the smaller states. The motion was voted
down as of a nature to reveal to the country the convention's peril; but it had doubtless served its real
purpose as a warning and reminder. Wilson, in a
long speech, then assailed the reasoning of Ellsworth.
With skill and force he rang the changes on the great
injustice and unwisdom of a federal arrangement.
Should the men in the convention who represented
three-fourths of the people yield to those who served
but one-fourth? In the government to be established,
should two-thirds submit themselves to one-third?
For whom were gentlemen forming a government?
Was it for *men*, or for imaginary beings called
states? No one had yet offered any explanation of
the danger of the large states' combining. It was all
illusive and imaginary. On the other hand, it was
true that the false majority in the second branch
could not carry measures over the majority in the
first; but they could prevent measures. And was it

not to remedy that very weakness the convention had
been called?

Ellsworth, rejoining immediately, was true to
Pierce's account of him; he struck at once at what
was strongest in his adversary's speech.

" The capital objection of Mr. Wilson, that the
minority will rule the majority, is not true. The
power is given to the few to save them from the many.
If an equality of votes had been given to them in both
branches, the objection might have had weight. Is it
a novel thing that the few should have a check on the
many? Is it not the case in the British Constitution,
the wisdom of which so many gentlemen have united
in applauding? Have not the House of Lords, who
form so small a proportion of the nation, a negative on
the laws, as a necessary defence of their peculiar rights
against the encroachments of the Commons? No instance of a confederacy has existed in which an equality of voices has not been exercised by the members
of it. We are running from one extreme to another.
We are razing the foundations of the building, when
we need only repair the roof. No salutary measure
has been lost for want of *a majority of the states* to
favor it. If security be all that the great states wish
for, the first branch secures them."

Even on the danger of a combination of the large
states, the weakest part of his contention, this rejoinder
was not entirely ineffective. It proves, at any rate,
that Ellsworth was ready and resourceful.

" The danger of combinations among them is not
imaginary," he declared. " Although no particular
abuses could be foreseen by him, the possibility of them
was sufficient to alarm him. But he could easily con-

ceive cases in which they might result from such combinations. Suppose that in pursuance of some commercial treaty or arrangement three or four free ports, and no more, were to be established: would not combinations be formed in favor of Boston, Philadelphia, and some port in Chesapeake? A like concert might be formed in the appointment of the great officers."

He appealed again to the obligations of the federal pact, which was still in force, and which had been entered into with so much solemnity, persuading himself that some regard should still be paid to the plighted faith under which each state, small as well as great, held an equal suffrage in the general councils. And he doubtless gave a greater moral force to his contention by adding: " His remarks were not the result of particular or local views. The state he represented held a middle rank."[1]

Madison, rising immediately, "did justice to the able and close reasoning of Mr. E.," and strove to weaken its effect. Catching at Ellsworth's assertion that in all confederate governments there was equality of suffrage, he cited instances to the contrary. But in replying to the plea for "antecedent plighted faith " he fell into a worse blunder himself: he attacked Connecticut as of all the states the last that should have made the plea. Turning to the real issue, he argued, wisely enough, that the antagonism truly to be feared was not between the great states and the little, but between the Southern and the Northern. Yet he had no plan to propose by which the two sections could be balanced.

[1] Madison and Yates, collated.

Ellsworth's quick rejoinder must have been effective both as debating and as oratory. For once, his old labors at the Pay Table brought him a reward.

" My state," he said,[1] " has always been federal, and " — turning to Washington — " I can with confidence appeal to your excellency for the truth of it during the war. The muster rolls will show that she had more troops in the field than even the state of Virginia. We strained every nerve to raise them; and we spared neither money nor exertions to complete our quotas. This extraordinary exertion has greatly distressed and impoverished us, and it has accumulated our state debts. We feel the effects of it even to this day. But we defy any gentleman to show that we ever refused a federal requisition. We are constantly exerting ourselves to draw money from the pockets of our citizens as fast as it comes in; and it is the ardent wish of the state to strengthen the federal government. If she has proved delinquent through inability, it is no more than others have been, without the same excuse."

Sherman clinched the refutation by again pointing out that Madison's object required him to prove the *constitution of Congress* at fault: he had only proved the states at fault. What was really needed was to give more power to the government. As others came into the discussion, it grew every moment keener and more anxious. Davie of North Carolina was much moved by Ellsworth's speeches, and showed plainly enough his discontent with the replies to them. Beyond question, the Connecticut idea was gaining favor. For the first time, Wilson offered a slight concession, agreeing that the smallest state, Delaware, ought under

[1] Yates, in Elliot's " Debates," I, 469, 470.

any ratio to have at least one representative in the second branch. He and Rufus King of Massachusetts displayed, however, a strong resentment at the half-threat of the small states that without equality in one branch they would not confederate at all. Wilson firmly declared that if this were so he was for letting them withdraw. King was of the same temper, and seemed to warn the opposition that this was their last chance to come into the Union. Gunning Bedford of New Jersey, angered by this language, went still farther in retorting. If, he said, the plan of the majority should go forth to the people, this would prove, truly enough, the last moment for a fair trial in favor of good government. But he was under no apprehensions. " The large states dare not dissolve the confederation," he declared. " If they do, the small ones will find some ally of more honor and good faith, who will take them by the hand and do them justice." Before he took his seat, however, he tried to soften this threat; and before he could be answered, Ellsworth, rising for the third time, spoke again, replying to a question King had put to him.

" I am asked," he said,[1] "by my honorable friend from Massachusetts, whether, by entering into a national government, I will not equally participate in the national security. I confess I should; but I want domestic happiness as well as general security. A general government will never grant me this, as it will not know my wants or relieve my distress. My state is only one out of thirteen. Can they — the general government — gratify my wishes? My happiness depends as much on the existence of my state government as a

[1] Yates, in Elliot's "Debates," I, 473.

new-born infant depends upon its mother for nourishment. If this is not an answer, I have no other to give."

But Bedford did not escape. King, an eloquent speaker, scored him severely; and with this exchange the sitting ended. At the next, July 2, without any more debate, Ellsworth's motion was put. The vote was a tie. For the first time, the national, large-states majority was broken.

It was Georgia that had changed. Her vote, hitherto regularly given to the majority, was this time divided.[1] It was, in fact, one man only that had changed, and that man was Abraham Baldwin, a native of Connecticut, a graduate and sometime tutor of Yale, and but recently become a citizen of the state which he now sat for. The facts countenance a conjecture that the personal influence of the three leading men of his native state may have helped to turn him;[2] but he may also have felt, as Georgia was the last state to vote, and had but two representatives, that he and his colleague had to decide whether the convention should continue in existence. He had said that he thought the second branch ought to be an aristocratic body, and his votes, both before and after this particular division, show that he was favorable to the national view. The chances are that to save the convention he had for the time being sacrificed his own opinions.[3]

The question now was, Would the majority yield? The two Pinckneys at once brought forward an

[1] Maryland also was divided, on account of Mr. McHenry's absence. Luther Martin, in Elliot's "Debates," I, 349.

[2] A close student of the literature of the convention declares, "It is ten to one Ellsworth managed him."

[3] See Martin, in Elliot's "Debates," I, 356.

impossible plan for the proportional representation, not of states, but of sections. A committee was proposed. Sherman said: "We are now at a full stop. Nobody, I suppose, meant that we should break up without doing anything." He favored a committee. Gouverneur Morris, still for making the second branch the stronghold of property, also favored it. Wilson, disappointed and unreconciled, and Madison, still distrustful, both opposed it. A grand committee of one from each state was, however, chosen by ballot. From Connecticut, Ellsworth was taken, and the convention had the good sense to put on Dr. Franklin from Pennsylvania. Everything was so plainly in suspense until the great point should be decided that the convention adjourned over from Monday to Thursday, July 5, to wait for the report.

When it came, it had the form of a compromise; but a compromise in which, obtaining all that they themselves had fought for, the federal men offered to the national men something they had not demanded. The committee recommended that in the second branch each state should have an equal vote, and that bills to raise and appropriate money and to pay official salaries should originate in the first branch and should not be altered or amended in the second. The specific plan was Franklin's. Ellsworth had not served on the committee; a note of Madison's tells us that he was kept away by indisposition and that Sherman took his place. Madison also reports that in the committee Sherman proposed another plan. He moved, " That each state should have an equal vote in the second branch, provided that no decision therein should prevail unless the majority of states concurring should also comprise a majority of the inhabitants of the United States;" but the motion was not seriously entertained. This was substantially the same plan that Sherman had proposed more than ten years earlier for the Articles of Confederation.

The national men had suffered a defeat; but the federal men had not yet won their victory. Wilson said the committee had exceeded their powers. Madison argued that the concession in the matter of money bills was valueless, and that it would lead to conflicts between the houses. Others attacked the proposal on other grounds. Ellsworth merely remarked that he had not attended the meetings of the committee, but was ready to accede to the report. "Some compromise was necessary, and he saw none more convenient or reasonable." George Mason of Virginia thought it at least preferable to an appeal to the world by the different sides. His deep anxiety was obvious. A country gentleman, and far from home, he vowed that he would bury his bones in Philadelphia rather than leave his country to the fate that awaited it if the convention failed. Gerry of Massachusetts spoke in the same tone; while on the other side there was not a sign of yielding. For ten days longer, the fate of the compromise was still in doubt. On July 10, Washington wrote to Hamilton:[1] "When I refer you to the state of the counsels which prevailed when you left the city, and add that they are now, if possible, in a worse train than ever, you will find but little ground on which the hope of a good establishment can be formed. In a word, I almost despair of seeing a favorable issue in the proceedings of our convention, and do therefore

[1] Sparks, "Writings of Washington," IX, 260.

repent having had any agency in the business." [1] It seemed as if, the longer the whole subject of the constitution of the legislature was up, the more the members differed about it. One new question after another continued to be raised. Should the ratio of representation in the first house be based on population, or property, or both? At what intervals should censuses be taken? Until the first was taken, what should be the ratio? Should new states be admitted to an equality with the old? In estimating population, should negro slaves be counted? Once this last inquiry came before the convention, it found itself engaged, at the same time, with two most difficult antagonisms. Morris increased the confusion with a motion that taxation should be apportioned according to representation. Several of these questions were referred to committees. In dealing with them all, Ellsworth seems to have been governed chiefly by a steady purpose to carry through the programme of adjustment. On July 7, by a vote of six to three, the clause conceding equality in the second branch was kept in the report. But that was not the end. At every opportunity, Wilson and Madison and Morris and others were battling with the drift toward Connecticut's position. Saturday, July 14, when Martin called for the question on the whole report, they tried to substitute another plan of Pinckney's, which gave to each state a fixed number of representatives in the second branch. When they had again recounted all the old objections to the federal convention, Ellsworth merely rose and asked two questions. He asked

[1] "We were on the verge of a dissolution, scarce held together by the strength of a hair." Luther Martin, in Elliot's "Debates," I, 358.

Wilson whether, in the old Congress, he had ever
seen a good measure fail for want of a majority of
states; and he asked Madison whether a negative
lodged with a majority of the states, even the smallest,
could be more dangerous than a qualified negative
lodged in a single executive magistrate, who must
be taken from some one state.

Pinckney's motion was defeated, and on Monday,
the 16th, without any more debating, the division was
taken. This time, Georgia was against the plan of
compromise; but Caleb Strong and Elbridge Gerry
voted " ay," dividing Massachusetts, and North Carolina passed over to the ays. New York was absent.
The vote was five to four in favor of the compromise,
and the decision proved to be final. One week later,
Morris and King moved that the voting in the second branch should be *per capita*, and only Delaware
objected. Ellsworth remarked that he had always
been in favor of voting in that mode. The same day,
the number of senators from each state was fixed at
two. The constitution of the Senate was determined.

However, the vote of the 16th was no sooner
taken than Randolph, deeply vexed, spoke of an adjournment. Paterson, taking him to mean adjournment *sine die*, challenged him to move it. But the
men from the big states were not ready to go that far.
They did indeed show, plainly enough, that they were
bitterly disappointed. The next day, before the hour
of meeting, they held a conference, and some of them
at that time talked of forming a union of their own,
without the smaller states. But others were frankly
for giving up the fight. The conference merely convinced the victors that they need not be afraid.

And this, no doubt, was what the men who made the compromise had counted on. They had judged rightly of the lengths to which each side would go. It was the state-rights extremists who were really dangerous. Some of these, even now, were far from satisfied. Yates and Lansing of New York had already left the convention. Before the end, Luther Martin of Maryland also withdrew. Neither, as the event proved, had the state-rights sentiment among the people been overestimated. As it was, the extraordinary advocacy of Hamilton hardly succeeded in overcoming the state-rights party in New York. In other states, the fight for ratification was nearly as close. Rhode Island and North Carolina held out several years. Ellsworth and his party had been remarkably near the truth in all their calculations.

If, now that a hundred years and more have passed, we try to form a judgment of their course in all its bearings, with all its consequences, we shall, I think, conclude that it was wise. Ellsworth was right when he declared both that a compromise was necessary and that no other compromise was possible. To perpetuate the union, a nation must be formed; but it had to be a federal nation. Nor is necessity the only ground on which we can defend the convention for leaving the federal principle in the government. It has, no doubt, cost us heavily to keep it there. For many of our tasks and opportunities, a government completely national might have been much better. It may be argued, even, that but for this concession to the states we never should have had the Civil War. That, however, is extremely questionable. The true causes of the Civil War were institutional; and constitutions

do not, as a rule, alter institutions — they are more
often made and altered by them. At any rate, nine
out of ten of us would probably now decide that the
federal principle is worth far more than it has ever
cost. And as for the union of the two principles in
one government, it is hard to overestimate the value,
to us and to mankind, of that invention or discovery.
To those who made it, the world owes such a debt as
that it owes to the illustrious men who from time to
time have revealed to their fellows some new law or
some new energy of nature. Their place in the history
of government is much like Newton's in the history of
science, or Darwin's, or Galileo's. And if, in nature,
we seek for a harmony of warring principles to match
with this of theirs in government, we find it nowhere
short of that immense and noble equilibrium which
throughout the entire solar system holds each satellite
loyal to its star, and keeps the stars, in all their mighty
circling, obedient to the suns.

Of Ellsworth's part, or any other one man's part,
in this most epochal achievement, it is not possible
to speak with perfect confidence. The material is not
sufficient. By a sort of consensus of historians, however, the chief part in it was either his or Sherman's.
It is quite probable that from first to last these two
were acting together to the same general end; and
others may have shared their counsels. By those who
feel that Sherman was the leader, it is pointed out
that ten years earlier he had taken much the same
position. It was he, too, who offered the first motion
looking to a compromise. He made more speeches
for it, perhaps, than any other. And later on, after Ellsworth left, it was he who first proposed to guarantee to

each state forever, even against amendments properly proposed and ratified, an equal representation in the Senate.[1] Yet to one who with an open mind follows all the motions and the speeches it will appear, I think, that Ellsworth's speeches were the stronger. His position was also closer than Sherman's to the final stand of the convention, and he spoke, almost from the beginning, with a kind of authority, as one who not only knew his own mind, and felt that he was right, but saw his way to victory. When, after many reverses, victory came, the fight was on his motion, the debate centred about his speeches, the leaders of the other side behaved toward him as if he were the leader. In Sherman's first reference to the particular plan which finally prevailed, he did not speak of it as if he were himself the author of it; on the contrary, almost to the end, he said that he preferred an appreciably different plan. When a committee was appointed, Ellsworth was chosen for Connecticut. Although he was indisposed, and Sherman served in his place, it was not Sherman who suggested the form of the report.

But these two long-dead statesmen were always, while they lived, the best of friends. After Sherman died, Ellsworth never failed, when he went to New Haven, to pay a visit to the other's grave. Perhaps we do them both a wrong to drag them into a posthumous rivalry for glory they were both content to share.

From this achievement of the two Connecticut leaders we must turn to another chapter of the con-

[1] See letter of George Frisbie Hoar — a grandson of Sherman — printed as an appendix to H. C. Lodge's "A Fighting Frigate, and Other Essays."

vention's history in which they are seen by no means at their best. The differences over the ratio of representation had led, almost at once, to a controversy over slavery, and on that issue they took a stand which it is now hardly possible to approve.

On the question of how negro slaves should be treated, whether as men or as property, Sherman and Ellsworth had both adhered to the arrangement first proposed in April, 1783, when Ellsworth was in Congress. Utterly illogical as it was, the plan of treating five slaves as equivalent to three free white men had got already a wide acceptance. It had, therefore, a certain advantage over every other plan proposed. Advancing from it as from a concession already made to her interests, South Carolina now demanded representation for all the slaves. Gouverneur Morris and one or two other members protested bitterly against recognizing slavery in any way, but from the first it seems to have been felt that their uncompromising view could not prevail. The practical question being merely how much should be conceded in order to keep Georgia and the Carolinas in the Union, Ellsworth, who stood committed to the three-fifths ratio as a basis for taxation, was for making it the basis of representation also. After Morris had carried through his resolution " that direct taxation ought to be proportioned to representation," and after Morris and Davie of North Carolina had exchanged strong language over slavery, Ellsworth moved the three-fifths rule, to hold until a census should be taken. Randolph wished to make the rule perpetual, and this substitute Ellsworth readily accepted. July 12, Pinckney's motion, that all the slaves be counted, was voted down, Randolph's proposal was adopted, and from that time the three-fifths rule never seems to have been in any real danger. It was accepted as a part of the great compromise.

It was late in August before Ellsworth spoke again on slavery. The resolutions, shaped now into a formal constitution, were passing the third time in review. The powers of Congress were under discussion, and two proposals, not apparently related, were, nevertheless, quickly associated by the spirit of compromise and bargain. The New England states were for giving Congress complete control of foreign commerce, with power to pass a navigation act; and the opponents of slavery were for giving it power to prohibit the foreign slave trade. In this second proposal Virginia heartily concurred; she had already prohibited the traffic. But Georgia and the Carolinas stood out against the plan. These two states, having little or no shipping interest of their own, were also opposed to a navigation act. Fearing that the Eastern ship-owners might acquire a monopoly of the carrying trade, they were quite willing to continue to make use of foreign bottoms. The draft of the Constitution then before the convention denied to Congress the power to prohibit the slave trade and gave it the power to pass a navigation act by a two-thirds vote of both houses. Luther Martin had moved to grant Congress control over the slave trade also, and Rutledge had answered him, when Ellsworth rose.[1] The true question, Rutledge had bluntly declared, was whether the Southern states should or should not be parties to the union. He put the matter wholly on the ground of

[1] August 21, "Documentary History of the Constitution," III, 584.

interest; religion and humanity, he declared, had nothing to do with it.

Ellsworth seems to have agreed with this contention. He was for leaving the clause as it stood. " Let every state import what it pleases," he said. " The morality or wisdom of slavery are considerations belonging to the states themselves. What enriches a part, enriches the whole, and the states are the best judges of their particular interest. The old confederation had not meddled with this point, and he did not see any greater necessity for bringing it within the policy of the new one."

The next day, the debate grew general and heated. Sherman indorsed Ellsworth's position, and a noble speech of George Mason of Virginia contrasted strangely with the language of these two New England representatives. Mason bitterly bewailed the fact of slavery, and upbraided sternly all who still engaged in the "nefarious traffic," sparing neither the shipowners of the East nor the planters of the lower South. No better arraignment of the whole system was ever made.

It is impossible to read Ellsworth's reply with any satisfaction. As he had never owned a slave, he said, he could not judge of the effect of slavery on character. If, however, it was to be considered in a moral light, the convention ought to go farther and free those already in the country. " As slaves also multiply so fast in Virginia and Maryland that it is cheaper to raise than import them, whilst in the sickly rice swamps foreign supplies are necessary, if we go no farther than is urged, we shall be unjust toward South Carolina and Georgia. Let us not intermeddle. As population increases, poor laborers will be so plenty as to render slaves useless. Slavery in time will not be a speck in our country. Provision is already made in Connecticut for abolishing it. And the abolition has already taken place in Massachusetts. As to the danger of insurrection from foreign influence, that will become a motive to kind treatment of slaves."

The sarcasm, if that was what he meant his opening for, was wasted on a character like Mason's. The intimation that Virginia was merely seeking her own interest as a breeder of slaves was also unjust; Washington and Madison, as well as Mason, have left on record too many proofs that they were, from conviction and from conscience, antislavery men. The appeal for "justice" to the "sickly rice swamps" is even less defensible. Nowadays, in fact, it is the disposition of moralists to condemn any statesman who at any period, on any grounds, declined to consider slavery as a moral question. A biographer of Gouverneur Morris, pointing out the striking contrast between the sentiments of Mason and those of the New England members, impetuously attacks the entire New England delegation, and singles out Ellsworth's speech for particularly severe dispraise.[1]

Much, of course, can be said, and has been said, for Ellsworth and those who saw the question as he did. Quite probably, General Pinckney was right when he declared that if he and his colleagues were to go home and use all their influence, they could not persuade their people to accept the Constitution without some protection for the slave trade. Ellsworth was by this

[1] Roosevelt's "Gouverneur Morris" (American Statesmen series), 138–139.

time fully committed to the general scheme of the
Constitution and anxious to see it adopted and ratified.
That same day he declared that he was for the plan
as a whole. The widening of opinion, he said, had a
threatening aspect. If members would not agree on
this middle and moderate ground, he was afraid they
would lose two states, with such others as might
be disposed to stand aloof, and fly into a variety of
shapes, most probably into several confederations,
and that not without bloodshed. Concerning another
disagreement, he had remarked:[1] "We grow more and
more sceptical as we proceed. If we do not decide
soon, we shall be unable to come to any decision."

There were also, it must be granted, many signs to
justify his hope that slavery might, before many years,
shrink into unimportance. Economic laws were working to that end; the antislavery feeling, North and
South, was strong and growing. No one, of course,
foresaw the invention of the cotton-gin and the rise of
the cotton kingdom. Of course, too, on any moral
question, something must be pardoned to the standards of another age. But if, to prove the wisdom of
the first great compromise, we consulted the outcome,
we are driven by the same reasoning to grant that it
was neither wise nor righteous to spare the slave trade;
that the convention lost a precious opportunity to
promote the cause of human freedom. The chances
were that if Georgia and South Carolina withdrew
North Carolina as well as Virginia would refuse to
follow them. The line between slavery and freedom
might thus in a few years have been pushed a thousand miles southward. An independent Southern

[1] August 15, when the President's veto power was under discussion.

confederacy of two states would not have been dangerous, and would probably have been short-lived. The Civil War might have been averted. The darkest and bloodiest pages in all our history might never have been written.

But neither the moral scruple nor a forecast of the long future determined the convention's course. The matter was disposed of by another compromise. It is possible that even while Ellsworth was replying to Mason the terms of a bargain between New England and the lower South were already substantially agreed upon. The clauses on the slave trade and on navigation acts were both referred to the same committee of one from each state. They reported in favor of giving Congress the power to pass navigation acts and forbidding it to impose any restriction on the slave trade, other than a duty at the average rate, before the year 1800. When the report came up for consideration, General Pinckney of South Carolina moved to strike out 1800 and insert 1808, and Gorham of Massachusetts seconded him. The motion was passed by the votes of all the New England states and all the Southern states except Virginia and Delaware. By the same vote, the amended part of the report was then accepted. It is no wonder that Charles Pinckney took occasion later to praise the New England delegates for " their liberal conduct toward the views of South Carolina." That there was an understanding on the subjects of navigation and slavery, Madison tells us in so many words. Johnson was the Connecticut member of the committee, but it is idle to suppose that Ellsworth or any other New England member was ignorant of the bargain.

Indeed, there were probably few important things done in the convention, after the great compromise, that Ellsworth did not have a hand in. By his part in that arrangement he had, as an individual member, proved his case with his fellows; and when it was adopted he and others who had seemed to be in opposition became at once keenly desirous that the convention should succeed. When the resolutions had passed through the second revision, they were given over to a committee of five, chosen by ballot, with instructions to report a constitution; and of these five Ellsworth was one. This was a great honor and a great responsibility. The other four were Rutledge, Randolph, Gorham, and Wilson. For ten days these men had in their hands the entire scheme of the proposed government. Of what they said and did in committee we have no record, but they did not confine themselves to questions of mere form; in many important respects, the instrument which they reported differed from the resolutions it was based on. This was particularly true of those provisions which related to the judiciary. The resolutions had been vaguer concerning that department than on any other subject. The shaping of it was left to the committee; and in this work, no doubt, Ellsworth took much interest. Curiously enough, however, hardly any of his speeches in the convention dealt with the judiciary. When the method of appointing judges was up, he urged that instead of giving the Senate a negative on appointments by the executive the convention should give the initiative to the Senate and the negative to the executive; but to both these arrangements he preferred an absolute appointment by

the Senate.[1] His only other reference to the department was made incidentally, when he favored Wilson's
motion to associate the Supreme Court judges with the
executive in the revision of laws.[2] He himself later
moved for an executive council of which the Chief
Justice should be a member.[3]

But his contributions to the discussion of other
subjects, particularly after his service on the committee, were numerous. He often spoke three or
four times in a single sitting, usually in defence of
some clause as it stood, and somewhat in the manner
of a congressman in charge of a bill on its passage.
Yet there were some amendments which he warmly
favored.

Though for a long time strongly opposed to paying
members of the legislature out of the national Treasury, on this point he finally changed his mind.[4] But
he never would consent to give Congress a negative
on state laws. That concession, he observed, would
mean either that all state laws, before taking effect,
should be submitted to Congress, or that Congress
should have the right to repeal them, or else that
the general government should appoint the state
executives and these should have the veto power.[5]
He was against Mason's proposal of national sumptuary laws;[6] and he remained firm also against the
plan of taking away from the states the right to fix
the qualifications for the suffrage in all cases. It was
a tender point, he said, and each state was the best
judge of the temper and the circumstances of its own

1 "Documentary History of the Constitution," III, 401.
2 Ibid., 391.   4 Ibid., 531, 534.   6 Ibid., 567.
3 Ibid., 559.   5 Ibid., 602-603.

people.[1]   If property or other qualifications were to be imposed, uniform rules would prove unequal in their application; each state ought to fix its own qualifications.[2]   To other clauses dealing with the legislature he applied observations drawn from his own experience. He did not, for instance, overvalue the concession to the first branch of the right to originate money bills.[3] He was against the proposal to fix minimum quorums for both the houses, preferring the majority rule;[4] and when it was moved to give every member a right to call for the yeas and nays, he agreed with Sherman that yeas and nays never did any good.[5]   He preferred winter sessions.[6]   He was willing to give up a clause requiring each house to keep and publish a journal, feeling that public opinion would secure publicity.[7]   He wished the disqualification of congressmen for all other offices extended a year beyond their terms of service.[8]   This, he thought, would not deter ambitious men from serving, and there was a danger that too many honors would go to members.   But on the other hand he was for requiring only a short term of residence in any particular state to qualify a man for representing it.[9]   This principle he applied also to foreign-born citizens.[10]   He was against the sweeping disqualification of all public debtors,[11] and he was for permitting governors to fill vacancies in the Senate when these should occur between sessions of the legislatures in the states concerned.[12]   On most of these questions, but not on all, time has confirmed his judgment.

1 "Documentary History of the Constitution," III, 464, 565.

2 *Ibid.*, 494–495, 496.   6 *Ibid.*, 460, 462.   10 *Ibid.*, 485.

3 *Ibid.*, 480, 482.   7 *Ibid.*, 503.   11 *Ibid.*, 441–442

4 *Ibid.*, 499.   8 *Ibid.*, 529.   12 *Ibid.*, 476.

5 *Ibid.*, 501.   9 *Ibid.*, 464, 465.

When it came to fixing the powers of Congress, and particularly when there arose proposals to enlarge them at the cost of the state governments, his opinions were decided, and on several of these issues he stood out stoutly for state-rights. In view of Connecticut's behavior during the War of 1812, it is particularly interesting to find that he and Sherman fought harder than any of the delegates except, perhaps, Gerry of Massachusetts, to retain for the states the control of the militia. When it was first moved to give the control mainly to the general government, Ellsworth would have amended the motion with such provisos as to take away its force. He thought that if this authority should pass from the state governments they would pine away to nothing, and that the general government, on the other hand, "could not sufficiently pervade the Union for such a purpose, nor could it accommodate itself to the local genius of the people."[1] The states, besides, would never submit to uniform militia laws. "Three or four shillings as a penalty would enforce obedience better in New England than forty lashes in some other places."[2] The subject was referred, along with the question of state debts, to another grand committee, which reported back the provision finally adopted.[3] Ellsworth carried a motion to table the report, and when it was again taken up he and Sherman tried to emasculate the clause; they proposed to give Congress the power merely to make rules which the states should execute.[4] Fortunately, Connecticut was the only state that voted for their substitute. The second war with Great Britain has not been the only

---

[1] "Documentary History of the Constitution," III, 562.
[2] *Ibid.*, 563. [3] *Ibid.*, 575. [4] *Ibid.*, 594–598.

occasion when there has been good cause for regret that even fuller control was not given to the national authorities. When the power of Congress to suppress rebellion in any state was under consideration, Ellsworth had also favored a proviso that this should be done only on the call of the state legislature if it could meet.[1] On the troublesome question of state debts, however, he seems to have favored assumption by the general government.[2] For reasons which he himself called "solid," as they were, he was against the taxing of exports by Congress, but he seemed to think that there was no necessity to forbid the states to do it.[3] "The attempts of one," he argued, "to tax the exports of another passing through its hands will force a direct exportation and defeat themselves." He was also — as who, with his experience, would not have been? — for withholding from Congress the power to emit bills of credit.[4] He wished to improve the good opportunity to "shut and bar the door against paper money. The mischiefs of the various experiments which had been made were," he said, "fresh in the public mind and had excited the disgust of all the respectable part of America. By withholding the power from the new government more friends of influence would be gained by it than by anything else. Paper money can in no case be necessary. Give the government credit, and other resources will follow. The power may do harm, never good."

Nor did he oppose the denial of this power to the states. His general notion of the proper relation between the Union and the states is perhaps best re-

---

[1] "Documentary History of the Constitution," III, 551–552.
[2] *Ibid.*, 557, 576.   [3] *Ibid.*, 543, 578–579.   [4] *Ibid.*, 547.

vealed in two or three short speeches on the treason clause and on the question of how the Constitution should be ratified.[1] When Madison pointed out that the same act might be treason against the United States and also be punishable as treason under the laws of a particular state, Ellsworth thought the national government was in no danger, since its laws were paramount. But a discussion at once arose over sovereignty, and Johnson was one of those who thought that sovereignty was lodged in the Union. Ellsworth, however, declared: "The United States are sovereign on one side of the line dividing their jurisdictions — the states on the other. Each ought to have power to defend their respective sovereignties." These were words, one fancies, from which comfort might have been drawn by the planners of a New England Confederacy twoscore years later, and by the builders of the Southern Confederacy. It is not surprising to find also that Ellsworth apparently never did conceive of the people of the whole country either as the true constituency of the convention or as the source of authority for the new government. At one stage in the gradual development of the Constitution he moved to refer it for final ratification to the legislatures of the several states, instead of conventions. Mason objected that the legislatures had no authority, and that their successors might rescind their acts. "As to the second point," Ellsworth answered, "he could not admit it to be well founded. An Act to which the States by their legislatures make themselves parties becomes a compact from which no one of the parties recedes of itself. As to the first point, he observed that a new set of ideas

---

[1] "Documentary History of the Constitution," III, 569, 570, 572.

seemed to have crept in since the Articles of Confederation were established. Conventions of the people, or with power derived expressly from the people, were not then thought of. The legislatures were considered as competent. Their ratification has been acquiesced in without complaint. To whom have Congress applied on subsequent occasions for further powers? To the Legislatures; not to the people. The fact is that we exist at present, and we need not inquire how, as a federal Society, united by a charter, one article of which is that alterations therein may be made by the Legislative authority of the States. It has been said that if the confederation is to be observed, the States must *unanimously* concur in the proposed innovations. He would answer that if such were the urgency and necessity of our situation as to warrant a new compact among a part of the States, founded on the consent of the people, the same plea would be equally valid in favor of a partial compact, founded on the consent of the Legislatures." To this keen dialectics Gouverneur Morris made an even keener reply, and Ellsworth's motion was voted down. But it is not improbable that the majority of his fellows were as slow as he was to understand how far they were actually moving away from the theory and practice of the confederation.

In more than one eulogy of Ellsworth, John C. Calhoun is quoted in his praise. Calhoun's words are worth quoting, and his praise worth having; but it is quite probable that Ellsworth himself, a little farther on in his career, would have relished an emphasis on what he did in the convention to turn the confederation into a real Union better than reminders of what he did to keep the Union from acquiring too great strength. Calhoun's tribute is in a speech delivered in the Senate in 1847.[1] " It is owing," he said, " mainly to the states of Connecticut and New Jersey that we have a federal instead of a national government — the best government instead of the worst and most intolerable on the earth. Who are the men of these states to whom we are indebted for this excellent form of government? I will name them. Their names ought to be written on brass, and live forever. They were Chief Justice Ellsworth and Roger Sherman of Connecticut, and Judge Paterson of New Jersey. The other states further south were blind; they did not see the future. But to the coolness and sagacity of these three men, aided by others not so prominent, do we owe our present constitution."[2]

Ellsworth had taken a lively interest in the clauses relating to the executive; and he seems to have had clearer notions about it than most of the delegates. This was the subject on which the convention was, from first to last, most at sea. In discussing it, the members did not, it is true, divide by states and sections quite as they did over the legislature; but there was the widest diversity of opinion, particularly over the method of election. In the course of the first two months, as Mason pointed out, no less than seven different plans were suggested.[3]

[1] Congressional Globe, 2d Session, 29th Congress, 466.

[2] It is worth recalling that Calhoun, after being graduated at Yale, remained a year or two longer in Connecticut studying law. It is not likely that he failed to learn what he could of the little state's more famous representatives in public life, and it is said that he was well acquainted with members of Ellsworth's and Sherman's families. See G. F. Hoar's " Autobiography," I, 8.

[3] " Documentary History of the Constitution," III, 432–433.

One of them actually included the expedient of a lottery. Ellsworth was one of the first to commit himself to the plan of a choice by electors.[1] July 19, he moved to strike out the original provision, for appointment by the national legislature, and substitute the words, "to be chosen by electors appointed by the legislatures of the States in the following ratio: to wit — one for each state not exceeding 200,000 inhabitants, two for each above that number and not exceeding 300,000, and three for each state exceeding 300,000."[2] After a little discussion, the convention voted by good majorities in favor of the plan, but without the ratio. It was very much closer to the plan finally adopted than any other that had been proposed. The same day, Ellsworth favored a six years' term. He argued that if the term were made too short, the executive would not be firm enough. There must be duties which would render him unpopular for the moment, and every administration would be attacked and misrepresented. Six years was agreed to. But the convention changed its mind more than once before it reached the final decision of these questions. Five days later, the subject was reconsidered, and by a vote of seven to four[3] the method of appointment by the national legislature was again preferred. It was also proposed to reinstate a provision that the executive should not be eligible for a second term, and this Ellsworth briefly opposed.[4] To many minds, he admitted, it seemed a necessary

---

[1] June 2, in committee of the whole house, Wilson had proposed an electoral college, to be chosen by districts, without reference to state lines. It was voted down with very little discussion. "Documentary History of the Constitution," III, 41–42.

[2] *Ibid.*, 379–380.   [3] *Ibid.*, 414–417.   [4] *Ibid.*, 417.

corollary to the choice by the national legislature; but he felt that a good executive ought in any case to be reëlected. The hope of an indorsement would lead him to deserve it. Eminent characters might be unwilling to assume the trust if they must always expect a degradation after a fixed period of service. The next day, he opened the discussion with a new motion, offering a compromise between the two methods of choice.[1] It would have permitted the national legislature to elect, but not to reëlect, the choice passing to electors whenever the question of a second term should arise. The special object of it was to avert what many dreaded — too great dependence of the executive on the legislature. Madison, in an elaborate speech, favoring an election by the whole body of the people, Ellsworth firmly objected.[2] Like so many of his fellows, he was still obsessed with the idea of an opposition between the two classes of states, and nobody seems to have foreseen the part which political parties were to play. But it cannot be said that his objection was entirely mistaken. Parties do as a rule prefer candidates from states which are at once doubtful and populous. Ellsworth's compromise proposal failed,[3] and on Mason's motion the resolution went to the committee of detail as it had been reported from the committee of the whole. Incorporated that way in the first draft of the Constitution, it was retained until very near the end. When Ellsworth's plan of a choice by electors was, with some changes, finally accepted, he himself was gone.

The last appearance of his name in Madison's jour-

[1] "Documentary History of the Constitution," III, 423.
[2] *Ibid.*, 427.　　　[3] *Ibid.*

nal is under the date August 23. That day he made
two speeches. Four days later, on his way home,
he paid a visit to President Stiles of Yale at New
Haven.[1] One suggested explanation of his departure
is that he and Sherman could not both neglect any
longer their duties on the bench.[2] He had no part in
the closing scenes of the convention, and lost also the
chance to sign the Constitution. That circumstance
may perhaps have helped to obscure his share in framing it. According to his unvarying habit of reticence
and modesty, he himself seems never to have claimed
that it was a great share. But when due allowance is
made for his entirely unrecorded labors on the committee of five,[3] not more than two or three men can
well be ranked above him for true effectiveness in the
convention; and nearly all of those who had played
parts comparable to his were men who, when the work
began, were better known than he was. By sheer force
of will and of sagacity, he had risen in that remarkable assembly to influence and to leadership. He had
stamped forever with the imprint of his mind and purpose his country's fundamental law. He had helped to
shape the life of a great republic for centuries to come.

The convention's rule of secrecy was, no doubt, wise;
but we would gladly know more of these men's thoughts
and feelings while they were about their epoch-making
business. When it was all finished, Washington, as

[1] Stiles's "Literary Diary," III, 279. See also J. F. Jameson, in
Annual Report of American Historical Association, 1902, I, 160.
[2] Jeremiah Evarts's "Sherman," in Sanderson's "Lives of the Signers,"
II, 44.
[3] It is a reasonable inference from the only utterance that we have of
Ellsworth about his work in the convention that he thought this committee service the most important part of it. See *post*, pp. 169-170.

he tells us in his diary, "retired to meditate upon the momentous work which had been executed." Only George Mason ever put into words what it meant to be a member of that illustrious company. "For my own part," he wrote to his son, "I never before felt myself in such a situation, and declare I would not, upon pecuniary motives, serve in this convention for a thousand pounds per day. The revolt from Great Britain and the formation of our new government at that time were nothing compared with the great business now before us. There was then a certain degree of enthusiasm which inspired and supported the mind; but to view through the calm, sedate medium of reason the influence which the establishment now proposed may have upon the happiness or misery of millions yet unborn is an object of such magnitude as absorbs, and in a measure suspends, the operations of the human understanding."[1] Ellsworth, as silent in statesmanship as ever any captain was in war, has left not a single self-revealing word about his own share in this immense experience. Even of his impressions of his fellow-delegates we know nothing. The only exception is a remark he once made to his son, Oliver Ellsworth, Jr., in a manuscript from whose hand this entry occurs: "One day, upon my reading a paper to him (in his illness), containing an eulogium upon the late Gen. Washington, which among other things ascribed to him the founding of the American Government, . . . he (Judge E.) objected, saying that President Washington's influence while in the convention was not very great; at least not much as to the forming of the present Constitution of the United States in 1787.

[1] Miss Rowland's "Mason," II, 128.

Judge E. said that he himself was one of the five who
drew up that Constitution."

It remained to get the instrument ratified. Whether
the necessary nine states could be brought into line
for it was very doubtful, and nowhere was the outlook
darker than in New York, Massachusetts, and Rhode
Island, the three next-door neighbors of Connecticut.
But in Connecticut, though there was serious opposition,
the friends of the new government did not, it appears,
need to make a very strenuous exertion. The work of
Ellsworth and Sherman at Philadelphia had paved the
way for victory with the people. When Sherman came
home, they two sent from New London to Governor
Huntington a copy of the Constitution and in a brief
and matter-of-fact letter[1] enumerated the chief differences between the proposed new system and the government under the Articles. Calling attention to the
ways in which state-rights were guarded, they pointed
out, what the tenth amendment afterward formally declared, that the new government, like the old, was to be
a government of strictly defined powers. "The particular States," they phrased it, "retain their sovereignty
in all other matters."[2] They summarized the whole
proposal thus: "The convention endeavored to provide for the energy of government on the one hand
and suitable checks on the other hand, to secure the
rights of the particular states, and the liberties and

---

[1] Elliot's "Debates," I, 491–492 ; Boutell's "Sherman," 168–170.

[2] It is interesting to compare the ways in which different state-rights
men estimated the extent of the concessions that had been made to the
national principle. See, for instance, Luther Martin's speech before the
Maryland legislature, denouncing the Constitution, and Patrick Henry's
speeches before the Virginia convention, and also in 1798, when, the Constitution being the law of the land, he could find no basis in reason or in

properties of the citizens. We wish it may meet the approbation of the several states, and be a means of securing their rights, and lengthening out their tranquillity."

The convention to reject or ratify met at Hartford in January, 1788. In the meantime, Sherman had been more conspicuous than Ellsworth in advocating the Constitution; but it was Ellsworth who now, at the opening of the convention, rose first to explain and defend it. In this particular assembly the leadership was clearly his.[1] An eye-witness wrote: "Mr. Ellsworth was a complete master of the subject. He was armed at all points. He took a very active part in defending the Constitution. Scarcely a single objection was made but what he answered. His energetic reasoning bore down all before it."[2] But once again incomplete and imperfect reporting denies us the privilege of observing for ourselves Ellsworth's powers in debate. Even the most expert stenographer might have been occasionally baffled by his extraordinarily vehement and rapid elocution. Only two of his speeches are preserved at all, and when the first was printed in the *Connecticut Courant* he himself wrote

honor for the claim of sovereignty for the states. On the other hand, Wilson, in the Pennsylvania convention, emphasized the national character of the instrument in a way that contrasts strongly with his own bitter speeches against the federal plan in the convention. Sherman and Ellsworth appear once more to have found the right and reasonable middle ground.

[1] Jackson Ms. For this particular part of Ellsworth's career, Jackson's narrative is excellent, though Wood's is somewhat fuller.

[2] Letter of Perkins to Simeon Baldwin. In a contemporary published account, "his energetic reasoning" appears, by contrast with "the learning and eloquence of a Johnson" and "the genuine good sense and discernment of a Sherman," as "the Demosthenian energy of an Ellsworth." Wood Ms.; Flanders, 156.

to the editor that the report was incorrect.[1]   Yet these
two speeches are the best material we have for an
estimate of his oratory.[2]

The first, his opening speech, is mainly given to a
plain and forcible arrayal of the reasons for a stronger
union.   It was necessary, he argued, for safety; divided, the American states would be, like any other
loose collection of small powers, the easy prey of foreign intrigue and of foreign arms.   It was necessary
for economy; a competent central government could
serve the common interests at far less cost than many
separate establishments.   It was necessary for peace
among the states themselves.   It was necessary for
" commutative justice."   Was not Connecticut, under
the existing system, already a tributary to her rapa-
cious neighbors?   Would she not thus be " like Issachar
of old, a strong ass crouching down between two
burdens "?   It was necessary because there must be
greater energy in government; with merely advisory
powers, Congress could not do the work that was
expected of it.   Did Connecticut need to be told that

---

[1] MESSRS. HUDSON AND GOODWIN : The few cursory observations
made by me at the opening of the convention were not designed for a
newspaper ; and what you have published as the substance of them, from
some person's minutes, I suppose, is less proper for me than the observations themselves were.   It is particularly erroneous with regard to some of
the historic facts alluded to, which are stated in a manner which neither
the observations nor history will justify : the deviations do not go to circumstances very material to the argument itself.

I am, Gentlemen, yours, &c.

OLIVER ELLSWORTH.

Jan. 10, 1788.

Connecticut Courant, Jan. 16, 1788.

[2] Both are given in Frank Moore's " American Eloquence," I, 404–409,
and in Elliot's " Debates," II, 185–197.   Flanders, 144–156, gives the
bulk of both, but not the whole of either.

the states could not be trusted to fulfil their mutual obligations without compulsion or restraint? Was there not, in a little state close by, "injustice too bare-faced for Eastern despotism" — "a spirit that would make a Tophet of the universe"? True, we had once done well without any union. But that was under different conditions. The British government discharged for us then functions that now could only be discharged by a strong central government of our own. Other confederacies had found it wise to use coercion. But why talk in such a general way, when all men knew that from want of energy in Congress we had fallen into injustice toward each other, into deceit and bankruptcy, into a shameful inability to perform our treaties with foreign nations? Recurring once again to the tribute Connecticut was paying to New York and Massachusetts, he asked, "If this is done when we have the shadow of a National Government, what shall we not suffer when even the shadow is gone?" And with question after question he laid barer and barer the utter hopelessness of the old system. "If we go on as we have done, what is to become of the foreign debt? Will foreign nations forgive us this debt because we neglect to pay? or will they levy by reprisals, as the law of nations authorizes them? Will our weakness induce Spain to relinquish the exclusive navigation of the Mississippi, or the territory which she claims on the East side of that river? Will our weakness induce the British to give up the Northern posts? If a war breaks out, and our situation invites our enemies to make war, how are we to defend ourselves? Has Government the means to enlist a man, or buy an ox? Or shall we rally the remainder of our old army? The European nations, I believe to be not friendly to us. They were pleased to see us disconnected from Great Britain; they are pleased to see us disunited among ourselves. If we continue so, how easy it is for them to portion us out among them, as they did the Kingdom of Poland! But, supposing this is not done, if we suffer the Union to expire, the least that may be expected is, that the European powers will form alliances, some with one State and some with another, and play the States off one against another, and that we shall be involved in all the labyrinths of European politics. But I do not wish to continue the painful recital; enough has been said to show that a power in the General Government to enforce the decrees of the Union is absolutely necessary."

There was, however, a quite respectable opposition in the convention, led by Colonel Wadsworth. It represented mainly the most decidedly democratic elements of the population of the state, and it quickly fastened on the clause conveying and defining the power of the new Congress to levy taxes. Of all the strictures on the Constitution, the objections to that clause seemed, both to its opponents and to its supporters in Connecticut, much the most formidable. In the second of his reported speeches, Ellsworth undertook to answer them. This speech, given as it was in the course of a general debate, is perhaps the best of all his utterances to represent him in his relation to the founding of the government.[1] Pierpont Edwards, a member of the convention, probably had it especially in mind when he afterward tried to describe

[1] See Appendix B.

the effect of Ellsworth's oratory. He himself, it appears, had made a speech before Ellsworth rose, and put his best into it; but when Ellsworth had finished he felt "like a lightning bug in broad daylight."[1] And it is hard in fact to overpraise Ellsworth's luminous exposition of the new relation between the states and the Union, between the Union and the individual citizen, between the national and the state judiciaries. In the most famous of the countless later discussions of these topics, his words were quoted by the greatest of all forensic defenders and expounders of the Constitution. In the course of the long debate of 1833 over nullification, Daniel Webster, replying to Calhoun, praised Connecticut as "that State so small in territory, but so distinguished for learning and talent," and read to the Senate extracts from the speeches made in her convention by Johnson and Ellsworth — "a gentleman, sir, who has left behind him, on the records of the government of his country, proofs of the clearest intelligence, and of the utmost purity and integrity of character."[2] Webster is said, indeed, to have paid an even higher tribute to the Connecticut statesman. One day, about the time of the reply to Hayne or the later battle with Calhoun, Ellsworth's son, then a member of Congress, went to him and thanked him for defending the Constitution against the nullifiers. "Where do you think," answered Webster, "I got my ideas on the subject? Among the most important sources of my knowledge have been the two speeches of your father before the Connecticut Convention. I value them so highly that when I met with them several years ago in a book

[1] Wood Ms.　　　　[2] Webster's Works, III, 485–486.

which I could not purchase I had them copied out in manuscript and keep them to this day among my papers."[1] No one has claimed for Ellsworth the first place among the founders of the government; but he enjoys among them one unique distinction. Calhoun and Webster, though they were the champions of entirely contrary views of the Constitution, agreed upon the soundness of his. Alone of all that famous company, he seems to have won the equal homage of those opposed intellects.

[1] Jackson Ms. Jackson was the son-in-law of Hon. W. W. Ellsworth (M.C., 1827–1834), and tells us in his diary that he got many of his facts and incidents from the lips of his father-in-law.

CHAPTER V

ELLSWORTH's quality was by this time known to the foremost men in the country; and to them as to us it must have been evident chiefly from what he had done and helped to do. We may feel, therefore, reasonably sure of the kind of esteem in which they held him. A phrase which is often employed nowadays, in business, war, politics, athletics, conveys very well the judgment of him which his work compels from any careful student of his career, and must have compelled also from those who knew him in the flesh. He was "a good man," —"a good man" at the bar and at the pay table, "a good man" in Congress, "a good man" on the bench, "a good man" when it came to blocking out and rounding into shape a constitution of government. He should serve even better than if he were a man of genius for an encouraging example of how much, with will and conscience, the citizen of a free country can do with his life.

When it was known that the new system would certainly be tried, Connecticut chose him and Johnson to be her first two senators, and he thus became a member of the assembly whose form and character he had done so much to determine. Sherman was at first sent to the House of Representatives, but in two years Johnson retired to become the president of King's College, whose name had been changed to Columbia, and then for a single session Sherman was once again Ellsworth's colleague. But in the recess of 1793 the old patriot died.[1] It is conjecturable that his lack of a collegiate training may have been one of the reasons why he was not in the first instance elected to the Senate.

Ellsworth and Johnson were two of the eight senators who were present in New York on March 4, 1789, the place and date appointed for the opening of the new Congress.[2] Neither house, however, had a quorum. Fisher Ames, the young Massachusetts orator, the successful rival of Samuel Adams in the Boston Congress district, had come to New York eager for acquaintance with the famous leaders of other states, and in his impatience he wrote back home that the new government was like to be forgotten before it was born. After waiting a week, the senators who had arrived sent a circular letter to their tardy fellows; but at the end of a fortnight there was still no quorum, and another more urgent call was despatched. It was not till April 6 that Richard Henry Lee of Virginia, the twelfth senator, appeared, and a messenger informed the House of Representatives, which had organized on April 1, that the Senate was ready to proceed to business. The first business was to count the ballots for President and Vice-President, and inform Washington and Adams of their election.

[1] At the opening of Congress in December, 1793, Stephen Mix Mitchell took Sherman's place. Ellsworth's last colleague (1795–1796) was Jonathan Trumbull, a son of the Revolutionary governor.

[2] Senate Journals, 1st Sess., p. 1. For Senate proceedings I have compared the official journals in the original published form with Gales and Seaton's "Annals of Congress" and Benton's "Abridgment of the Debates of Congress."

It was the end of April before Washington was inaugurated; but meanwhile the two houses had gone ahead with legislation necessary to set the wheels of government in motion. The House of Representatives took up first the question of revenue, and proceeded to devise a tariff and a bill for tonnage duties. The Senate led the way in framing rules for the legislature and making plans for the other departments. In this, no other senator was more active than Ellsworth.

He was doubtless more at home and at ease with his fellows in the Senate than he had ever been at his entrance into any other legislative body. The number was so small that on a chilly day they all left their seats and gathered near the fire.[1] When he looked about him, there were few strange faces. Of the twenty-two members and members-elect, a majority were men whom he had already encountered in the old Congress or the Constitutional Convention, and there was no one among them of whom he needed to stand in awe. Certainly no one from New England outclassed him or his colleague. Of the men from the Middle states and the South, Morris and Lee were probably the most influential. Madison, defeated by the state-rights party in the Virginia legislature, had with difficulty secured a seat in the House of Representatives. Hamilton was not in Congress at all. New York, in fact, had not yet chosen her senators. When she did choose, one of them was Rufus King, who had recently moved from Massachusetts to New York City. Nor did any of the new men reveal a commanding fitness for leadership. To one of these, however, William

[1] The Journal of William Maclay (ed. by Edgar S. Maclay, 1890), 21.

Maclay, Morris's colleague from Pennsylvania, we are indebted for our most intimate view of the Senate and of Ellsworth during the first two sessions.[1] It is not a very charitable view, nor is it unbiassed, for Maclay was a democrat of the suspicious kind, distrusting everything that savored either of authority or intrigue. He judged men's motives severely, for the most part, and he seems to have had a strong dislike for Yankees — stronger even than was common in the Middle and Southern states. Many of his criticisms of men and measures are decidedly carping, and nearly all his comments and characterizations must be taken with a grain of salt. But one feels, nevertheless, in reading his diary, that though narrow he was honest; and sometimes his accounts of actual happenings yield peculiarly vivid and photographic glimpses of the way men looked and acted, and the way things were done, while the first Congress was making precedents for its successors, and the first President was setting a standard to which none of his successors has ever quite come up. At times, Maclay was deeply grieved even at Washington's behavior, and there was scarcely one of his fellow-senators whose course did not sooner or later plunge him into the gloomiest reflections concerning human depravity. What he tells us of their frailties and perversities ought not, however, to be entirely disregarded. Much of it is doubtless true, and there is a certain comfort in knowing that these founders and first administrators of the government, so far from being faultless, were perhaps reasonably like the public men of our own time; for we see now that their work

[1] Maclay's Journal, as above. The edition of 1890 is much fuller than the first edition, published ten years earlier.

OLIVER ELLSWORTH.

From a miniature by Trumbull, in the possession of Yale University.

was on the whole good. Maclay's diary is priceless, for during these early sessions the Senate's doors were closed and the debates unreported, and the journals are as meagre as those of the old Congress of the Confederation. Ellsworth was one of the last to favor public sessions. The motion to open the doors, often proposed, was not finally passed until February, 1794.[1] It took effect at the next session, but the debates did not actually begin to be reported and published until Ellsworth's service was ended. Maclay, though he spared the Connecticut statesman no more than any other of the leaders, has rendered, nevertheless, a valuable service to his memory, for the diary makes it plain that from the first he was a very real leader indeed.

So much, perhaps, might be inferred even from the journals. It was Ellsworth who, the day a quorum appeared, went to inform the House of Representatives that the Senate was ready to count the votes for President and Vice-President. The next day, the 7th, the first vote was, " That Mr. Ellsworth, Mr. Paterson, Mr. Maclay, Mr. Strong, Mr. Lee, Mr. Bassett, Mr. Few, Mr. Wingate, be a committee to bring in a bill for organizing the Judiciary of the United States "; and immediately afterward Ellsworth was set at the head of another committee to prepare rules for the Senate and for conferences between the two houses, and to take thought also on the subject of chaplains.[2] During the next few weeks he was much engaged with questions of form and procedure. He helped prepare the certificates of election which were sent to Washington and Adams, and waited on Adams

[1] Senate Journals, 3d Cong., 1st Sess., 55–56.   [2] *Ibid.*, 10.

to consult about his inauguration. He reported the
first set of Senate rules, and considered a plan for
printing the journals. He headed the committee
which divided the senators into classes with different
terms of service. He served on the committee on titles
for the President and Vice-President, and frequently
discussed that much-vexed subject.[1] Historians of the
period have not failed to exhibit the comical aspect of
the Senate's troubled concern over matters of etiquette,
and the House of Representatives won much favor
with the populace by its democratic stand against all
titles. John Adams was so keen about them that he
disgusted Maclay and other of the senators, and Maclay set down Ellsworth as one of those who humored
and supported him.[2] But it is only just to remember
that these men felt that they were making at every
turn precedents which might hold for many years.
The new government was a very bold and radical
departure, and they wished to neglect nothing that
might help to link it with the past and to give it dig-

[1] Journals, 5, 10, 13, 19, 26, 31, 32, 34, 35 ; Maclay, 3, 22–24, 29, 33, 35,
37, 39.

[2] One day, shortly before the inauguration of Washington, Adams made
a fairly piteous appeal to the Senate to tell him how he ought to behave on
that occasion — whether as Vice-President, as President of the Senate, or
as President of the United States *in posse.* " I wish gentlemen to think
what I shall be," he ended, in much distress. Maclay says that in the
solemn silence which followed the profane muscles of his own face were in
tune for laughter.

" Ellsworth, however, thumbed over the sheet constitution and turned it
for some time. At length he rose and addressed the chair with the utmost
gravity : —

" 'Mr. President, I have looked over the Constitution (pause), and I
find, sir, it is evident and clear, sir, that wherever the Senate is to be,
there, sir, you must be at the head of them. But further, sir (here he
looked aghast, as if some tremendous gulf had yawned before him), I shall
not pretend to say.' " Maclay's Journal, 2–3.

nity. In this regard, Washington was as gravely cautious as any one. Ellsworth's committee would have called the President "his Highness, the President of the United States, and Protector of their Liberties," and the House of Representatives threw out the proposal with successful ridicule. But at this time most Englishmen still looked back with something like horror to the years when England had been so radically republican as to substitute a Lord Protector for a King; and America had broken away from England to be independent, not to set up a democracy. Neither had the constitutional movement that was now being consummated aimed at democracy, but rather at strength, stability, efficiency. There were plenty of men, and some of them important characters in the government, — as Jefferson, on his return from France, soon remarked, — who augured nothing but ill from the democracy already worked into the system. Hamilton and Adams, in different ways and different degrees, were both exponents of that view.[1] But Maclay was probably wrong in supposing Ellsworth to be of their party in the sense that he leaned toward monarchy, as Hamilton certainly did.[2] Ellsworth was, beyond question, zealous and resolute in all things that tended to make the new government strong and respectable. He did not share at all the apparent reaction from the national impulse which soon carried over Madison, the house leader, from Hamilton's side

[1] See a curious note by Adams to his own Davila essays, concerning a resolution in praise of the Constitution offered by Ellsworth. "I was obliged to put the question and it stands upon record. . . . John Adams alone detested it (*i.e.* the Constitution)." Adams's Works, VI, 323.

[2] See Maclay's Journal, 23, 112, 114, for speeches of Ellsworth that Maclay particularly disrelished on this account.

to Jefferson's.   On the contrary, from this time to the end of his career, he remained a consistent Federalist. When the French Revolution broke out, he soon showed that he was not thrilled by any sympathy with its radical ideas and methods.   But in these conservative opinions he was never violent or extreme, and there is nothing to indicate that he ever lost faith in the kind of democracy he had always known in Connecticut.   In this moderation his career contrasts very favorably indeed with that of his more partisan Federalist friends, particularly when they went out of power.   There were doubtless more brilliant minds than his in the government in its early days, but scarcely one better balanced or more steadfast and judicious.

These broad questions were not, however, immediately broached, save as the disputes about forms and titles may have involved them.   There were too many tasks of a constructive nature that must at once be undertaken, and one of these, as fundamentally important as any, was peculiarly Ellsworth's.   Hamilton is not more clearly responsible for committing the government to permanent policies in finance than Ellsworth is for setting the judiciary in the course of development which it has followed ever since.

The fact that he was chairman of the Senate committee to bring in a bill to organize the courts is by no means the only evidence that he was the responsible author of the measure.   Maclay's testimony on that point is abundant; and Maclay was himself a member of the committee.   "This vile bill," he one day observes, "is a child of his (Ellsworth's), and he defends it with the care of a parent, even with wrath and anger."[1] Nearly fifty years later, Madison wrote to Wood, " It may be taken for certain that the bill organizing the judicial department originated in his (Ellsworth's) draft, and that it was not materially changed in its passage into law."[2] Madison had already, several years earlier, written to Edward Everett, to correct an impression that he himself was the author of the law, " The bill originated in the Senate, of which I was not a member, and the task of preparing it was understood, justly I believe, to have been performed by Mr. Ellsworth in consultation probably with some of his learned colleagues."[3] A few letters that passed between Ellsworth and certain of his friends show that for all his modesty he felt himself charged with the main responsibility for the bill. One of them shows also that as early as the end of April — that is to say, by the time Washington was inaugurated — he had worked out the general scheme of courts which the committee afterward adopted. Yet it was not till twelve days later that the committee named a subcommittee to draft a bill.[4] His substantial author-

[1] Maclay's Journal, 91–92. " Ellsworth hath led in this business, backed with Strong, Patterson (*sic*), Read often, Bassett seldom." *Ibid.*, 101.

One afternoon, Morris, Rufus King, and Pierce Butler called on Maclay. " The talk was all about the judiciary. Mr. Morris said that he had followed Ellsworth in everything; if it was wrong he would blame Ellsworth." *Ibid.*, 152.

[2] " Letters and Other Writings of Madison " (ed. 1865), IV, 428. The letter is dated Feb. 27, 1836.

[3] *Ibid.*, 220–221, letter dated May 30, 1832. See also Madison to Doddridge (June 6, 1832), *ibid.*, 221–222. Madison was peculiarly careful and accurate on all such questions as this about past events.

[4] July 9, 1789, Fisher Ames wrote to a Massachusetts correspondent: " The Judiciary is before the Senate, who make progress. Their committee labored upon it with vast perseverance, and have taken as full a view of their subject as I ever knew a committee take. Mr. Strong, Mr.

ship of it, asserted by his biographers, is conceded by historians of the period, and indeed does not seem to be questioned by any one.[1]   He had, of course, a great interest in the subject, and his experience on the old committee of appeals, in the great convention, and on the bench, gave him an exceptional equipment for the work.

No complete history of the bill can now be written, but there is enough in the journals of the two houses and in the debates of the House of Representatives to sustain Madison's impression that it went through without any radical changes.   It was introduced on June 12 by Lee;[2] but Lee can hardly have had much share in framing it, for he soon tried to amend it radically, and he was one of the six who voted against it when it passed the Senate.[3]   His amendment expressed the strongest opposition which the measure encountered, for it would have prevented the setting up of any inferior federal tribunals whatever, except for admiralty and maritime cases.

Whether to set up a complete system of federal courts or to assume for the federal establishment, in

Ellsworth, and Mr. Paterson, in particular, have their full share of this merit." Works, I, 64.

[1] Flanders stated (1857) that the original draft of the bill, in Ellsworth's handwriting, was "still preserved in the archives of the Government," and that "it passed with but little alteration from the original draft." But he gives no reference and does not state that he himself had seen the document.   Van Santvoord (1854) supposes that Paterson, an able lawyer, had a share in the work, and adds: "It is said that he (Ellsworth) was assisted also by the valuable aid of his colleague, Mr. Johnson. To Ellsworth, however, was assigned the chief share of the labor, and the draft of the bill was undoubtedly from his pen." Flanders, 159; Van Santvoord, 238.   See also Schouler's "History of the United States," I, 96; Carson, "History of the Supreme Court," I, 129, 186; Mr. Justice Field, in *Ex parte Virginia*, 100 United States Reports, 313.

[2] Senate Journals, 1st Sess., 50.   [3] *Ibid.*, 64.

all but a few categories of cases, a merely appellate jurisdiction, was probably the first question the committee had had to consider. To understand the precise nature of their task, little is necessary beyond a careful reading of the brief third article of the Constitution.[1] For models and object lessons they had of course the judicial establishments of England and the

[1] ARTICLE III

Section 1. The judicial power of the United States shall be vested in one Supreme Court, and in such inferior courts as the Congress may from time to time ordain and establish. The judges, both of the Supreme and inferior courts, shall hold their offices during good behavior, and shall, at stated times, receive for their services a compensation which shall not be diminished during their continuance in office.

Section 2. The judicial power shall extend to all cases, in law and equity, arising under this Constitution, the laws of the United States, and treaties made, or which shall be made, under their authority; — to all cases affecting ambassadors, other public ministers, and consuls; — to all cases of admiralty and maritime jurisdiction; — to all controversies to which the United States shall be a party; — to controversies between two or more States; — between a State and citizens of another State; — between citizens of different States; — between citizens of the same State claiming lands under grants of different States, and between a State, or the citizens thereof, and foreign states, citizens or subjects.

In all cases affecting ambassadors, other public ministers and consuls, and those in which a State shall be party, the Supreme Court shall have original jurisdiction. In all other cases before mentioned, the Supreme Court shall have appellate jurisdiction, both as to law and fact, with such exceptions and under such regulations as the Congress shall make.

The trial of all crimes, except in case of impeachment, shall be by jury; and such trial shall be held in the State where the said crimes shall have been committed; but when not committed within any State, the trial shall be at such place or places as the Congress may by law have directed.

Section 3. Treason against the United States shall consist only in levying war against them, or in adhering to their enemies, giving them aid and comfort.

No person shall be convicted of treason unless on the testimony of two witnesses to the same overt act, or on confession in open court.

The Congress shall have power to declare the punishment of treason, but no attainder of treason shall work corruption of blood, or forfeiture, except during the life of the person attained.

several colonies, and possibly some of them were acquainted also with the systems of continental Europe. They can scarcely have failed to foresee from the beginning that there would be jealousy of the new establishment, since it would bring the fresh power of the central government home to the people more intimately, perhaps, than any other department. But on the other hand there was the history of the committee of appeals to show that unless the central government had efficient courts of its own it could not be sure of successfully asserting its judicial authority. Ellsworth, in particular, can hardly have forgotten the case of the sloop *Active* and the still unsatisfied claim of Olmstead and his fellows. To the establishment of inferior courts with original jurisdiction of maritime causes there seems in fact to have been no serious objection from any quarter. But the committee decided also that there must be inferior federal courts for all causes to which, according to the Constitution, the judicial power of the central government extended. There could scarcely be a briefer statement of the scheme of courts which was then adopted than the following, from a letter written by Ellsworth on April 30 to Judge Richard Law of the Connecticut Superior Court:[1]

"NEW YORK, April 30, 1789.

"DEAR SIR: The following are outlines of a judiciary system contemplating before a committee of the Senate.

"That the Supreme Court consist of six judges, and hold two stated sessions annually at or near the seat of government.

---

[1] Wharton's State Trials, 37-38.

"That there be a District Court with one judge resident in each State, with jurisdiction in admiralty cases, smaller offences and some other special cases. "That the United States be divided into three circuits. That a court be holden twice annually in each State, to consist of two judges of the Supreme Court and the District Judge. This court to receive appeals in some cases from the District Court, to try high crimes, and have original jurisdiction in law and equity, in controversies between foreigners and citizens and between citizens of different states, &c., where the matter in dispute exceeds two thousand dollars. I wish to be favored with your thoughts on this important subject, as particularly as you please. Mr. Larned will be able to gratify your curiosity as to what has been done and is doing here."

Nor could there be a much briefer statement of the reasons for the decision to set up inferior tribunals than the following,[1] written early in August to the same correspondent:

"NEW YORK, Aug. 4, 1789.

"DEAR SIR: I thank you for two letters received since my late return from Connecticut, and am glad to find your opinion favorable toward the Judiciary Bill, which has been the result of much deliberation in the Senate. To annex to State Courts jurisdictions which they had not before, as of admiralty cases, and, perhaps, of offences against the United States, would be constituting the judges of them, *pro tanto*, federal judges, and of course they would continue such during good behavior, and on fixed salaries, which in many

[1] Wharton's State Trials, 38.

cases would illy comport with their present tenure of office. Besides, if the State Courts, as such, could take cognizance of these offences, it might not be safe for the General Government to put the trial and punishment of them entirely out of its own hands. One federal judge, at least, resident in each State, appears unavoidable; and without creating any more, or much enhancing the expense, there may be Circuit Courts, which would give system to the department, uniformity to the proceedings, settle many cases in the States that would otherwise go to the Supreme Court, and provide for the higher grade of offences. Without this arrangement there must be many appeals or writs of error from the Supreme Courts of the States, which by placing them in a subordinate situation, and subjecting their decisions to frequent reversals, would probably more hurt their feelings and their influence, than to divide the ground with them at first, and leave it optional with the parties entitled to federal jurisdiction, where the causes are of considerable magnitude, to take their remedy in which line of courts they pleased. I consider a proper arrangement of the Judiciary, however difficult to establish, among the best securities the Government will have, and question much if any will be found at once more economical, systematic, and efficient, than the one under consideration. Its fate in the House of Representatives or in the opinion of the public, I cannot determine. But being after a long investigation satisfied in my own mind of its expediency, I have not hesitated, nor shall I, to give it the little support in my power. As to the District Court in Connecticut, I should be well satisfied with its sitting alternately at New Haven and New London." [1]

But apart from the decision to have inferior courts, and the scheme of districts and circuits, it was no simple business to carry out in a practical fashion the general directions of the Constitution. The longer one examines the third article of that potent instrument, the more one admires its condensation, its comprehensiveness, its wise elasticity. It is perhaps the very best specific instance of the founders' wisdom and foresight. The definition of the limits of federal jurisdiction is perfectly clear and perfectly logical, and the two or three rules concerning the way it shall be exercised leave to the legislature a discretion ample for all conceivable changes of conditions. But the bill cannot have been an easy one to draft. Provision must be made for ten classes of cases, the jurisdictions of the Supreme, Circuit, and District courts must be carefully delimited, and the judicial authority of the several states no further invaded than was necessary to assert fully the judicial authority of the Union. The device of concurrent jurisdiction and the expedient of transferring cases from one court to another had to be freely employed — perhaps more freely than ever before in the history of jurisprudence. But it would again be difficult to detail the way in which the various problems were solved in fewer or simpler words than those of Ellsworth in the bill itself. [2]

Had Lee's amendment carried, the bill would have

[1] Among some Ellsworth papers in the Public Library of the city of New York there is a brief letter written the same day to Pierpont Edwards, telling him that Judge Law thought well of the proposed judiciary system.

[2] For the text, without amendments, see "Statutes at Large" (edited by R. Peters), I, 73–93.

lost its character as a complete fulfilment of the constitutional mandate, and the new government would
have surrendered at the outset a great part of its
authority. To leave unexercised the power to create
inferior tribunals would have been conceding too much
to a destructive anti-Federalist sentiment. While the
Constitution was before the people, its adversaries had
with much success inveighed against it as threatening to overthrow the state judiciaries. Lee himself,
in his " Letters of a Federalist Farmer," had skilfully
taken that line of attack. In this, although he probably did not know it at the time, he was merely
following the lead of Rutledge, Butler, and others in
the Constitutional Convention. Four of the delegates
who would not sign the Constitution — Randolph,
Mason, Gerry, and Martin — had mentioned among
their objections the extensive jurisdiction given to the
federal courts. Senators who had served in the convention were probably not surprised, the day the bill
was introduced, to hear Pierce Butler of South Carolina set upon it forthwith in such a " flaming " speech
that he had to be called to order by the chair.[1] But
it now seems perfectly clear that Ellsworth and the
majority of the committee were wise to yield not at
all to these natural but illogical fears. They were
sustained by the Senate, for Lee's motion was voted
down. In the debate over it, as in all the debates
while the bill was on its passage, Ellsworth acted as
its manager and principal defender: so much at least
we learn from Maclay. And it appears that he was a
jealous defender, *tenax propositi*, and none too gentle
in his handling of objections and adversaries.

[1] Maclay's Journal, 74.

Taken up in committee of the whole on June 22, the bill was before the Senate much of the time until July 17, when it passed. In the debate by clauses, Ellsworth successfully resisted the attempt to reduce the number of judges of the Supreme Court. " He enlarged on the importance of the causes that would come before them, of the dignity it was necessary to support, and the twelve judges of England in the Exchequer chamber were held up to view during the whole harangue, and he seemed to draw conclusions that twelve were few enough." [1] But Maclay's amendment to permit affirmations instead of oaths carried,[2] and so did another to change a clause, not specified, " where Ellsworth in his diction had varied from the Constitution," — notwithstanding that Ellsworth " kindled, as he always does when it (the bill) is meddled with." [3] On the motion to strike out a clause requiring a defendant, on oath, to disclose his knowledge of the cause, there was much feeling displayed. " Up now rose Ellsworth, and in a most elaborate harangue supported the clause; now in chancery, now in common law, and now common law again, with a chancery side." But the amendment was passed, and a rage of speaking caught the Senate. Instead of consenting to strike out the clause, Ellsworth would have met the objections to it by applying the rule to the plaintiff also. But this did not satisfy the opposition, and they continued to press him the next day. So again " up rose Ellsworth and threw the common

[1] Maclay's Journal, 87.

[2] " Ran Ellsworth so hard, and the other anti-affirmants, on the anti-constitutionalism of the clause that they at last consented to have a question taken whether the clause should not be expunged, and expunged it was." *Ibid.*, 89. [3] *Ibid.*, 91–92.

law back all the way to the wager of law, which he
asserted was still in force." Strong of Massachusetts
taking the other side, " Ellsworth's temper forsook him.
He contradicted Strong with rudeness; said what the
gentleman asserted was not fact; that defendants were
admitted as witnesses; that all might be witnesses
against themselves. Got Blackstone; but nothing
could be inferred from Blackstone but such a thing by
consent." According to Maclay, Ellsworth lost his
own amendment, and lost the clause.[1] There was
another stiff contest over the section — the sixteenth
— which prohibited suits in equity in cases where a
remedy could be had at law,[2] and another over the
judges' powers to apprehend, bail, and commit,[3] Ellsworth each time leading for the bill as it stood. Maclay himself was somewhat daunted in his opposition
when he learned that the foremost lawyers of Pennsylvania — the Chief Justice, James Wilson, Judge Peters,
and Tench Coxe among them — had indorsed the
plan of it.[4] Ellsworth growing somewhat more ac-
commodating, and standing firm against enlarging the
scope of chancery, — Maclay's pet aversion, — the suspicious old democrat began to think a trifle better of
him also. They two stood together, in a contest with
nearly all the lawyers of the chamber, against admitting any more equity proceedings than the first draft
allowed; and it seems that they won their fight.[5]

[1] Maclay's Journal, 92–94.   [3] *Ibid.*, 98–99.
[2] *Ibid.*, 94–95.   [4] *Ibid.*, 102–103.
[5] Maclay says that on the 13th Ellsworth made a motion, practically
identical with a clause lost on the 11th, which, from the context, was evidently the anti-equity clause; and the Senate Journal (p. 63) shows that
a clause stricken out on the 11th was restored on the 13th. For the whole
discussion, *ibid.*, 103–109.

" Ellsworth has credit with me," Maclay concedes; and again, " Ellsworth . . . has credit with me on the whole of this business. The part he has acted in it I consider as candid (bating his caballing with Johnson) and disinterested." But on the final vote Maclay was against the bill as a whole, and when it passed he was again visited by the gloomiest misgivings, fearing that all the state judiciaries were going to be swallowed up.[1]

A kindred spirit in the House of Representatives was Livermore of New Hampshire. " For my part," he said, " I contemplate with horror the effect of the plan; I think I see a foundation laid for discord, civil war, and all its concomitants."[2] This was on August 24, for it was more than a month before the bill was taken up in the House. Up again on August 29 and 31, it slumbered the next week while the House engaged in what Fisher Ames describes as "this despicable grog-shop contest, whether the taverns of New York or Philadelphia shall get the custom of Congress."[3] Debated from September 8 to 15 in committee of the whole, it was many times amended, though probably in unimportant ways, then reported back to the House, which promptly passed it, with the amendments. But what the amendments were does not appear, for the proceedings in committee are given only for the first three days, when none were adopted.[4]

The discussion during those three days was over Livermore's motion, substantially identical with Lee's

---

[1] Maclay's Journal, 117–118.   [2] Annals of Congress, I, 784–785.
[3] Ames's Works, I, 80.
[4] Annals of Congress, 782–894; House Journals, I, 120–131.

in the Senate, to give up all the inferior tribunals except the courts of admiralty. The fight against the bill was vehemently waged by Livermore, by Tucker, Burke, and Sumter, of South Carolina, by Jackson of Georgia, and by Stone of Maryland. Stone's criticisms were the strongest and best tempered. He made a fair retort to the contention that Congress had no authority to invest state courts with a jurisdiction which the Constitution expressly conferred on federal courts, pointing out that this was actually done in the bill for causes involving small amounts ; and he argued well from mere policy against going at once the full length of the constitutional grant of authority.[1]   Jackson, the *enfant terrible* of the first House, clamored against the inconvenience, expense, and tyranny of the plan.[2] People would not submit, he thought, to be dragged great distances from their homes to be tried by strangers. The principal defenders of the bill were the foremost men in the chamber, — Madison, Sherman, Ames and Sedgwick, of Massachusetts, Benson and Lawrence, of New York, and William Smith of South Carolina. Smith put particularly well an argument which Maclay had made in the Senate, viz. that the Constitution was really mandatory in respect of the setting up of inferior courts, since it directed that the judicial power be vested only in them and the Supreme Court. But it was felt all along that the bill would pass, substantially as it was.[3]

[1] Annals of Congress, 809–812, 822–827.

[2] *Ibid.*, 801–804, 813–815.

[3] Ames wrote, September 6, " The Judicial slumbers, and, when it shall be resumed, will probably pass as an experimental law without much debate or amendment, in the confidence that a short experience will make manifest the proper alterations." Works, I, 71.

Ellsworth, who headed the Senate committee on the House amendments, reported in favor of disagreeing to four, amending one, and agreeing to the rest,[1] and in this compromise the House concurred.[2] The bill was signed by John Adams on September 22. Two days later, Washington signed it, and immediately sent to the Senate the nominations of John Jay to be Chief Justice, and of Rutledge, Wilson, William Cushing, and John Blair to be associate justices of the Supreme Court. February 2, 1790, at New York City, in a room provided at the Exchange, the court was organized, and the Judiciary Department of the government went into full operation. It is hard to see how any one could have disputed with Ellsworth the distinction of having had the chief part in creating it. Apart from his authorship of the law, his appointment to the first place on the committee strengthens the conjecture that it was he who, on the committee of five in the Constitutional Convention, had drafted the article on the judiciary.

Three other laws were passed by the first Congress to supplement the judiciary act, and two of these also were apparently from Ellsworth's hand; for he headed the committees which severally reported an act additional to the judiciary act and an act to define crimes and offences cognizable under the authority of the United States.[3] He also helped to frame the third supplementary law, which regulated

[1] There were at least fifty-two, as one of those agreed to was the fifty-second.

[2] Senate Journals, 137–140, 143. Carson ("History of the Supreme Court," Ch. 2) gives a history of the bill, drawn from authorities already mentioned.

[3] Journals, 2d Sess., 12, 16, 17, 63.

processes in the courts.[1]   There were no standing
committees during these early years of the Senate;
but so long as he remained a senator he continued
to serve, usually as chairman, on all special committees charged with business relating to the judiciary.   He had, therefore, a part, and doubtless still
the chief part, in such changes and extensions of his
handiwork as in actual operation it seemed to need.
These, however, were neither many nor radical.   His
scheme stood the test under which the vast majority
of laws made, as this was, out of the whole cloth, usually come to grief.   It worked.   One of his committees was appointed to consider certain improvements
recommended by the members of the Supreme Court
in a joint letter to the President, but these, too, were
comparatively unimportant.   It was ten years before
the first really radical change in the judiciary was
made, and that was made, partly at least and probably mainly, from partisan motives.   Beaten in the
elections of 1800, and about to go out of power, the
Federalists passed an act which largely increased
the number both of districts and circuits, relieved
the Supreme Court justices of all circuit duties, and
provided, instead, for three circuit judges for every
circuit.   The act created twenty-three new judge-
ships in all, and this at a time when the business of
the courts was actually decreasing.   President Adams,
on the very eve of his retirement, filled all these new
places with Federalists.   But one of the first acts of
the Republicans on coming into power was to repeal
this law entirely, throwing the new judges out of
office, and leaving the Ellsworth law again in force.

[1] Senate Journals, 1st Sess., 153.

It proved sufficiently elastic to serve, with extensions to keep pace with the growth of the country, but with no real changes, until 1869, when the great increase of business led again to a provision for circuit judges, which finally relieved the Supreme Court justices of all circuit duties. This modification of the system was followed in 1891 by an act still farther to relieve the Supreme Court by setting up a Circuit Court of Appeals, to have final jurisdiction in certain classes of cases formerly appealable to the Supreme Court.

But even these changes can hardly be considered a departure from Ellsworth's general scheme of the courts. Most of the great judicial structure he devised still remains intact. He has, therefore, to this day, a hold on the life of his countrymen such as few even of the most illustrious minds of his own time have kept. Makers of mere laws are sometimes belittled by comparison with poets and artists and founders of creeds. But there are laws, particularly those which plant institutions capable of growth, that go very deep into the life of civilized societies and exert for ages true compulsions and restraints; and such a law is the act of 1789 "to establish the Judicial Courts of the United States."

It will always remain the most conspicuous monument of Ellsworth's legislative career. But his labors in the Senate, entirely apart from the judiciary, were nothing less than prodigious. To give the mere list of the committees he served on and the measures he framed or helped to frame would require several pages. The reader would be little enlightened, and certainly wearied, with the lifeless journal entries that constitute, in many instances, the sole record and evidence of the share he had in legislation which, by reason of its fundamental, semi-constitutional character, stands apart from all that later Congresses have done, save when they have either adopted amendments to the Constitution, or set up new departments, or in other ways struck out entirely new policies. It was he who reported back from a conference committee the first twelve Constitutional amendments which Congress submitted to the states,[1] ten of which were ratified. When North Carolina came into the Union, ceding her Western lands to the new government, he helped to frame the measure that welcomed her and accepted the cession;[2] and a little later he reported the act to provide a government for all unorganized territory south of the Ohio.[3] When Rhode Island, at the end of a year, still declined to come in, it was he, apparently, who found the means to force her in. The means was a non-intercourse act; and a few weeks later Ellsworth wrote of it:[4] " Rhode Island is at length brought into the Union, and by a pretty bold measure in Congress, which would have exposed me to some censure had it not produced the effect which I expected it would, and which, in fact, it has done. But ' all's well that ends well.' The Constitution is now adopted by all the States, and I have much satisfac-

---

[1] Senate Journals, 1st Sess., 142, 145.

[2] *Ibid.*, 2d Sess., 18-20, 29, 33; Maclay, 202-203, 226, 236.

[3] Journals, 2d Sess., 55, 56-59.

[4] June 7, 1790, — " to a friend," Flanders, 163; Journals, 2d Sess., 63, 75-76; Maclay, 259, 264, 266. " Ellsworth spoke with great deliberation, often and long," says Maclay; and again, ". . . Ellsworth spouted out for it."

tion, and perhaps some vanity, in seeing, at length, a great work finished, for which I have long labored incessantly." He dealt with the question of salaries for the President and Vice-President and other officials, and he reported at the end of the year the sums due to himself and his brother senators for mileage and attendance — a fairly strong proof in itself that he was trusted by his fellows.[1] He fought for and carried a joint rule that at the beginning of a new session of Congress all business should be taken up *de novo*.[2] He wrote the first act concerning the consular service.[3] He helped to make the first plans for the military establishment,[4] the postal service,[5] and a census.[6] While the departments were being organized, he took a firm stand on an important question over which the President and the Senate have more than once fallen into violent contention. In July, 1789, there was a heated debate over the power

[1] Journals, 1st Sess., 87; 3d Sess., 122; 4th Sess., 49; Maclay, 140, 144, 147. Ellsworth seems to have crossed Adams by favoring low pay for senators.

[2] Journals, 2d Sess.,13–15; Maclay, 179, 181–183, 185. Maclay implies that the rule was adopted to get rid of some action already taken on the question of residence.

[3] ". . . And, of course, he hung like a bat to every particle of it." *Ibid.*, 368.

[4] Journals, 2d Sess., 98; Maclay, 239, 241–245, 250–251.

[5] Journals, 1st Sess., 132; 2d Cong., 1st Sess., 96, etc.; 2d Sess., 150.

[6] *Ibid.*, 1st Sess., 26. Johnston (of North Carolina) "had said something against the bill as it stood, but when Ellsworth made his motion, he got up to tell how convincing the gentleman's arguments were, and that they had fully convinced him. . . . I got a hard hit at Ellsworth. He felt it and did not reply. The bill was immediately afterward committed and the Senate adjourned. Ellsworth came laughing to me; said he would have distinguished with respect to the point I brought forward. I said, 'Ellsworth, the man must knit his net close that can catch you; but you trip sometimes.' So we had a laugh and parted." Maclay, 195–197.

of removal from appointive offices, and John Adams, seeing the importance of the subject, entered in his diary some notes of the speeches. This is his report of Ellsworth's: [1]

" Ellsworth. We are sworn to support the Constitution. There is an explicit grant of power to the President, which contains the power of removal. The executive power is granted; not the executive powers hereinafter enumerated and explained. The President, not the Senate appoints: they only consent and advise. The Senate is not an executive council; has no executive power. The grant to the President is express, not by implication." [2]

And yet he found the time and energy to enter into the discussion of the four subjects over which the first Congress divided with the greatest heat. These were, the revenue, the seat of government, the debt, and the bank.

The first tariff bill that came up from the House of Representatives had originated with Madison, and Ellsworth must have recognized it as the consummation of the plan for a permanent revenue which he and Madison and Hamilton had commended to the states in April, 1783. The duties were not high, but many articles had been added to Madison's original list, and some of the duties were specific. The principle of protection had been introduced, and the interests of different states and sections had been drawn

---

[1] Adams's Works, 409.

[2] See also Maclay, 144, for the same speech, and 112–114, 116, for Ellsworth's part in the controversy. He seems to have felt very strongly, indeed, on the whole question of the power and independence of the President, fearing that the system would fail because the executive arm was not made strong enough.

at once into controversy. New England representatives had fought for high duties on rum and low duties on molasses, that they might continue to import the one in order to manufacture and export the other; and they had also, in the interest of the fisheries, opposed the duty on salt. On this last item, Ellsworth, unlike most New England men, did not follow the lead of eastern Massachusetts. At first, he was also against any discrimination in favor of our own merchant vessels engaged in the tea trade with the East; and by changing his mind on that subject he convinced Maclay that he, like others, was " governed by convenience or cabal." [1] In the end, he headed the committee which reported the Senate's decision on the question,[2] and he rendered a like service on the question of trade relations with the West Indies and other parts of America.[3] He stood out against the proposal to discriminate, both in the tariff bill and in the tonnage bill which followed it, in favor of France and other nations with which we were in treaty;[4] and he served on the committee of conference which gave to both these essential measures their final character. So concerned was the Senate over this particular conference that while it lasted no other business was taken up.[5] Throughout the discussion, Ellsworth appears as one of those whose chief anxiety was for the actual success of the revenue measures, not for the special interests which they might endanger or advance. At the second session, when Hamilton, who was now at the head of the Treasury

[1] Maclay, 57, 60, 61, 68.
[2] *Ibid.*, 71 ; Journal, 1st Sess., 46.
[3] *Ibid.*, 87 ; 2d Sess., 26.

[4] Maclay, 89.
[5] Journals, 1st Sess., 55.

Department, recommended an increase of the revenue, Ellsworth seems to have championed even more zealously the bill which carried out the secretary's desire.[1] At the third session, when an excise bill, aimed particularly at whiskey, was sent up from the House, he had the courage to be the Senate manager of that unpopular measure, which eventually caused the so-called " Whiskey Rebellion." [2]

On the question of the seat of government, he took in the first session a decidedly Eastern stand. For the permanent seat he favored the Susquehanna as against any point farther southward; and for a temporary seat he stood out for New York as against Philadelphia. Later, he did once vote for Baltimore for the permanent seat; but probably only in preference to a site on the Potomac, for he was against the bill that finally passed. This would seem to indicate that his was not one of the votes that were changed to carry out the famous bargain by which Hamilton secured the assumption of the debts of the states in return for the concession of the capital to the South.[3] But from this it must not be inferred that Ellsworth was lacking in ardor either for assumption or for a firm and national policy with all the different schedules of the debt. Holding that they were all parts of the price of independence, he was for acknowledging the entire obli-

---

[1] Journals, 2d Sess., 190, 194–196.

[2] *Ibid.*, 3d Sess., 43, 47, 88; Maclay, 381. "Ellsworth could not rest a moment all this day (Jan. 27, 1791). He was out and in, in and out, all on the fidgets. Twice or thrice was an adjournment hinted at, and as often did he request that it might be withdrawn, expecting the excise bill to be taken up."

[3] Journals, 1st Sess., 147–149; 2d Sess., 97–99, 127–128, 131, 134, 141, 144; Maclay, 158, 275, 293, 308, 313, 395.

gation and taking measures to fund it, principal and interest, and for providing the means to carry it and eventually discharge it. It seems, in fact, that he was again peculiarly responsible for the way in which the subject was finally disposed of; for the funding bill as it passed, including the provision for assumption, originated in a resolution which he offered in the Senate early in July, 1790. At that time, the seat of government was not yet chosen, assumption had been defeated in the House, and a House funding bill, with no provision for the debts of the states, was in the hands of a Senate committee of which Ellsworth was a member. It is entirely probable that he knew of the agreement by which, in return for Jefferson's help in passing the assumption bill, Hamilton was to procure enough votes to fix the capital on the Potomac.[1] Ellsworth's resolution was, " That provision be made the next session of Congress for loaning to the U.S. a sum not exceeding twenty-two millions of dollars, in the certificates issued by the respective states for service or supplies for the prosecution of the late war, the certificates which shall be loaned to stand charged to the respective states by whom they were issued until a liquidation of their accounts with the United States can be completed." [2] Laid on the table until the residence bill, which passed the House two days later, had also passed the Senate, this resolution was then referred to a committee which soon reported it

[1] For a good account of the status of the two measures, showing the relation of Ellsworth's motion to the compromise, see Hunt's " Life of Madison," 197–200.

[2] Journals, 2d Sess., 104, 108. He had given notice the day the House funding bill came up. See also Maclay, 288. Maclay's record indicates that Ellsworth was the first to propose assumption in the Senate.

back lengthened into a set of resolutions. These being in turn committed along with the funding bill, both were finally reported in the form of a bill dealing with the entire debt. Ellsworth was a member of both committees, as he was also of the committee and the conference committee which handled the old accounts with the states.[1] He spoke repeatedly on the funding bill, both before and after the assumption was incorporated in it. According to Maclay, he was trying "to reconcile the secretary's (Hamilton's) system to the public opinion and welfare."[2] But from another source we learn that on at least two not unimportant details he differed with Hamilton. July 20, Oliver Wolcott, Jr., a son of Ellsworth's old friend and colleague in the Continental Congress, and now, probably by Ellsworth's influence, auditor of the Treasury, wrote to his brother Frederic:[3]

"The great question is now respecting interest. Our friend, Mr. Ellsworth, in the Senate, has been of opinion that it was not expedient to fund the public debt at a higher rate of interest than four per cent. That this sum, punctually paid, would answer the expectations of the creditors, the requirements of justice, and would better secure the public honor than a promise of a higher provision, which would, under the circumstances of this country, be attended with great risk of failure.

"He has also been dissatisfied with the secretary's

---

[1] Journals, 2d Sess., 147, 154.

[2] Maclay, 290. For Ellsworth's connection with funding and assumption, see also *ibid.*, 287–291, 298, 300–301, 314, 325–328; Journals, 2d Sess., 142, 145, 147, 149, 173.

[3] Gibbs, I, 49. In the same volume (20, 22) are two letters from Ellsworth concerning the appointment of Wolcott to the auditorship.

proposal of leaving one-third of the debt unfunded for ten years, as this measure would tend to encourage speculations, and would leave, after ten years, a great burden upon the country, with little advantage to foreigners, who would purchase that part of the debt at a low rate.

" These opinions have been supported by him with all that boldness and reason which give him a predominant influence in the Senate. He has, however, been warmly opposed, and a compromise, it is said, has been made to fund the principal of the domestic debt in the following manner: For every $100 principal, $66\frac{2}{3}$ to be funded presently at 6 per cent, and $26\frac{88}{100}$ after ten years at the same rate. The indents and all arrearages of interest, which amount to about one-third of the debt, to be funded at 3 per cent. This, it is said, will give about 4s 3 per cent interest for the entire debt.

" A resolution has passed the Senate for funding the state debts at the same rate as the continental debt; but all these things may, and probably will assume a different modification before the session is completed."

But Wolcott's information concerning the compromise arrangement proved correct. Within a month, the funding bill, including assumption, was carried through both houses substantially as he described it. All that was then needed to complete Hamilton's general scheme of finance was a bank; and in this step also Ellsworth, from his experience in the old Congress, could render valuable aid. When the secretary's report on the bank was received, the first Congress being then in its third session, he served on the committee which considered it and prepared a bill, and he spoke and voted for the bill itself,[1] which passed with no radical amendments.

By these bold, firm measures the new government accomplished at the outset an immense gain of prestige, won the propertied class to its support, raised its credit, and by the quick success of its policies soon stimulated industry to a great revival all over the country.   For all this Hamilton is chiefly to be praised; but he could never have achieved his designs without skilful and courageous management in Congress; and all the evidence we have goes to indicate that in the Senate no man did more to carry through the programme than the junior senator from Connecticut.   It is doubtful if any other senator did so much.

Ellsworth's first term ended with the life of the first Congress, but he was reëlected to serve until 1797. After 1791, however, there is no Maclay's diary to give meaning and life to the journal record, and it is impossible to follow with any assurance of a right comprehension the votes and other officially recorded acts of any senator.   Save as Ellsworth is revealed to us in contemporary letters and the recollections of his associates, we must rest content with the salient facts of his undiminished energy and ceaseless activity, his maintenance of the leadership already established, and the stands he took on the greater questions of the time. Besides his watchful interest in all that pertained to the judiciary, there were certain routine duties of the Senate, nowadays the province of standing committees, with which, at each successive session, his name is

[1] Journals, 3d Sess., 21, 33, 35; Maclay, 370–371.

regularly associated. He was one of the senators who revised the annual appropriations as they came from the House.[1] He concerned himself particularly with the regulation of the consular service.[2] Again and again he considered the cases of persons applying for pensions.[3] When the right of Albert Gallatin to sit for Pennsylvania was challenged, he served on the first Senate elections committee and helped to prepare a report against the claim of the brilliant young Swiss.[4] On one occasion, near the end of a session, as chairman of a special committee, he took charge of four not unimportant subjects, and the next day reported three bills to dispose of them.[5]

But his time and energy were more and more absorbed by questions which owed their interest to party controversy quite as much as to their own intrinsic importance. For the second Congress was but a few months old when Fisher Ames could write, truthfully enough, that the opposition to the policies of the administration had become "a regular, well disciplined party."[6] So much, at least, Jefferson had accomplished within a year to offset the brilliant achievements of Hamilton in the actual working of the government. In 1791, George Cabot of Massachusetts came to join Ellsworth, King, and Strong, leaders of the administration party in the Senate; but at the same time Aaron Burr's name was entered on the roll. It was not long before Langdon of New Hampshire went

[1] Journals, 2d Cong., 1st Sess., 269; 3d Cong., 1st Sess., 191; 4th Cong., 1st Sess., 58.

[2] Ibid., 2d Cong., 1st Sess., 31.

[3] Ibid., 109, 149; 2d Sess., 32, 68, etc.

[4] Ibid., 3d Cong., 1st Sess., 16, 29, 61, 62.

[5] Ibid., 147, 149.   [6] Works, I, 118.

over to Jefferson's following, which in the third Congress controlled the House of Representatives, and on several occasions, but for the casting vote of Adams, would have deadlocked the Senate. The true sources of the strength of this opposition cannot here be analyzed. It is enough to say that its attacks were made first on the financial policy of the administration, then on its foreign policy. But the outcry against the assumption and the bank gradually lessened with the coming of prosperity, and the discontent with the revenue measures was speedily put out of countenance by the low character, the trifling proportions, and the swift and easy suppression of the Whiskey Rebellion in Pennsylvania. In this episode, the readiness of Hamilton and the firmness of Washington turned what might have been a fatal revelation of the government's weakness into a proof of its strength and a means of discomfiting its opponents.

Readiness and firmness in the legislature also were needed, and these qualities the Federalist senators and congressmen at once displayed. They took measures promptly to strengthen the military establishment, passing acts to build magazines and arsenals, and to encourage recruiting,[1] and they upheld Washington's hands with their addresses to the President and with speeches in the chambers. In the summer of 1794, while the so-called insurrection was in progress, Ellsworth wrote from Windsor to the younger Wolcott, whose office kept him in Philadelphia, that he thought the use of the militia indispensable; and that Washington — " who seldom mistakes, and as we believe

---

[1] See, for Ellsworth's part in these activities, Senate Journals, 3d Cong., 1st Sess., 43, 92, 117, 153, 157, etc.

never "— could count on the steadfast support of Connecticut, and indeed of all New England. But at the end he added: "Pray keep me well informed of this rebellion, which I hope to see brought to a good issue. And tell me as much as you may of what Mr. Jay writes — I think the two subjects are related."[1]

The remark is a good index to Ellsworth's view of the political situation, and indeed of the entire state of our affairs. That summer, Jay was in England, and to follow the train of causes which had sent him thither would be to write the political and diplomatic history of the five years that went before.

The mission was the immediate outcome of a plan which had originated with Ellsworth and his Senate confrères rather than with Washington. The warlike measures they had prepared in accordance with the President's recommendations had not been aimed chiefly at the malcontents at home. Washington had been deeply concerned over our relation to the contest between England and France. Notwithstanding that his whole desire was for peace and an honorable neutrality, he had urged Congress to prepare for a possible foreign war. The opposition, siding openly with France, had seemed bent on forcing the administration into a complete break with England; while the extreme Federalists had been brought into a mood of intense hatred for France and of too marked partiality for Great Britain. Genet, the light-headed minister of the new French republic, had done all that could be done by tactlessness, and by an utter disregard of our neutral rights, to drive us either to a subservient alliance or to a rupture with his government.

[1] Gibbs, I, 158–159.

But England, on the other hand, by a course hardly less contemptuous and even more damaging to our interests, seemed to be doing her best to offset the folly of Genet and the intemperate behavior of his American admirers. The discontent of the Southwest, and the threatening attitude of Americans in that quarter toward the Spanish in New Orleans, increased the tension. There was a widespread conviction that we should soon have a war, the only uncertainty being, with which of the powers we should fight. In this predicament, the whole course of politics turned on our foreign relations, to an extent that now passes belief. Even Ellsworth became for a time completely absorbed in international questions.

As usual, however, he kept his head. He was one of the few who in their anger with opponents at home and their indignation at foreign outrages never forgot their patriotism, and who in their patriotism never once lost sight of the main chance — the real and permanent interests of the country. Zealously supporting the administration in making ready for war, he was yet firm for peace; and he never despaired of it. Quite out of sympathy with the enthusiasm for the French notion of liberty, he made, as early as 1790, a speech in which he ridiculed France's claim to our gratitude.[1] He voted later to soften some over-ardent resolutions congratulating France on the adoption of a republican form of government, he supported the bill denying her the use of our ports for prizes, and he seconded Cabot's motion to strike out the phrase, "that magnanimous nation," from another set of resolutions thanking her

---

[1] Maclay, 405, calls the speech "a burst of abuse . . . against the French in the most vituperative language that fancy could invent."

for a gift of colors.[1] He was also against a temporary embargo which passed, and against a bill to prohibit all importations from Great Britain, which was beaten only by Adams's vote.[2] But he went into no excess of partisanship for the British. The governing consideration with him seems to have been that friendship and trade with England were worth more to us than anything France could offer. In January, 1794, when the Republicans were clamoring for war with England, and many who opposed it thought it unavoidable, he wrote to his friend, Judge Law:[3] "As to the war between this country and England, so much dreaded by some and wished for by others, *I think it will not take place.* Complaint of Mr. Genet has been made to his Court, with a request of his recall. The answer is, that they disapprove of his conduct, and will immediately recall him. The fact however is, that he has not done but part of the mischief he has been sent to do." And early in March he wrote to his brother David:[4] "As to war, sir, I still think that we shall avoid it, notwithstanding all the difficulty and danger attending our condition. Should I at any time think it advisable for you to sell the whole or part of your stock I shall certainly tell you of it." A few weeks later, writing to the elder Wolcott about Madison's resolutions for discriminating against all nations not in trade with us, he agreed with his correspondent that they could, if passed, produce nothing but mischief. The debts of the South were, he thought, a principal factor in creating the situation " by opposing compul-

[1] Journals, 2d Cong., 1st Sess., 155; 3d Cong., 1st Sess., 118–119; 4th Cong., 1st Sess., 44.

[2] *Ibid.*, 3d Cong., 1st Sess., 118–119, 165.

[3] Jan. 20, 1794, Wood Ms.; Flanders, 168–169.   [4] March 4. 1794.

sive energy of the government, generating mist and irritation between this country and Great Britain, and, of course, giving a baleful ascendancy to French influence." But he added: " I hope in a few days we shall see the business turned into a channel of negociation, and a respectable envoy sent to London, on the subject of commercial spoliations. A negociation of this kind, with proper interior arrangements to give weight, would, I presume, save us from war."[1]

When Ellsworth expressed such a definite hope as this, the chances were that it was already by way of being realized. From the letters of two or three other Federalist leaders, as well as from his own cautious outgivings and the recollections of the members of his family, we know that he did not speak of the mission to England until he and a small group of his friends had taken steps to bring it about; he may even have had it in mind as early as his letter to his brother.[2] At any rate, the mission was first considered about the beginning of March, when Madison's anti-British resolutions and other proposals in the House put an end to all friendly relations between the two countries. The son and biographer of Hamilton has asserted that the first suggestion of it came from him, and this may very well be true; but the proof is wanting.[3] What seems fairly certain is that the plan was first proposed to Washington by Ellsworth.

[1] April 5, 1794, Gibbs, I, 134–135.

[2] It is interesting to compare his correspondence at this time with his speeches in the Constitutional Convention before the so-called Connecticut compromise was accepted. Both illustrate his coolness and balance.

[3] J. C. Hamilton's " History of the Republic," V, 532–535 ; H. C. Lodge's " Life of George Cabot," 67, and note.

On March 10, Ellsworth, King, Strong, and Cabot had held a conference and considered the whole situation. It was plain that the House of Representatives was partial to France and hostile to England, and there were many signs that the country was with the House. England, by her disregard of our rights as a neutral, — her orders in council, her seizures of our ships and impressments of our sailors, — was daily feeding the popular wrath against her. France, though guilty of equal outrages, had the sympathy of the populace, and the skilful advocacy of Jefferson and other Republican leaders. Even in the Senate, the slight Federalist majority could not be depended on;[1] and the Genet episode had showed that the great prestige of Washington might not long suffice to uphold a policy the masses detested. There could be no doubt that we were really in danger of drifting into war, and that England, rather than France, would be the enemy. The outcome of the conference was a unanimous decision that an envoy extraordinary ought to be sent to England to negotiate a treaty of commerce, and Ellsworth was chosen to go at once and lay the matter before the President.

He accordingly sought an interview. When he had gone over the situation, dwelling on the crisis in our foreign relations, and pointing out that it was sure to aggravate our domestic difficulties, Washington asked him what was to be done. Ellsworth replied by proposing to send an envoy or envoys to England, and mentioned Hamilton and Jay as men whom he and his friends had agreed to recommend. The President, it seemed, was taken completely by surprise. Although

[1] H. C. Lodge's " Life of George Cabot," 95.

the two discussed the project at length, he would not at once commit himself. At the end of the interview, he said merely, " Well, sir, I will take the subject into consideration."[1]

But it did not take him many weeks to make up his mind; and somehow a rumor soon got about that he was going to make Hamilton the envoy. James Monroe heard it, and at once wrote to remonstrate, for to the Republicans there was no other name quite so obnoxious as Hamilton's. Washington, in reply, asked for a statement of the objections to Hamilton, and this Monroe failed to give. But it was decided, and no doubt wisely, that to appoint Hamilton would provoke an unavoidable opposition to the mission. Washington turned, accordingly, to John Jay, who had not yet been drawn into the more violent party controversies; and this choice Hamilton heartily approved.[2] To Jay himself, however, the call was most unwelcome, for he foresaw that the service would make him unpopular.[3] The following, from a letter to Wolcott, written April 16, 1794, may indicate that Ellsworth was one of those who helped Jay to see that it was his duty to accept:[4]

" In a late letter I suggested to you the idea of turning our grievances into a channel of negotiation. I now venture to assure you that Mr. Jay will be sent as special envoy to the Court of London, with

[1] Wood Ms.; O. E. Wood, in *New York Evening Post*; Lodge's "Cabot," 67; Lodge's Address on Ellsworth, in " A Fighting Frigate and Other Essays," 86–87 ; " Life and Correspondence of Rufus King " (ed. by C. R. King), I, 517–518.
[2] Hamilton's Works, IV, 536.
[3] " The Correspondence and Public Papers of John Jay," IV, 2–4.
[4] Gibbs, I, 135.

such powers and instructions as probably will produce the desired effect. His nomination will come forward this day or to-morrow. He is now here, and has this moment informed me of his determination to accept the appointment if it shall be made. This, sir, will be a mortifying movement to those who have endeavoured by every possible means to prevent a reconciliation between this country and Great Britain. The British instructions of the eighth January, which I sent you, begin to operate favourably in the West Indies. The embargo, I trust, will not be continued beyond the thirty days for which it was laid. It ought not to have been laid at all."

The day this letter was written, Washington sent to the Senate the nomination of Jay. After a violent debate of three days,[1] the Senate confirmed it. Early in May, the envoy sailed for England. It is no wonder that throughout the trying summer that followed, and late into the autumn, Ellsworth showed the deepest anxiety for news of his success. It is significant that on November 19, the day the treaty was signed, besides letters to Washington and to Edmund Randolph, Secretary of State, Jay wrote to Hamilton, King, and Ellsworth. To each of these three in turn, recognizing their common interest in the mission, he made a kind of brief report.[2] The results of the mission were in truth by no means brilliant, but they were all, perhaps, that could reasonably have been expected. Jay had failed to obtain compensation for the negro slaves carried off by British troops after the Revolution, or any agreement to stop the impressment of our seamen.

[1] "Life and Correspondence of Rufus King," I, 521–522.
[2] Jay's "Correspondence and Public Papers," IV, 132–144.

To obtain a slight measure of freedom of trade with the British West Indies he had consented to humiliating and damaging conditions. But a date was fixed for the surrender of the Western posts, which the British had held ever since the Revolution; boundary disputes were referred to commissioners; another commission was to sit on claims for damages to individuals; rules were framed to govern all questions of the right of seizure at sea; and we gained something in the matter of the restrictions on our commerce with India. The claims commission was doubtless the most important concession Jay had obtained, for it enabled him and his friends to feel that they had accomplished their principal object, — to avoid war without positive dishonor.

But the hardest part of the fight for peace was still ahead. Ellsworth had been right in his prophecy that the mission would prove "a mortifying movement" to the opposition. The treaty did not reach Philadelphia until the day after the short session of Congress came to an end. In June, the Senate was convened in special session to consider it. The opposition senators fought it bitterly. They succeeded in striking out the twelfth article relating to trade with the West Indies. But on June 24, by a bare two-thirds majority, the rest was approved. A few days later, the substance of the whole was revealed to the public; and at once, while the President was considering it, there broke upon the administration quite the most furious storm of crimination, slander, and abuse that ever arose even in those early years of the party system, when men still treated political opponents as enemies and traitors to the country. One of those who made themselves conspicuous by their violent opposition was John Rutledge, Ellsworth's associate in many earlier labors, whom Washington had recently chosen to be Jay's successor on the bench — a circumstance that had an important bearing on the future of Ellsworth himself.

There were reasons enough why Washington should hesitate before he signed the treaty, and he held it seven weeks — a period which gave the opposition an ample opportunity for protest. The opportunity was not neglected. Hamilton, rising to address a public meeting in New York, was driven from the rostrum with stones and curses. Jay was burned and hanged in effigy, lampooned in the public prints, denounced in public meetings, damned and double-damned in public and in private. Washington declared, "I have never since I have been in the administration of the government seen such a crisis." The worst of the business was not known to him, however, until one day when Wolcott, now promoted to be Secretary of the Treasury in place of Hamilton, who had resigned, put in his hands a document which seemed to show that Edmund Randolph, Jefferson's successor in the State Department, had been conspiring secretly with the minister of France, perhaps for pay, to compass the defeat of the treaty. This shameful episode, which is not even yet completely understood, may possibly have induced Washington to decide at once; and a few days later, on August 15, he signed the treaty.

Meanwhile, at his home in Windsor, Ellsworth had been pacing the hall in the most intense anxiety. For several nights he scarcely slept at all. For once, it seems, he had misdoubted Washington's firmness and

courage. Himself thoroughly convinced of the wisdom of accepting the treaty, he feared lest Washington
should bend before the tempest of popular disapproval.
The very day the treaty was signed, he wrote to Wolcott: " If the President decides wrong, or does not
decide *soon, his good fortune will forsake him.* N. E.
I think is tolerably quiet, and will be more so, as the
subject becomes more understood. But I am to be
responsible only for Connecticut. That E. R.[1] should
not act at all is less surprising than that J. R.[2] should
act like the D——. I wait for the unravelling, when
more is to be known. . . ." Even when he got Wolcott's letter, telling him the treaty was signed, he was
not content. August 20, he wrote again: " I am glad
the President has done at last, what I am unwilling to
believe he ever hesitated about, and the delay of which
has not been without hazard and some mischief. The
crisis admits not of the appearance of indecision, and
much less of steering any course but one.

" There is less reason to be anxious for the Eastern
quarter than there was some weeks since. The attempt of a few Lawyers, taking their tone from New
Haven, to agitate the state, has been unsuccessful,
and must be abandoned. Rhode Island and Vermont
I apprehend to be out of danger, though my information is not so full as might be wished. The current, I
believe, is turning in Massachusetts, though you may
perhaps hear of some more obscure Town Meetings.
The declarations of the Boston Merchants and the
President's letter to the Selectmen are good dampers,
and together with able defences now circulating, will

[1] Probably Edmund Randolph, possibly Edward Rutledge.
[2] John Rutledge.

produce an effect. As I hear nothing from New Hampshire except of the first impression at Portsmouth, I infer that Brother Langdon's argument and explanation, that ''tis a damned thing made to plague the French,' has by repetition lost its force. This is all I can tell you about New England. And I very much wish you, when you have leisure, to tell me how general and how violent the opposition is in all the States south of this, and what effects are to be expected from it.

"It is not certainly owing to laziness, that nothing more formal has been here written on the side of the Treaty. We thought it best to stand prepared for defence if an attack should be here made, which has not yet been the case, and in the meantime perhaps to scrap and squib a little, just to keep the humour the right way, and to see to the publishing of what is well written elsewhere."

Evidently, his whole heart was in the business, and he felt deeply his own share of the responsibility for it. He was right to fear that the danger from the opposition was not yet over. The House of Representatives was still to be reckoned with, for money must be appropriated to carry the treaty into effect. Throughout the whole of the following winter at Philadelphia, interest centred in the opposition's efforts to defeat the appropriation and the virtual claim of the House to a revisionary control over the exercise by the Senate and the President of their right to conclude treaties. The tide of national feeling and opinion was near its ebb, and for one reason or another the strongest men of the strong government party were passing from the scene. On his return from Europe, Jay resigned his place on the bench to become again the governor of New York. The cabinet places were already given over to second-rate characters. At this session of Congress, King, Cabot, Strong, and Ellsworth sat together for the last time in the Senate. From the other house, Fisher Ames, the most brilliant orator in Congress, was also about to retire, for a wasting disease had checked almost at the outset a career which otherwise would surely have been long and brilliant. His strength hardly enabled him to stand while he poured out in defence of the treaty a speech of extraordinary eloquence — the one really great oration of the Federalist period. Before the House finally voted the appropriation, Ellsworth also got an opportunity to render one more service to the cause of peace with England. The House had asked the President to lay before it the instructions to Jay, and the correspondence and other documents relating to the treaty. While Washington and his cabinet were considering the demand, Ellsworth was requested to give his opinion, and he drew up an argument to show that the House had no constitutional right to the documents.

This opinion was not rendered by Ellsworth the senator, but by the Chief Justice of the United States. His work as a lawgiver had come to an end. March 8, in a letter on another subject to the elder Wolcott, who was now governor of Connecticut, he wrote: " It is, sir, my duty to acquaint you that I have with some hesitation accepted an appointment in the judiciary of the United States, which of course vacates my seat in the Senate. This step I hope will not be regarded as disrespectful to a state which I have so long had the honor to serve, and whose interests must forever remain precious to my heart." [1]

But before we turn to Ellsworth the Chief Justice we should like, if it were possible, a better acquaintance with Ellsworth the Senator. According to one competent and intimate observer, the years of his senatorial service — notwithstanding that one of them was his fiftieth — were a period of remarkable growth. He met the many demands of his new place with a fresh access of energy and a display of gifts and powers which surprised even his intimates. It was doubtless his first colleague, Johnson, who to the best of Ellsworth's early biographers made this statement.[2] It is of a piece with the report of other of his associates within and without the closed doors of the Senate. It accords also with the reasonable inference from the multitudinous activities recorded in the journals and with a tradition which may linger in the Senate even to the present day[3] — a tradition that Ellsworth's influence with his fellows was, as Wolcott said, "predominant." Such an estimate of his rank is not inconsistent with his failure to attain a wide celebrity; for it frequently happens that the leaders in this peculiar chamber, even nowadays, when its debates are published, are less well known to the public than men whose actual weight in legislation is but slight. Neither is it inconsistent with the testimony of Maclay. In spite of all Maclay's carping at Ellsworth, he conveys a distinct impression of a powerful intellect and will, of a quite extraordinary energy and effective-

[1] Gibbs, I, 306.
[2] *Analectic Magazine*, III, 392.
[3] See G. F. Hoar's "Autobiography of Seventy Years," II, 45.

ness. Unlike the unknown commentator on Wood's manuscript, he considered Ellsworth eloquent. " Elsworth, who is a vastly better speaker than I am "; " he explained everything with a clearness and perspicuity which I seem quite incapable of "; " Mr. Elsworth did the subject justice "; " Elsworth is really a man of ability "; " this man has abilities "; " all powerful and eloquent in debate "; and again, " Elsworth, a man of great faculties and eloquent in debate " — such tributes to a man he was almost constantly opposing more than outweigh the strictures. There is also an involuntary tribute in the confession that once, under a fierce attack from Ellsworth, Maclay himself fairly fled the chamber. The strictures, however, are certainly severe. Bored by an excessively long and tedious argument, he proposes " endless Ellsworth " for a nickname. Of Ellsworth's obstinacy there is constant complaint, and he is also set down as " the most conceited man in the world." Worse still, Maclay could not believe in his integrity. " It is really surprising to me the pains he will display to varnish over villainy and to give roguery effect without avowed license." " He will absolutely say anything, nor can I believe he has a particle of principle in his composition." He is able, " but abilities without candor and integrity are the characteristics of the devil." " I can in truth pronounce him one of the most uncandid men I ever knew possessing such abilities. I am often led to doubt whether he has a particle of integrity: perhaps such a quality is useless in Connecticut." But fortunately these severe animadversions are usually accompanied with a recital of the incidents which provoked them; and these are such passages as not infrequently occur between opponents heated in debate. On the particular occasion when Maclay was driven before the blast of Ellsworth's invective, he returned to the charge, with fresh ammunition gathered from the other's record in the old Congress, and cited one of the many reports signed by Ellsworth, Madison, and Hamilton. There follows an amusing and very human picture of the effect of his retort: "Elsworth took a great deal of snuff about this time. He mumped, and seemed to chew the cud of vexation. But he affected not to hear me, and indeed, they were all in knots, talking and whispering. Mr. Adams talked with Otis (the secretary) according to custom. . . . I am too sparing; I should have read that part of the report with their names."

Aaron Burr was another senator who must have seen much of Ellsworth, for they served together on many committees. They were, apparently, leaders of the opposing sides in the Senate on party questions, as in the bitter fight, sectional as well as partisan, that arose over the act to fix the ratio of representation in the House after the first census had been taken.[1] In all probability, therefore, Burr was an unfriendly critic, and we know how he could hate an adversary. Yet he, too, paid tribute to the other's formidable strength. "If," he said once, "Ellsworth had happened to spell the name of the Deity with two d's, it would have taken the Senate three weeks to expunge the superfluous letter."[2] Another political opponent who, though not

[1] Senate Journals, 2d Cong., 1st Sess., 42, 51, 60–61, 145, 152, 159, 162.

[2] "Old Time Notables," by John Blair Linn. This writer remarks: "The ablest advocate of the administration, Oliver Ellsworth of Conn., on account of his great ability and efficiency in the conduct of business, was yielded precedence in the Federal ranks in the Senate."

a senator, might be supposed to have known Ellsworth well, was Madison. But in the letter which he wrote to Wood, long after the death of Ellsworth, he said that he had but a limited acquaintance with the Connecticut senator, and that no epistolary correspondence ever passed between them. The letter goes on: " As we happened to be thrown but little into the familiar situations which develop the features of personal and social character, I can say nothing particular as to either — certainly nothing that would be unfavorable. Of his public character I may say, that I always regarded his talents as of a high order and that they were generally so regarded. As a speaker his reasoning was clear and close, and delivered in a style and tone which rendered it emphatic and impressive. In the convention which framed the Constitution of the United States, he bore an interesting part, and signed the instrument in its final shape,[1] with the cordiality verified by the support he gave to its ratification. Whilst we were contemporaries in the early sessions of Congress, he in the Senate and I in the House of Representatives, it was well understood that he was an able and operative member." [2]

It is not a very warm tribute; but Madison was always discriminating in his encomiums. Had he and Ellsworth remained of the same party, it is likely that he would have had more than hearsay to tell concerning the other's work in the Senate. It is not unreasonable to suppose that some sectional feeling may also have contributed to keep them apart. For we know

[1] A singular mistake for Madison to make; but at this time (1836) he was a very old man, close to his end.
[2] " Letters and Other Writings of Madison," IV, 428.

that in this period sectional feeling ran very high. Madison was consorting more and more exclusively with men of his own party and of the Southern states; and the only picture we have of Ellsworth in any particular social circle at Philadelphia while he was a senator associates him only with other New England characters.[1] There is no record of his taking part in the fierce debate that arose over the Quaker anti-slavery petition to the first Congress, nor can anything of a general nature be positively said about his relations with Southerners. But he felt, as we have seen, that the debts of the South were a main source of friction with England. There is also a story that once, in his vehement advocacy of some measure in the Senate, he much offended that well-named senator, Gunn of Georgia, who threatened to call him out; but that certain other Georgians in Congress, sympathizing with Ellsworth, and knowing that he could not conscientiously fight a duel, offered to take his place, and Senator Gunn desisted. These facts are not enough to show that Ellsworth felt as some other Federalists did — his friend, Cabot, for instance — concerning the South.

But on this point a curious bit of testimony has lately come to light. In the spring of 1794, a time, as we have seen, of much perturbation over malice domestic and much apprehension of foreign levies, John Taylor of Virginia, better known as John Taylor of Caroline, was perhaps the most extreme

[1] "When I mention such names as Ellsworth, Ames, Griswold, Goodrich, Tracy, &c., you may imagine what a rich and intellectual society it was." From a letter of Judge Joseph Hopkinson of Philadelphia, quoted in Gibbs, I, 162–163. Hopkinson indicates that this circle met oftenest at his own house and Wolcott's.

representative in the Senate of the Southern, the
state-rights, the anti-Federalist, the anti-English sentiment. A paper in his handwriting, dated May
11, prepared for James Madison, preserved among
the Madison papers, and now, after more than a
century, given to the public,[1] records an interesting
interview which occurred on May 8 or 9 between
Taylor on the one hand and King and Ellsworth,
Federalist leaders, on the other. Taylor, it seems,
had been violent in his opposition to the measures of
the Federalists, particularly to their course with the
debt, to the setting up of the bank, and to the proposal
to send an envoy to England. A few days before, he
had moved with a bitter speech to sequester all British
debts. Defeated, he had declared that he meant to
resign. Matters were in this train when King invited
him into a committee room and there began to talk to
him about a dissolution of the Union. According to
Taylor's memorandum, King said that the Union simply
could not continue. The East and the South could
not agree, and the South was clogging every movement
of the government. When the two Federalist senators
from South Carolina should give way to anti-Federalists, Southern interests would prevail, and the East
would not submit. Better, then, peaceably dissolve at
once. Ellsworth coming in about this time, apparently
by accident, — though Taylor thought from concert, —
King, protesting that he had not mentioned the matter
to him before, repeated what he had said, and Ellsworth
concurred. " K. was throughout the chief spokesman,

[1] " Disunion Sentiment in Congress in 1794. A Confidential Memorandum hitherto unpublished, written by John Taylor of Caroline for James
Madison." Edited by Gaillard Hunt, Washington, 1905.

tho' E. occasionally joined him, and appeared entirely
to concur with him." Taylor, taken aback, argued for
a plan to pay the debt by reducing army expenses and
selling Western lands, as in his judgment the debt
was the main source of the sectional divisions. But
to this King would not agree. There were, he
thought, other essential subjects of difference. South
and North would never think alike. He was particularly concerned about the course of Madison,
believing him to harbor some "deep and mischievous
design." He ended as he began. Taylor, after reflection, was quite convinced that here was a fully matured
plot to break up the Union. The words and the
countenances of King and Ellsworth forbade him to
doubt it. More still: he feared that at the bottom of
the business some British interest lurked. Perhaps
the full plan was, to dissolve first, then bring the East
and England together, and finally, by this union, force
the South to terms.

But on the memorandum of these facts and opinions
which Taylor had written out for Madison's benefit,
Madison himself merely wrote, "The language of K.
and E. probably *in terrorem*"; and everything we
know of Ellsworth is in keeping with this interpretation of the incident. He was a bold as well as a
shrewd politician, not easily frightened, never inclined
to overrate the strength of his opponents. So much
is amply shown by his course in the Constitutional
Convention, as well as in the Senate. Quite likely, he
and his associates felt that it was time to give the
violent anti-Federalists a bit of tit-for-tat. It all
looks very like the present-day game of politics as
it is played behind the scenes — and not unlike a

certain thoroughly American game at cards. It does not convince one that Ellsworth and King, who were working night and day to strengthen the Union, had any real design to break it in two, — and leave George Washington in the other half ! [1]

The estimates of Ellsworth by the members of his own group of Federalist leaders are naturally higher than those of even the more magnanimous Republicans. The letters of King and Cabot reflect the intimacy of the ruling coterie in the Senate. Jay also wrote of him in terms of complete respect and of strong friendship. Allusions to his character in the letters of other Federalists are nearly always commendatory. " He is a good man, and a very able one," wrote Congressman Jeremiah Smith of New Hampshire, on hearing of his appointment to the bench ; "a man with whom I am well acquainted, and greatly esteem." [2] About the time of his retirement from the Senate, Fisher Ames praised him in signal fashion. Christopher Gore, writing from London, had inquired earnestly about the leadership of Congress when Ames himself should be gone ; and Ames replied : [3] " As to my absence from the House, the loss will be nothing as to

---

[1] Mr. Gaillard Hunt, editor of the document, and biographer of Madison, thinks that " Madison was right." But he also thinks that King and Ellsworth were seriously contemplating disunion, and points to their intimacy with Cabot and Strong, who took later, during the War of 1812, a course that caused them to be charged with disaffection to the government.

[2] Elsewhere, Smith tells a story of a Philadelphia bookseller who had beguiled him and others into making purchases by flattery. The man would watch a possible customer turning over the leaves of a book and approaching with the remark, " Sir, I perceive you are a man of letters," proceed to recommend his wares. Smith saw him try this trick on Ellsworth, but it failed. " Life of Jeremiah Smith," by John H. Morrison, 91, 393.

[3] Oct. 5, 1796, Works, I, 203.

leading. I never had any talent in *that* way, and I have not been the dupe of such a belief. Few men are fit for it. Ellsworth, Hamilton, King, and perhaps John Marshall, would lead well, especially Ellsworth, —

> . . . *quo non praestantior alter*
> *Aere ciere viros, martemque accendere cantu.*

"His want of a certain fire that H. and K. have would make him the fitter as a *dux gregis*. The House will be like sheep without a shepherd. I never was more than a shepherd's dog." Rather curiously, John Adams takes much the same line in praising this senator translated to the bench. They two had not always escaped friction in their intercourse in the Senate chamber; but Adams, who from his President's chair had for seven years beheld Ellsworth dealing with all manner of public questions, was almost bitter with Washington for depriving him of such a supporter. He wrote in 1813 that at the time of the appointment the opposition had long been making plans to explode Washington, sacrifice Adams, and bring in Jefferson, and that Washington understood this. " But what had he done before he left the chair? Ellsworth, the firmest pillar of his whole administration in the Senate, he had promoted to the high office of Chief Justice of the United States; King he had sent ambassador to London ; Strong was pleased to resign, as well as Cabot ; Hamilton had fled from his unpopularity to the bar in New York ; Ames to that in Boston ; and Murry was ordered by Washington to Holland. The utmost efforts of Ellsworth, King, and Strong in the Senate had scarcely been sufficient to

hold the head of Washington's administration above
water during the whole of his eight years." And
after men of this stamp, Adams asks in wrath, "What
was my support in the Senate? Mr. Goodhue of
Massachusetts. . . . Had Ellsworth, Strong, and King
been there, the world would never have heard of the
disgraceful cabals and unconstitutional proceedings of
that body."

Here were indeed egregious calls for Hector. That
in such a state of parties Washington decided to take
Ellsworth for the bench may show that he was himself
less of a partisan than some of his biographers would
have us believe ; but it also shows that he, too, had
noted Ellsworth for "a good man." There is no
evidence that Ellsworth was one of the very few who
ever were on terms of anything like intimacy with
Washington, who was himself hardly the sort of Southerner to thaw the ice of a New Englander's reserve.
But Ellsworth did have Washington's friendship and
esteem. They had known each other for ten years at
least, probably for twenty, and Washington had had
good opportunities to judge the other for himself. At
least once, he had been Ellsworth's guest at Windsor.
October 21, 1789, being then on his tour of New England, he wrote in his diary: " By promise was to have
breakfasted at Mr. Ellsworth's at Windsor on the way
to Springfield, but the morning proving very wet and
the rain not ceasing until ten o'clock, I did not set out [1]
till half after that hour. I called however on Mr. E.
and stayed there near an hour." [2]   That, we may be

---

[1] From Hartford.
[2] The Diary of George Washington from 1789 to 1791 (ed. by Benson
J. Lossing), 27.

sure, was quite the greatest hour in the history of Windsor and of the Ellsworth household. Had the New England tour served no political object whatsoever, many an old New England house would still be richer by a priceless association. The homes Washington visited were thenceforth forever distinguished, and with a distinction not less than that the visitations of a monarch confer upon the seats of his subjects. It were no mean superstition to hold that a child born in a house across whose threshold that great figure had once passed could never be false to his country or heedless of a call of patriotism.

Tradition has generously lengthened out, and embellished with incidents of an old-fashioned, patriotic flavor, the single hour of Washington at Elmwood. There is the story of the errand of one of Ellsworth's young sons to the Wadsworth Mansion at Hartford, to present the invitation; of his trepidation at the thought of facing the greatest man in the world; and of his surprise, relief, and disappointment to find only a quiet old gentleman, dressed very much like his father. Hardly reconcilable with this is the story of an aide-de-camp of Washington who came to Elmwood to announce the visit, mistook Mistress Ellsworth, who answered his knock herself, for a servant, and never recognized her when he came again and saw her dressed for company.[1] And there is the story of Washington's taking on his knees the youngest twain of the Ellsworth children and singing them the ancient

[1] Both stories seem inconsistent with an entry in Washington's diary for the day before the visit. "Tuesday, 20th. After breakfast, accompanied by Colo. Wadsworth, Mr. Ellsworth and Colo. Jesse Root, I viewed the woollen manufactory at this place (Hartford), which seems to be going on with spirit." Diary of George Washington.

ballad of the Derby Ram. If Ellsworth's hard-working statesmanship had been compensated with more such pleasant interludes, his biographer would willingly turn antiquary to learn the details of them.

There is Washington's own hand to prove that he felt a real affection for this strong New England prop of his administration. The day before he left the seat of government to go into his final retirement, he wrote:

"PHILADELPHIA, 8th Mar. 1797.

"DEAR SIR: Before I leave this City, which will be within less than twenty-four hours, permit me, in acknowledging the receipt of your kind and affectionate note of the 6th, to offer you the thanks of a grateful heart for the sentiments you have expressed in my favour, and for those attentions with which you have always honored me. In return, I pray you to accept all my good wishes for the perfect restoration of your health, and for all the happiness this life can afford.

"As your official duty will necessarily call you to the Southward, I will take the liberty of adding, that it will always give me pleasure to see you at Mount Vernon as you pass and repass. With unfeigned esteem and regard in w^hc Mrs. Washington joins me

"I am always — and affectionately yours,

"G⁰. WASHINGTON.

"OLIV^R ELLSWORTH, ESQ^R., Chief Justice."

But the intervals of work in Ellsworth's life were not all filled with such intercourse or such exchanges. In this letter to his wife, one sees another side of his high public employments:[1]

[1] Dated Philadelphia, Feb. 26, 1796. Original in the possession of Mrs. Henry E. Taintor of Hartford.

"As to amusements this winter, the city is full of them, but I participate in none. My pleasure consists in doing the business of the day, and, when I sit alone in my chamber in the evening, in thinking of my family, to all of whom I always say something.

"Olle I suppose is gone back to College, and Martin I suppose is getting ready to go as fast as he can. Daddy wants to see all his little children very much, and he wishes mamma to let them have one plate of plums now every week until he comes home, and pay for them with Daddy's money."

Something like commiseration mingles with our respect for this New England nature, for this tireless public servant, pursuing so steadfastly, and with so little relief, his hard, masculine tasks. Not, however, that Ellsworth was of an unsocial disposition, or habitually denied himself social recreations, or that Philadelphia lacked good society. It was a lively and pleasant little capital; the men from the frontiers and the backwoods districts probably thought it a veritable Paris. But Ellsworth could never enjoy social or other pleasures until he had mastered whatever problem he had on his mind. His standard of thoroughness was unusual, his absorption in his work phenomenal. In his brief intervals of leisure he found children the best resource for amusement and refreshment — certainly a happy preference. His oldest daughter, "Nabby," accompanied him to New York for the winter session of 1790, and perhaps also to the first session in Philadelphia; but sometimes he was hard put to it for the companionship he liked best. One session, he wrote to his wife:

" The family in which I live have no white children. But I often amuse myself with a colored one about the size of our little daughter, who peeks into my door every now and then, with a long story, which I cannot more than half understand.[1] Our two sons I sometimes fancy that I pick out among the little boys playing at marbles in the street. Our eldest daughter is, I trust, alternately employed between her book and her wheel. You must teach her what is useful, the world will teach her enough of what is not. The nameless little one I am hardly enough acquainted with to have much idea of; yet I think she occupies a corner of my heart. . . ."[2] Of another child, which died in infancy, he also speaks. " He who bore your countenance and my name — the world has never been the same to me since his death."[3]

His personal and family relations were all apparently of this American quality — a trifle stiff and formal, for the age was formal, but simple, genuine, sincere. He writes from Philadelphia to " Nabby ":

" Miss Wadsworth enjoys high health, which she takes much pains to preserve, walking frequently three or four miles before breakfast. The rest of the time she spends much as you spend yours — in seeing and being seen. She has some advantages — a richer and more fashionable father, and perhaps a

[1] "On one of his visits at New Haven the Judge (Ellsworth) met a little colored girl and patted it on its head and said, ' Just as happy as any child in the neighborhood now, but by and bye '— then shook his head and passed on." From a letter of Samuel Hoar, son-in-law of Roger Sherman, quoted in Jackson Ms.

[2] Quoted, without date, in " National Portrait Gallery " (1839), Vol. IV, sketch of Ellsworth.   [3] *Ibid.*

fonder one, tho' that is more than I admit, notwithstanding she gets a kiss or two from him every time
he comes in and goes out."[1]

He lived at a time when people were given to
writing letters, and extremely long letters at that.
Postal charges were too high for sending mere notes
by mail. Ellsworth's friend, Cabot, for instance, was incessantly favoring his correspondents with reams of political comment and prophecy and lamentations. Fisher
Ames wrote even more letters than Cabot, though he
cut them shorter, and made them much more readable. But not only were Ellsworth's political epistles
marvels of condensation; if in private correspondence
brevity were a model quality, his letters to his friends
and his family would be models also. The palm belongs to a missive that came to his wife at Windsor
when she had grown anxious over a silence longer
than was usual even with him. She adjusted her
spectacles, opened the packet, and read:

" One week and then
" OLIVER ELLSWORTH."[2]

[1] Copied by Mr. W. Irving Vinal from original in possession of Mrs.
Waldo Hutchins.
[2] Jackson Ms.

CHAPTER VI

THE SUPREME COURT

Ellsworth's commission as chief justice bore date March 4, 1796. Four days later he took his seat on the bench of the Supreme Court, and within a month, the court adjourning, he sailed for Savannah to go upon the southern circuit. He held his commission until November, 1800;[1] but his actual service lasted only until the autumn of 1799 — about three years and a half.

The appointment came as a surprise to many of his contemporaries, and perhaps also to him. In the summer of 1795, when Washington appointed Rutledge to succeed Jay, Congress was not in session; but the leading Federalists soon showed that they were highly vexed at the President's choice. Rutledge himself had been accounted a Federalist, and they could not condone his onslaught on the Jay treaty. Ellsworth's reference to the matter in his letter to Wolcott[2] was exceedingly mild in comparison with most of the Federalist comment. Some felt that Washington, when he read Rutledge's speech on the treaty, ought to have withheld the promised commission. The President rose easily above that low level of partisanship, and Rutledge received his commission and presided over the Supreme Court at the August term. But the Senate, when it met in December,

[1] Carson's "History of the Supreme Court," I, 191. [2] *Ante*, p. 220.

would not ignore partisan considerations. It refused to confirm the nomination, and solely for political reasons. However, there very soon came to light a quite sufficient reason why Rutledge should not have the place. Letters from South Carolina brought the painful news that his mind had failed him. He was, in fact, little better than a maniac. Once, a year or two later, the cloud seemed for a little while to have lifted;[1] but the great Southern patriot was never again fit for any public service.

Before Washington decided to take Ellsworth from the Senate, a number of other names were canvassed. Among the men considered for the place were at least three of the associate justices, and one of them was actually appointed. One day, at a state dinner, as the guests were being seated, Washington bowed to Mr. Justice Cushing of Massachusetts, and said, "The Chief Justice of the United States will take the seat at my right"; and the nomination of Cushing, sent the next day to the Senate, was readily confirmed. But the modest justice declined the promotion.[2] His associate, Iredell, regretted his refusal, feeling that it would now be necessary to pass over Justices Wilson and Chase in order to obtain a proper character.[3] On March 4, Iredell wrote to his wife, "I have this moment read in the newspaper, that Mr. Ellsworth is nominated our Chief Justice, in consequence of which I think it not unlikely that *Wilson* will resign." Ire-

[1] Griffith J. McRee, "Life and Correspondence of James Iredell," II, 527–528.

[2] Perhaps he felt that his health forbade him to accept. Justice Iredell had written to his wife two years before that Cushing had a cancer on his lip. *Ibid.*, 441.

[3] Iredell to Johnston, *ibid.*, 462.

dell himself had been mentioned, but a few weeks later he wrote: "Whatever other chance I might have had, there could have been no propriety in passing by Judge Wilson to come at me. The gentleman appointed I believe will fill the office extremely well. He is a man of an excellent understanding, and a man of business."[1] Here, perhaps, is a hint of the true reason why the President, to the disappointment of Adams and other Federalists, turned to the Senate for the new Chief Justice. To Wilson, notwithstanding his acknowledged eminence for learning and ability, there were, probably, insuperable objections. He was already involved in those speculations which in a few months ruined him completely. In 1798, a bankrupt, and in imminent danger of the debtor's prison, he took refuge at Iredell's home in North Carolina, and there, utterly broken by his shame and his misfortunes, he died.

Of Ellsworth's associates on the bench, Wilson was probably, on the whole, the most highly endowed; but they were all men of force. Cushing, who had been Chief Justice of Massachusetts, who in fact had spent nearly all his life in different judicial stations, was entirely worthy of the honor Washington had offered him. James Iredell, English by birth, Irish by descent, had done good service in winning over North Carolina to the Union. He was an excellent lawyer, and a man of fine and amiable character. His published letters, which are the chief source of our knowledge of what it meant to be a member of the Supreme Court in its early days, strongly commend him to one's liking and respect. The fourth justice in the order

[1] " Life and Correspondence of James Iredell," II, 463, 465.

of seniority was William Paterson, Ellsworth's old associate of the Cliosophic Society and the Constitutional Convention. The fifth was Samuel Chase of Maryland, able and eloquent, but self-assertive and often overbearing. Only two changes occurred while Ellsworth presided over the court. Bushrod Washington succeeded Wilson; and Iredell died in October, 1799. But before Iredell's successor appeared on the bench Ellsworth was elsewhere and otherwise employed.

There is an impression — chiefly due, perhaps, to Jay's resignation, and to his discontented utterances about the judiciary — that at this early period it was not thought a very high distinction to be a member of the Supreme Court, or even to be the head of it. It is true that certain eminent public men did prefer the highest places in the state governments to any but the highest in the federal establishment. It is true, also, that in all the earlier appointments of chief justices the office sought the man, and at least twice failed to win him. But Cushing, who declined it in 1796, remained an associate justice; and Jay, who in 1800 refused a reappointment, seems to have stood almost alone in his opinion that the judiciary needed a complete reorganization to give it dignity and strength. Rutledge, who accepted in 1795, was one of the very foremost characters in the whole country; and we have seen what a career in the Senate Ellsworth abandoned in order to take the place.

Yet he found it in many ways less attractive than his seat in the Senate. His new duties left him even less time to devote to his home and his family than he had hitherto enjoyed. Iredell's letters are full of regrets at the long separation from his wife and children, and of complaints — though never bitter or querulous — at the length of the circuits, the badness of the roads, and the other hardships of the life. There are indications that even Ellsworth's strong constitution was by this time showing some effects of his long and intense application to public business. At least twice he was prevented by illness from attending the Supreme Court at Philadelphia.[1] But there is, as usual, nothing from his pen that sounds like a complaint; indeed, there is hardly a word of any kind of comment on his new duties and experiences.[2] His starting so promptly on the southern circuit was entirely characteristic. He also at once set himself to repair any deficiencies in legal knowledge under which, from his long absorption in other subjects, he might be laboring. As Connecticut was still an agricultural state, his experience there as judge and as practitioner had given him no great familiarity with commercial law, and he had probably never studied international law at all. He accordingly undertook a severe course of study and reading.

The day John Adams was inaugurated President, he wrote to his wife, " Chief Justice Ellsworth administered the oath and with great energy." Contemporary sources yield us few similar glimpses of Ellsworth as Chief Justice. But his tall figure, his strong features, his clear, penetrating blue eyes, his resonant voice, and his simple manners made him

[1] "Life and Correspondence of James Iredell," III, 492, 519.

[2] I have found but one letter written by the Chief Justice to an associate on the bench — a brief and unimportant note to Iredell, from Raleigh. *Ibid.*, 576.

an impressive figure of a republican judge. By all accounts, he presided over the Supreme Court with perfect self-possession, and he knew how to assert the dignity of his office if any one, even one of his brethren of the bench, offended against it. Mr. Justice Chase, it appears, was sometimes wanting in the proper respect for his associates, and given to brow-beating counsel; and on one occasion Ellsworth, deeply provoked, took a severe method to show him his place. The incident occurred when they two were sitting together in a circuit court at Philadelphia. Jared Ingersoll of Philadelphia, who was of counsel in the cause on trial, had hardly entered on his argument when Judge Chase impatiently interrupted and told him that the point he was engaged on was well settled and he need not argue it. Vexed and disconcerted, Ingersoll proceeded to a second head of his contention, only to be again interrupted and told that he was wasting time. Mastering his anger, he began a third argument; and a third time Chase interrupted him. The indignant attorney folded up his notes and took his seat. Ellsworth took out his snuff-box, tapped it with his finger, and with plenty of emphasis said to Mr. Ingersoll: " The Court has expressed no opinion, sir, upon these points, and when it does you will hear it from the proper organ of the court. You will proceed, Sir, and I pledge you my word you shall not be interrupted again." And he turned upon his overbearing associate a look that made him fairly quail in his seat.[1] Yet when no sense of duty prompted the new Chief Justice to self-assertion he

[1] Wood, on authority of Uriah Tracy, senator from Connecticut, who witnessed the incident. Flanders, 187–188.

could be as entirely democratic and unpretentious as
his successor. On the passage to Savannah, the Duc
de Liancourt, who was travelling by the same ship,
marvelled much that the other passengers showed
so little deference to so great an official, and the
chances are that Ellsworth really preferred to be
treated with no particular consideration.[1] One other
glimpse of him displays not merely his democratic
spirit but the Yankee readiness and fertility in practical contrivances which he had got from his New
England life and training. Somewhere on the southern circuit, a coach breaks down, and one of the passengers, a tall and energetic man, promptly offers his
services and in a little while succeeds in mending it.
An observer, much impressed with his mechanical
skill, inquires, " Who is that gentleman who under-
stands everything, and is eloquent about a coach
wheel?" The reply is, "The Chief Justice of the
United States."[2]

The greater part of the duties of the justices, as
well, no doubt, as the harder part, — certainly, the
least agreeable part, — were those they rendered in
the circuit courts. At this period, neither of the two
sessions of the Supreme Court, which were held in
February and in August, lasted, as a rule, more than
two or three weeks. But to reach and then to travel
the southern district was a matter of months. Ellsworth uncomplainingly took his full share of these
duties, and as he began with the southern circuit he
had to travel it again before he left the bench. Sometimes, it is said, he took with him on his longer jour-

---

[1] Liancourt's " Travels," I, 553.
[2] " National Portrait Gallery," IV, article on Ellsworth.

neys some young boy of his neighborhood, who not infrequently rode behind him on horseback. From his training and temper, he found the duties of a *nisi prius* judge particularly congenial, and discharged them with distinguished success. It appears, too, from the letters of Jay and of Iredell, that these expeditions, trying as in many ways they were, offered some compensations. Perhaps no other officials of the new government had so good an opportunity as the justices to see the whole country and to become acquainted with the leading characters of all the sections. Wherever they went, the people treated them with much respect, and many hospitalities were offered them. The opening of a circuit court was always something of an occasion. The judge's opening charge to the grand jury was a formal address, written with care, and usually in the nature of a philosophical discourse on American institutions in general, and particularly on the place of the courts in the civil order. Frequently, it took a political turn, and it had sometimes a distinctly partisan character. All the early judges of the highest court seem to have been Federalists, and they naturally dilated on the duty of loyalty to the general government and the Constitution's virtues and beneficence. Ellsworth followed the custom, and his charges won much praise for their uncommon clearness and force. Several have been preserved, and among them the first, given at Savannah in April, 1796. The principal paragraph may serve to show that if Ellsworth hated and feared the pen it was not because he could not give to weighty thought a stately utterance. It reads:[1]

[1] Wood and Jackson Mss. All but a few sentences at the opening and the close are given here.

"Your duty may be deemed unpleasant, but it is too important not to be faithfully performed. To provide in the organization that reason shall prescribe laws, is of little avail, if passions are left to control them. Institutions without respect, laws violated with impunity, are, to a Republic, the symptoms and the seed of death. No transgression is *too small*, no transgressor *too great*, for animadversion. Happily for our laws, they are not written in blood, that we should blush to read them, or hesitate to execute them. They breathe the spirit of a parent, and expect the benefits of correction, not from *severity* but from *certainty*. Reformation is never lost sight of, till depravity becomes, or is presumed to be, incorrigible. Imposed as restraints here are, not by the jealousy of usurpation, nor the capriciousness of insensibility, but as aids to virtue, and guards to rights, they have a high claim to be rendered efficient. Nor is this claim more heightened by the purity of their source, and the mildness of their genius, than by the magnitude of the interests they embrace. The national laws are the national ligatures and vehicles of life. Though they pervade a country as diversified in its habits as it is vast in extent, yet they give to the whole harmony of interest and unity of design. They are the means by which it pleases Heaven to make, of weak and discordant parts, one great people, and to bestow upon them unexampled prosperity, and so long as America shall continue to have one will, organically expressed and enforced, must she continue to rise in opulence and respect. Let the man or combination of men who, from whatever motive, oppose partial to general will, and would disjoint their country to the sport of fortune, feel their impotence and error. Admonished by the fate of Republics which have gone before us, we should profit by their mistakes. Impetuosity in legislation, and instability in execution, are the rocks on which they perished. Against the former, indeed, we hold a security, which they were ignorant of, by a representative instead of the aggregate, and by a distribution of the legislative power to maturing and balancing bodies, instead of the subjection of it to momentary impulse, and the predominance of faction. Yet from the danger of inexecution we are not exempt. Strength of virtue is not alone sufficient, there must be strength of arm, or the experiment is hopeless. Numerous are the vices, and as obstinate the prejudices, and as daring as restless is the ambition, which perpetually hazard the national peace, and they certainly require that to the authority vested in the executive department, there be added liberal confidence, and the increasing coöperation of all good citizens for its support. Let there be vigilance, constant diligence, and fidelity for the execution of laws — of laws made by all and having for their object the good of all. So let us rear an empire sacred to the rights of man and commend a government of reason to the nations of the earth."

While Ellsworth presided over the Supreme Court, no great number of cases came before it. His own decisions are so few, and so extraordinarily brief, that they fill less space in the reports than many a single more elaborate opinion. But several of them deal with questions which were at once new and fundamental. Marshall certainly deserves the distinction he enjoys as the foremost judicial exponent of the Consti-

tution and as the great constructive statesman who
completed on the bench the work of nation-building
begun on the Revolutionary battle-fields and continued
in the great convention and the early Congresses.
But when Marshall came to the bench, Jay and Ellsworth and their associates had already done much
that was of a piece with his achievement.   It is
true that they had not yet exercised the utmost
authority of the judiciary; they had not yet pronounced any law of Congress to be null and void.
But the very day Ellsworth took his seat in the
Supreme Court, a case was on trial which could
hardly have been tried at all without a clear assumption by the court of the right to make such a decision.
It was the case of Hylton *vs.* the United States,[1] involving the constitutionality of a carriage tax imposed
by an act of 1794, and Alexander Hamilton appeared
before the court in favor of sustaining the law.   As
Ellsworth had not heard all the arguments, he took no
part in the decision.   In the case of Ware *vs.* Hylton
also, which was tried within a day or two, he delivered
no opinion; but apparently he did concur in the decision, and it was a decision to set aside a perfectly
plain provision of a state law.[2]

This famous and hard-fought cause, appealed from
a circuit court at Richmond, turned on the effect of a
clause in the treaty of peace with England which provided that British creditors should " meet with no lawful impediment in the collection of their just dues from
their American debtors."   During the war, Virginia
had sequestered all debts due from her citizens to
Britons, and in the lower court a great array of counsel,

---

[1] 3 Dallas, 171.   [2] *Ibid.*, 199; McRee's "Iredell," II, 395.

headed by the venerable Patrick Henry, had argued for
the validity of the law, the treaty to the contrary notwithstanding. John Marshall, who had been one of
Henry's fellow-counsel in the trial at Richmond, made
now before the Supreme Court an argument that convinced every one of his extraordinary powers. But
fortunately he failed to convince the court that the
treaty did not abrogate the law. Iredell, in his elaborate dissenting opinion, sustained Virginia's position;
but Chase, Paterson, Wilson, and Cushing, all in long
written opinions, took the other side. If Ellsworth
did not actually pass on the case, he certainly agreed
with the majority, for he had soon to pass on another
case involving substantially the same question, and
he then firmly sustained the principle established in
Ware *vs.* Hylton. Sitting in a circuit court in North
Carolina, he delivered an opinion, perhaps the most
elaborate of his that is now preserved, in which he fully
discussed the bearing of the treaty on the rights of
British creditors. The case on trial differed from
Ware *vs.* Hylton only in the circumstance that North
Carolina, instead of merely sequestering, had actually
confiscated debts due to Britons. In that part of his
opinion which dealt with the conflicting provisions of
the treaty and the law, the Chief Justice reasoned in
this broad fashion :

   " As to the opinion that a treaty does not annul a
statute, so far as there is an interference, it is unsound.
A statute is a declaration of the public will, and of high
authority; but it is controllable by the public will sub-
sequently declared; hence the maxim, that, when two
statutes are opposed to each other, the latter abrogates
the former. Nor is it material, as to the effect of the

public will, what organ it is declared by, provided it be an organ constitutionally authorized to make the declaration. A treaty, when it is in fact made, is, with regard to each nation that is a party to it, a national act; an expression of the national will, as much as a statute can be: and does, therefore, of necessity annul any prior statute, so far as there is an interference. The supposition that the public can have two wills, at the same time, repugnant to each other — one expressed by a statute and another by a treaty — is absurd." [1]

None of his learned and more experienced associates had put quite so clearly the truth that in sustaining the supreme law of the land against other laws of less authority the courts of the United States were doing, after all, only what all courts everywhere must do: that is to say, they were merely deciding and declaring what was the law. The British-debts cases were an important category of the business before the courts, as they were also an important factor in politics, but by their final effect in making plain the supremacy of the Constitution and of the national authority they no doubt amply repaid all the time and trouble they had cost.

It seems best, instead of following any chronological order, to group in two or three categories the other cases that Ellsworth helped to decide. One category — those cases, namely, that turned on purely legal issues, and which appeal, therefore, almost solely to a professional interest — we may quickly dismiss. Brown *vs.* Barry,[2] in which the arguments of counsel dealt mainly with a fine question of special pleading, and Clark *vs.*

---

[1] Flanders, 197–203, quotes the whole opinion "from a manuscript."
[2] 3 Dallas, 365.

Russell,[1] in which the issue was again abstruse and technical, are good examples of the class. It is worthy of remark, however, that in dealing with such cases Ellsworth showed the same disposition Marshall afterward displayed; his opinions, brief as always, strove to base themselves on reasoning that was broad and practical, to divest the controversy of its merely technical quality and set it in the plain light of justice and common sense. This characteristic of his judicial method appears very strikingly in the case of Irvine *vs.* Sim's Lessee,[2] in which counsel had discussed at great length the effect on certain Pennsylvania land titles of a treaty or agreement between that state and Virginia. In a single page the Chief Justice stated the facts of the case, and summarized broadly the reasons for the court's decision. Iredell, in a concurrent opinion, required nine pages to give his reasons.

Of those decisions which had both a permanent force or significance and an interest other than professional, most were jurisdictional. The courts had not yet fully defined their place in the federal system or fully asserted their entire authority. This, in fact, they could only accomplish gradually, as from time to time specific controversies led to an assertion or a disputation of their jurisdiction. Neither had they thoroughly adjusted their relations among themselves.

In three leading cases, Ellsworth and his associates of the Supreme Court considered its relations with the Circuit and District courts, and laid down rules of a far-reaching potency concerning writs of error and appeals.

[1] 3 Dallas, 415; McRee's "Iredell," II, 549.
[2] 3 Dallas, 425; McRee's "Iredell," II, 543–544.

In Wiscart *vs.* Dauchy,[1] an action in equity brought up by writ of appeal from a circuit court, the main question was, Could the Supreme Court go behind the record of facts sent up by the Circuit Court, examine for itself the testimony, — which in this particular instance had also been sent up, — and perhaps readjudicate the facts? Ellsworth, speaking for the majority, disposed of the issue in two short, oral paragraphs:

"If causes of equity or admiralty jurisdiction are removed hither, accompanied with a statement of facts, but without the evidence, it is well, and the statement is conclusive as to all the facts which it contains. This is unanimously the opinion of the court.

"If such causes are removed with a statement of the facts, and also with the evidence, still the statement is conclusive, as to all the facts contained in it. This is the opinion of the court, but not unanimously."

But Wilson, who dissented from the second ruling, argued first that it was not a correct interpretation of the judiciary act, and then that the Constitution of its own force granted to the Supreme Court appellate jurisdiction, always including the right to reëxamine evidence, in all maritime and admiralty causes. Ellsworth, in reply, denied that an appeal could be sustained without reference to a rule provided by Congress, and then went on to analyze closely the pertinent provisions of the law he had written, and to distinguish, in language that has many times been quoted, writs of error from appeals. "An appeal," he said, "is a process of civil law origin, and removes a cause entirely, subjecting the facts as well as the law to review and retrial; but a writ

[1] 3 Dallas, 240.

of error is a process of common law origin, and it removes nothing for reëxamination but the law." To Wilson's practical objections to the ruling, he opposed other considerations quite as practical; but he also sententiously observed that "it is of more importance, for a judicial determination, to ascertain what the law is, than to speculate what it ought to be."

In Jennings vs. the Brig Perseverance,[1] an admiralty case, in which the record sent up from the lower court contained the evidence, but left out the statement of fact, it was held, nevertheless, that the principle of Wiscart vs. Dauchy applied. "If," said Paterson, "there is no statement of facts, the consequence seems naturally to follow, that there can be no error." The rule stood until 1803, when Congress, by an amendment to the judiciary act, provided for appeals in equity and admiralty causes.

In Wilson vs. Daniel,[2] the court with equal clearness disposed of another question concerning its appellate jurisdiction. In a civil action in a circuit court for a very large sum of money, the jury had found for the plaintiff, but only in the sum of eighteen hundred dollars. The case being brought up on a writ of error, it was argued that the Supreme Court had no jurisdiction, since a civil action could not be removed from a circuit court unless the sum in dispute exceeded two thousand dollars. When the case was first argued, Ellsworth was absent; the justices divided, and no decision was rendered. But at a second hearing Ellsworth, speaking for the majority, held that to ascertain the matter in dispute it was necessary to go to the beginning of the action. He pointed out that if the

[1] 3 Dallas, 336.   [2] *Ibid.*, 401; McRee's "Iredell," 532–533.

first judgment should be the criterion, and this for any given case should be for less than two thousand dollars, the defendant would have no relief, but the plaintiff would have a right to a removal. From this ruling, based on common law usage, Iredell and Wilson dissented; and Iredell's opinion came in time to be accepted as the right construction of the law.

In Turner *vs.* the President, Directors, and Company of the Bank of North America,[1] Ellsworth, in the last opinion he ever rendered for the Supreme Court, dealt with still another question of jurisdiction. The decision turned on the residence of the parties to the action. Unless they were of different states, the case did not come within any provision of the Constitution or the law; and on this point the record was defective. One of the parties was described merely as " using trade or merchandise in partnership " at certain places. The court accordingly held that there was error, and on this ground reversed the judgment of the Circuit Court, which it would otherwise have affirmed, and thereby established the rule that in all such cases the record must state clearly the evidence of all the parties. " It is exceedingly to be regretted," Ellsworth remarked, " that exceptions which might be taken in abatement, and often cured in a moment, should be reserved to the last stage of a suit, to destroy its fruits."

In view of the origin of the federal judiciary, it is interesting to find that the courts were at this time frequently considering, along with these questions of jurisdiction *inter se*, questions of the extent of their maritime authority. With maritime cases, in fact, the new Chief Justice was occupied oftener than with any

[1] 4 Dallas, 8.

other kind. France and England were at war, privateers of both nations were scouring the seas, and neither showed much respect for America's rights as a neutral. During Ellsworth's first term, a case was argued that displays curiously enough the complicated character of the questions to which this international situation was giving rise.[1] The *Mary Ford*, an English ship, had been captured by the French, who relieved her of her crew and cargo, attempted to destroy her, and left her a derelict. In this state an American vessel found her, and she was brought into port at Boston and there libelled for salvage. But the British consul intervened for her original owners, and the French consul for her captors. The District Court awarded to the original owners two-thirds of the proceeds of the sale, and to the salvors the other third. The captors appealed, and the Circuit Court awarded the larger share to them. From this decree the original owners appealed, and the jurisdiction of the District Court was questioned. The Supreme Court now affirmed the District Court's original jurisdiction, but sustained the Circuit Court's decree.

Before Ellsworth came to the bench, the decision in the case of Glass *vs.* the Sloop Betsy[2] had established the jurisdiction of our admiralty courts in all cases of prizes and captures on the high seas. The case of *La Vengeance*,[3] argued on a writ of error at his second term, brought up the question of seizures within a port and also the novel question whether the admiralty court's jurisdiction extended over navigable waters within a county. *La Vengeance*, a French privateer, had been libelled for exporting arms from

[1] McDonough *vs.* Delancey, 3 Dallas, 188. [2] *Ibid.*, 6. [3] *Ibid.*, 297.

Sandy Hook, N.J., to a foreign country, contrary to
the neutrality law of 1794; and it was contended
that the cause, to be cognizable by federal tribunals,
must have arisen wholly on the high seas. This
objection, however, the Chief Justice brushed aside,
holding broadly that "transportation is entirely a
water transaction"; and the court sustained the forfeiture by the lower court. But in Moodie *vs.* the
Ship Phœbe Ann,[1] argued at the same term, Ellsworth
and his fellows — all, probably, anti-French in their
sympathies — showed that they would follow the law,
even when it worked favorably to France. A French
privateer having taken a British merchantman and
sent her into port at Charleston, the British consul, charging that the privateer had been illegally
fitted out in the United States, demanded restitution
of the prize. But the evidence showed that, though
the privateer had entered Charleston for repairs, she
had not there received any augmentation of her force;
and the court held that this did not constitute an
illegal fitting out. Counsel had argued against the
policy of suffering foreign privateers to equip in
American ports, and the Chief Justice replied: "Suggestions of policy and conveniency cannot be considered in the judicial determination of a question of
right; the treaty with France, whatever that is, must
have its effect."

The criminal causes Ellsworth had to pass on
may be treated together as a third category. Most
of them came before him in circuit courts, and several,
having an obvious bearing on the politics of the time,
excited much partisan feeling. Mr. Justice Chase's

[1] 3 Dallas, 319.

conduct of similar trials so enraged the Republicans
that a few years later, when they had come into
power, they attempted to remove him by impeachment. Ellsworth's course was never so severely cen-
sured. It did not inflame his opponents into such
a heat of anger that their criticism ever turned into
attacks upon his personal integrity. On the contrary,
scarcely another public character of the period stood
so well the ordeal of politically hostile criticism. Yet
his handling of legal questions that had a political side
was by no means timid, nor was he himself lukewarm
in his party loyalty. In what is probably the best
known of all his judicial utterances, he took a very
decided stand on a question over which opinions
were then much divided, and which has caused heated
controversies at later periods of our history.

The case itself was of a nature to stir up party sympathies and antagonisms. One Isaac Williams had
been indicted for accepting a commission in the French
navy, contrary to the treaty of amity and commerce
between Great Britain and the United States. He
was tried in a circuit court at Hartford, in which Ellsworth sat with his friend Law, who was now judge of
the Hartford district. The defence offered to prove
that Williams was a naturalized citizen of France, and
Law thought that the evidence of this fact ought to
go to the jury. But Ellsworth ruled it out, and he
based his ruling on the common law doctrine of perpetual allegiance, holding the common law to be part
of the law of the land.

Whatever may be thought of the justice, the wisdom, or the legal correctness of this stand, the boldness of it cannot be questioned. The federal courts,

it is true, had already asserted a common law jurisdiction in criminal cases. Jay had asserted it in a much discussed trial.[1] On this point, Ellsworth merely sustained a position clearly assumed by his predecessor. But in the very case in which the first Chief Justice had first taken this position, the jury had, nevertheless, acquitted a defendant charged with the same offence Williams was now charged with, and without Williams's defence of naturalization; and the verdict had been manifestly popular. As to the specific common law maxim, that "no man can throw off his allegiance," the Supreme Court had once, in Rutledge's day, avoided a pronouncement, in a case which certainly permitted the court to consider whether the rule had force in the United States. Ellsworth met the issue without the least attempt at quibbling, or the least sign of hesitation. He told the jury, in substance, that no American had the right to become a citizen of any other country. But though he drew the rule from the common law, he justified it by a theory quite unknown to the common law. For the common law doctrine of citizenship is clearly feudal, and had its origin in a distinctly feudal usage; and the American Chief Justice now derived it from the social compact — a curious instance of an occurrence not uncommon in history: one age taking the creed of another, but supporting it with entirely fresh reasoning, based on different customs. No member of the compact, Ellsworth argued, can dissolve his connection with the community unless he first obtain the community's consent. Counsel had pointed out that our own government naturalized

---

[1] The case of United States *vs.* Henfield, Van Santvoord, 55-56; Wharton's State Trials, 49.

OLIVER ELLSWORTH AND HIS WIFE.

From a portrait by Earle.

foreigners, and asked if that were not a sign of consent; but on this point he observed:

"Consent has been argued from the acts of our government permitting the naturalization of foreigners. When a foreigner presents himself here, and proves himself to be of good moral character, well affected to the Constitution and Government of the United States, and a friend to the good order and happiness of civil society; if he has resided here the time prescribed by law, we grant him the privilege of a citizen. We do not inquire what his relation is to his own country; we have not the means of knowing, and the inquiry would be indelicate; we leave him to judge of that. If he *embarrasses himself by contracting contradictory obligations, the fault and the folly are his own.* But this implies no consent of the government, that our own citizens should expatriate themselves. Therefore it is my opinion that these facts which the prisoner offers to prove in his defence are totally *irrelevant;* they can have no operation in law; and the jury ought not to be embarrassed or troubled with them; but by the constitution of the court the evidence must go to the jury."[1]

In accordance with this ruling, the jury convicted Williams. But the doctrine of the ruling began at once to be questioned. In a newspaper of the day, a writer who signed himself *Aristogiton*, and who was thought to be George Nicholas of Virginia, assailed it with much turgid but sincere rhetoric. The Chief Justice, he argued, "must either admit that according to the principles of our naturalization laws our citizens have a right to expatriate themselves, or that the

[1] Van Santvoord, 267-272, — the best account of this trial; Flanders, 194-197.

legislature of the United States, that body whose laws (when they are constituted) he is bound to expound and enforce, have been guilty of the most horrible of all crimes, and have given a sufficient cause of war to all the nations of the world." And already, a month before the trial of Williams, Jefferson had attacked the entire claim of the courts to a common law criminal jurisdiction as the most formidable of all the Federalist pretensions — "the audacious, barefaced, and sweeping pretension to a system of law for the United States, without the adoption of their legislature, and so infinitely beyond their power to adopt."[1] It was not many years before the Supreme Court abandoned the claim in the form and sense in which it was originally advanced; but after more than a century the chosen leader of Jefferson's own party, in the heat of a campaign for the presidency, commits himself to this so dangerous doctrine — and his successful opponent denies it![2] This reversal of the attitude of the parties throws a curious light upon the charge of partisanship against Ellsworth, which one of his biographers practically admits — and tries to extenuate by citing the example of Lord Mansfield. It is a charge that cannot be either proved or disproved.

[1] Writings, III, 425.

[2] See the speeches and letters of Parker and Roosevelt, accepting their respective nominations for the presidency in 1904. It seems curious that in this renewal of an old controversy more use was not made of Ellsworth's charge in the case of Williams, or of the contrary view set forth in United States vs. Hudson (7 Cranch, 32) and still more clearly in Wheaton vs. Peters (8 Peters, 591). The court's opinion in the latter case contains this language — doubtless a correct statement of the law: " It is clear that there can be no common law of the United States. . . . When, therefore, a common law right is asserted, one must look to the state in which the controversy originated."

Whatever the truth of it, and whatever the correct doctrine concerning the force of the common law in our federal courts, the ruling of Ellsworth concerning perpetual allegiance, though it stood for many years, was in the end completely overthrown. The considerations that finally prevailed against it were rather practical than legal. The government found itself again and again convicted of the inconsistency which *Aristogiton* had pointed out. It is remarkable, indeed, that this country should so long have succeeded in maintaining a claim upon its own citizens so utterly inconsistent with its practice in freely naturalizing the citizens and subjects of other countries. After countless controversies in which it firmly asserted its right to protect naturalized immigrants against the laws of their native lands, it still hesitated to admit that any American could throw off his allegiance. The courts were quite as slow as the other departments of the government to abandon our contention. In 1804, when the doctrine was again discussed before the Supreme Court, Marshall, following the example of Rutledge, avoided a decision.[1] Cushing, in 1808,[2] and Story, in 1822,[3] took the same course. A few years later, Story did, however, recognize the general principle contained in the common law maxim, though without attempting " to ascertain its precise nature and limits."[4] It is not unnatural to suppose that in this the courts were influenced by the stand of the executive and the legislature. The final abandonment of the whole contention did not come

[1] In Murray *vs.* Charming Betsey, 2 Cranch, 64.

[2] In McIlvaine *vs.* Coxe's Lessees, 4 Cranch, 209.

[3] In the case of the Santissima Trinidad, 7 Wheaton, 268.

[4] In Inglis *vs.* Sailor's Snug Harbor, 3 Peters, 156, and in Shanks *vs.* Dupont, *ibid.*, 242.

until some years after the Civil War. In 1868, the United States made with the North German Confederation the first of a series of treaties which now regulate our practice in all cases of naturalization. Two years later, England also, by a treaty with the United States, and by changes in her laws, accepted the modern doctrine.

This brief list comprises all the opinions of Chief Justice Ellsworth that are likely to be of much interest to a later generation. They are too few to warrant us in any positive estimate of his judicial career, or in assigning him a distinct rank and station among American judges. To competent critics, however, they have seemed to indicate, taken with the other proofs of his ability and integrity and of his extraordinary industry, that if he had been left to devote the rest of his life to the bench he would have built himself a great monument of juristic achievement and of fame as a judge. Beyond question, his intellect and his temperament were both eminently judicial. There is no reason to doubt that he found his duties congenial, that they stimulated his ambition, that he meant to give himself to his great office with the same singleness of purpose he had displayed in all the others he had held. At the time of Adams's election, eleven electoral votes had been cast for Ellsworth for President, but this hardly indicates that he himself aspired to the presidency, or that those who voted for him had the least expectation of ever seeing him at the head of the nation. Below that highest station of all there was none of greater dignity than the headship of the judiciary, offering, as it did, security of tenure and immunity from the countless hateful demands of politics which no President escapes. It is, therefore, safe to say that Ellsworth, who had discharged so well so many other public responsibilities, would not, had he remained Chief Justice, have fallen short of his own high standard of public service. It is also safe to say that if he, rather than John Marshall, had had the task of upholding the national theory against the separative tendencies in many of the states, against state-rights Congresses and Presidents and a dominant state-rights party, he would have been as firm as Marshall was. This is not saying that the republic could well have spared Marshall. One may well count it an extremely fortunate thing that a Southerner, and not a New England man, gave to the national theory its authoritative form and expression. Nor is it saying that Ellsworth equalled Marshall either as a statesman or a jurist. In certain qualities of mind Marshall doubtless surpassed every other American of his time; no one could possibly have filled his place. Yet the two men had much in common. They held the same general views on all the greater public questions. In temper, in habits of life, in ideals, they were very like. The likeness goes even farther. Few and brief as are Ellsworth's judicial opinions, they have a tone and style which strongly suggest the tone and style of his successor. The literary form of Ellsworth's is, however, additionally distinguished by a quite unequalled inclination and ability to pack his meaning into the fewest possible words. His extraordinary terseness of phrase would of itself make his style noteworthy. But it had also the always interesting quality that belongs to language stamped with a personality. The impression it invariably leaves is of energy and power, of intellectual integrity, of a grave intensity of purpose. It reminds one of still another American statesman's fashion with the pen. There are turns that set one thinking, not of Marshall only, but of Lincoln. We cannot, of course, regret that Ellsworth left the bench. We know how the vacancy was filled; we know, too, what the work was that he left the bench to do. But the judiciary was indeed fortunate if it gained by such a loss.

The charge in the case of Williams — granting that it reflected a conviction that was political as well as legal — does not stand alone to indicate the interest with which the Chief Justice continued to follow the political movements in which as senator he had been so deeply concerned. Party feeling under Adams had not relaxed from the intensity it reached during the second term of Washington; and to the antagonism of parties there was now added the still more bitter rancor of faction. Many Federalists had from the first regarded Hamilton, and not Adams, as their real leader. Adams, with all his claims to the gratitude of the country and the loyalty of his party, never had inspired the enthusiasm or won the affection of his following. He had some foibles that displease men more than graver faults. He had neither the tact of such a man as Madison, nor the compelling genius of Hamilton, nor the subtler gift of Jefferson. Negatively, he was to blame for the division among the Federalists. Positively, however, the men about him, and particularly the members of his own cabinet, were still more at fault. Apparently, every one of them preferred Hamilton to him, and Hamilton they followed. The letters of Wolcott and Timothy Pickering, Secretary of State, reveal an attitude toward the President which makes one feel that it was hardly honorable for them to remain members of his official family. For this state of affairs Hamilton himself must also be held partly responsible. Nothing else in his career does him so little credit as his behavior toward Adams. Nor can this judgment be averted either by pointing out that he had done his utmost — resorting even to questionable methods — to prevent the party from making Adams President, or by arguing that he was right and Adams wrong in their differences over questions of policy. The history of this old factional division does not inspire one with any profound admiration for Adams; but it leaves the reader's sympathy with him, rather than with his assailants and detractors.

Among these were several of Ellsworth's closest friends, but there is nothing to show that he himself ever had a part in their merely factional activities. The charge of partisanship is the strongest that can be brought against him; and his was a decidedly mild kind of partisanship for the times when New England ministers preached at Jefferson as a sort of anti-Christ, and when even that comparison would hardly have conveyed a Southern Democrat's hostility to either Hamilton or Adams. The worst that can be said of Ellsworth is, that he defended the Sedition Act of 1798, and perhaps also the Alien Act, passed at the same session, — two laws which, with a new law of naturalization, constituted the Federalist party's greatest blunder and the chief cause of its overthrow. An undated charge to a jury, which has been taken for evidence that he approved this legislation,[1] will hardly bear that

[1] Flanders, 191, after Wood Ms.

construction. He does not in this utterance refer especially to either of the acts, but merely insists upon the government's right to the loyalty and affection of all classes of its citizens, gravely deprecates the restless desire for novelty and change, and protests with a fully justified severity against the foreign influences which were operating to divorce the people from the government. The charge contains, moreover, positive evidence that the Alien and Sedition acts did not suggest it; for it refers to our "eight years' experiment" of the federal system and must, therefore, have been delivered before the summer of 1798, when the acts were passed. The only real proof that Ellsworth approved of either of them is a private letter to Timothy Pickering, written in December, 1798, when the Republicans in Congress were urging a repeal of the Sedition Act.[1] Two or three letters of earlier dates show also his opinion and his feeling concerning a course of events which soon drew him from his judicial labors to render, in the strange field of diplomacy, his last great service to his country.

Besides the factional division of the Federalists and the constant strife between the Federalists and the Republicans, the Adams administration was occupied mainly with foreign affairs. The contests of parties and of factions, and the rivalries of individuals, themselves turned chiefly on our relations with France and with England; but from the final acceptance of the Jay treaty the menace to our neutrality came from France rather than from England.

To succeed Monroe, who was thought much too French in his sympathies to be a proper representa-

[1] *Post*, p. 270.

tive of our interests at Paris, Washington had appointed Charles Cotesworth Pinckney, a Federalist. Adams had been but a few weeks President, and was planning to join with Pinckney some leading Republican like Madison and some important character from the East, and hoping thus to reach a better understanding with our old ally, when the news came that the French government had rejected Pinckney, and with very scant courtesy. The Directory, which now governed France, was enraged at the Jay treaty, it was strengthened in its entire foreign policy by the victories of French arms under Napoleon Bonaparte, and it was encouraged by the intemperate sympathy of the Democrats in America into a persistent hope of somehow coercing the American government out of its new friendship with England and perhaps out of its neutrality. Behind this hope and policy there may have been a sincere feeling that America owed to France more than the equal consideration which a friendly neutral owes to a belligerent, and for that sentimental view of the situation something might perhaps be said; but there is no defending the method which the Directory now took to assert it. A claim of sentiment soon loses its quality and its force when it is asserted by insults and blackmail; and these ugly terms are none too strong to apply to the conduct of Talleyrand, who undoubtedly had the Directory behind him.

Angry as Adams was at the treatment of Pinckney, and though the members of the English faction about him were angrier still, he clung to his plan of a joint embassy, and in October, 1797, John Marshall, Pinckney, and Elbridge Gerry arrived in Paris, with full powers to negotiate a treaty of amity and commerce

not unlike the Jay treaty with England. They remained there more than half a year; but they never
got beyond the first preliminary moves of a formal
negotiation. The details of their experience, which are
given at length in various books, and need not here
be recounted, make up the most exasperating episode
in all our diplomatic history. It is safe to say that if
to-day similar indignities were offered American envoys
in any capital in Europe, we should instantly go to
war to avenge them. Talleyrand, delaying on various
pretexts the proper reception of the embassy, tried by
three several go-betweens to browbeat and cajole the
three Americans into bribing the Directory and into
pledging their government to grant a money loan to
France. As the envoys firmly rejected his insulting
proposals, he went about to detach Gerry, who was a
Republican and seemed more pliable than the other
two, from his Federalist associates. When Marshall
and Pinckney at length withdrew from the embassy,
Gerry remained at Paris, and through him alone Talleyrand again sought his object.

When these extraordinary proceedings were reported
in America, hardly the most extreme Gallomaniacs
would have had the government keep Gerry at Paris
or in any way continue or reconstitute the embassy.
The cabinet was for declaring war at once — all unprepared as we were. Adams did not recommend that
course, but in a special message to Congress he did
recommend putting the country in readiness for fighting. Some months later, having in the meantime
sent to Congress the cipher despatches in which our
envoys told the story of their mission, he indignantly
declared, "I will never send another minister to France

without assurances that he will be received, respected, and honored as the representative of a great, free, powerful, and independent nation."[1]

There followed an inspiring outburst of national feeling which for some months gave Adams a popularity he had never known before, and which seemed to assure his party of a new lease of power. Congress responded with a series of acts which broke off all commercial intercourse with France, declared the old treaties between the two republics no longer binding, permitted American vessels, both of the navy and the merchant marine, to make reprisals for French depredations, provided for increasing the military and naval forces, established a department of the navy, and in fact looked straight toward war with France. Washington came from his retirement to take command of the new army. But the strife of parties and factions did not cease. The Republicans, though they took for the most part no decided stand against measures of defence, advocated caution, and would not concede that the last chance for an understanding with France was gone. The Hamilton faction among the Federalists, still discontent with Adams, forced him to give Hamilton a military rank second only to the aged Washington's — planning, perhaps, as Adams suspected, to make their leader the actual head of the army, in order to his succeeding Adams three years later. Hamilton himself, playing at this time both the politician and the soldier, seems to have lost his head. He counselled centralizing policies as radical as those he had advocated in the Constitutional Convention; he gave his ear to a wild scheme of expan-

[1] "Messages and Papers of the Presidents," I, 266.

sion by the forcible seizure of Spanish territory to the
southward; and he failed completely in his attempt to
manage the President.   On the contrary, he and his
following drove Adams into a fury of jealousy and
wounded self-esteem.

As if this division in the party were not enough to
work its ruin, the Federalist majority in Congress
chose this particular time for an unwise assault upon
the liberty of speech and of the press, and for taking
a narrow policy with the foreign-born.   By a new
naturalization law, they extended to fourteen years the
term of residence required of foreigners who desired to
become citizens.   By the Alien Act, they empowered
the President to deport foreigners whose presence here
he might deem dangerous to our institutions.   By
the Sedition Act, they threatened with severe punishments any who should combine to oppose government
measures, or should print any matter with intent to
bring into disrepute the government or its officials.

A final section of this act permitted the truth of any
such matter to be offered as a valid defence, and provided that in all trials for seditious writings the jury
should pass on the law as well as the facts; it was this
section that Ellsworth had particularly in mind when
he wrote to Secretary Pickering, the following December, concerning the attacks on the law:[1]

" I thank you for sending me the charge of that
painstaking Judge Addison, who seems to be a light
shining in darkness, though the darkness compre-
hends him not.   He is doubtless correct in supposing
that the Sedition Act does not create an offence, but
rather, by permitting the truth of a libel to be given

[1] Jackson Ms.; Flanders, 193–194.

in justification, causes that, in some cases, not to be an offence which was one before. Nor does it devise a new mode of punishment, but restricts the power which previously existed to fine and imprison. But as to the constitutional difficulty, who will say, negating the right to publish slander and sedition is abridging the freedom of speech or of the press, of a right which ever belonged to it? or will show us how Congress, if prohibited to authorize punishment for speaking in any case, could authorize it for perjury? of which nobody has yet doubted. If a repeal of the act is to take place this season, I think the preambles, in order to prevent misapprehensions, and withal to make a little saving for our friend Marshall's address, should read thus : — 'Whereas, the increasing danger and depravity of the present time require that the law against seditious practices *should be restored to its former rigor*, therefore, &c.' I congratulate you on the late success of the British; not that they had not power enough before, but because the French had too much; and, besides, if the latter had obtained the victory, they would not have thanked God for it."

With this defence of the law, as good, perhaps, as any ever offered, Ellsworth takes, of course, his share of his party's responsibility for it. On the question of the right course with France, his position up to this time had been decidedly cautious. He had merely communicated to Wolcott his impression that the government should not behave timidly from any fear that the people, particularly the people of New England, would not sustain vigorous measures.[1] We have

[1] In two letters written in May, 1797, after the news came that Pinckney had been rejected. Gibbs, I, 532, 540.

no further expression of his opinions until it became
necessary for him to accept or to decline the foremost
rôle in our diplomatic dealings with France.

It is hardly necessary to trace minutely the course
of events which finally led Adams to call for Ellsworth's services.   The President had never ceased
entirely to hope for peace, and it soon began to appear that the French government, impressed by the
warlike tone of the American, had come to see its
mistake.   Talleyrand detained Gerry at Paris as long
as he could, and endeavored, through him and others,
to efface the impression made by the treatment of our
envoys.   From Americans in France, and from other
sources, there came to Adams many evidences of the
change of heart of the Directory.   Finally, through
M. Pichon, *chargé d'affaires* at the Hague, Talleyrand sent to the American minister there, William
vans Murray, the assurance without which Adams
had declared that he would never appoint another
minister to France.

When Murray's letter containing Talleyrand's message arrived, Adams, thoroughly enraged with Hamilton, and distrustful of his own political household,
heartily welcomed it.   How far personal ambition
and personal resentments governed him, and how far
purely patriotic motives, cannot, of course, ever be
determined.   But on February 18, 1799, without a
word to his cabinet, and to the utter dismay of the
war party, he sent to the Senate the nomination
of Murray to be minister to France, promising, however, that the minister should not proceed to Paris
until the French government should agree to receive
him in character and appoint a minister of equal rank

to negotiate with him a treaty covering all the controversies between the two republics.

To Hamilton, who was really at the head of the army, and still more to such consistent partisans of England as Pickering, Wolcott, and Cabot, this sudden turn meant political and personal discomfiture. It meant that the President had resolved to be the real head of his administration; and it also vetoed the wide-reaching schemes of national aggrandizement which had for some time filled Hamilton's mind. The Senate, which these men really controlled, delayed action on the nomination, and the party leaders convinced Adams that he must strengthen his proposal. Again without consulting the cabinet, he on February withdrew the nomination of Murray to be minister and sent, instead, the nomination of Oliver Ellsworth, Patrick Henry, and William vans Murray to be envoys extraordinary and ministers plenipotentiary. This nomination the Senate confirmed, but until the day the envoys sailed Pickering, Wolcott, Cabot, and their faction, including as it did a majority of the cabinet, were continually striving to delay and to defeat the mission. Murray accepted his appointment promptly, and with evident pleasure; Ellsworth reluctantly, and solely from a sense of duty — according to Pickering, "from the necessity of preventing a greater evil." [1] Henry declined, pleading his advanced age, and Adams named in his place William R. Davie of North Carolina, who was, like his colleagues in the embassy, a Federalist.

Adams kept his word. While his Federalist opponents sought about for means to defeat his purpose,

[1] Pickering to Cabot, Feb. 26, 1799, Lodge's "Cabot," 233–234.

he was studying the course of events in Europe to make sure that his envoys would be properly received. Ellsworth, meanwhile, was attending to his judicial duties. His friends of the English faction brought pressure to bear on him, but it was not strong enough to make him reconsider his acceptance. During the spring and summer, and well into the autumn, Pickering, Cabot, Wolcott, and perhaps other anti-French extremists, were in constant correspondence about the embassy. They, too, were constantly looking to Europe, hoping that the instability of the French government or the defeat of the French armies, perhaps the restoration of the Bourbons, might deter Adams from resuming negotiations with the Directory. But when it came to reading the signs of European politics Adams had an advantage over his opponents. From his long residence in Europe he understood better than they the forces playing in that field. He showed, therefore, as always, plenty of confidence in his own judgment. ˙At the end of July, a letter from Talleyrand brought the assurances he had required. But the news of the revolution of Third Prairial, which reconstituted the Directory, coming about the same time, caused the President more hesitation. Meanwhile, however, he and Pickering were at work on the letter of instructions to the envoys; and a draft of this document reached Ellsworth in September, while he was on the eastern circuit.

Ellsworth's position was extremely delicate. Between the President, on the one hand, and his friends of the English faction — Wolcott, Pickering, Cabot, King, Hamilton — on the other, he felt the strain of two contending loyalties. His friends were urging him to advise the President to give up the mission. He himself inclined to agree with them, and he looked forward with anything but pleasure to the voyage to France. Yet he would not shirk his duty. "This excellent man," Pickering wrote of him to Cabot, "when he was here in August, saw no alternative *but he must go.* The subsequent changes in Europe, and especially in France, I think, must change his ideas. I wish you would write him upon it, and propose his attempting to dissuade the President from the pursuit. I also will write him. There is nothing in politics he more dreads than the mission, and nothing in nature he more dreads than the voyage across the wide Atlantic."[1]

A few days later, Cabot wrote to Pickering:[2]

" If anything could be done at this hour, it would be by an able display of the subject in a private letter to Ellsworth, which might engage him to expostulate strongly with the President, and refuse to go."

And the next day, having received Pickering's letter, Cabot wrote again:[3]

" I had written to Mr. Ellsworth through the medium of Governor Trumbull, and received his answer before your suggestion. I rejoice to find he thinks practically as we do on the general merits."

Ellsworth's own letters show that he favored a postponement; but they show also that he was already, in his usual businesslike way, studying the requirements

---

[1] September 13, Lodge's "Cabot," 237. " I am told the Chief Justice goes sorely against his will. *The whole measure is very nauseous to the friends of the government.*" Rufus King to Troup, " Life and Correspondence of Rufus King," III, 92.

[2] September 22, Lodge's "Cabot," 238.

[3] *Ibid.*, 242.

of his new rôle. On September 17, he writes to Pickering:[1]

"I have this day written a letter to the President from which he will easily collect my opinion concerning a temporary suspension of the mission to France, tho' I have endeavored to write in a manner that would not give offense." The letter to the President ran as follows:[2]

"SIR: If the present convulsion in France, and symptoms of a greater change at hand, should induce you, as many seem to expect, to postpone for a short time the mission to that country, I wish for the earliest notice of it. The Circuit Court in this state and Vermont fell through last spring from the indisposition of Judge Chase, and must now fall through from the indisposition of Judge Cushing, unless I attend them. I am beginning the Court here, and should proceed to Vermont, if I was sure of not being called on, in the meantime, to embark. It is, Sir, my duty to obey, not advise, and I have only to hope that you will not disapprove of the method I take to learn the speediest intimation of yours."

Rather to Ellsworth's surprise, the President's reply indicated that he also felt it best to wait.[3] The recent change in France, and the prognostics of a still greater change, would certainly, he said, induce him to postpone the mission for a longer or shorter time; and he indicated that the envoys would probably sail on October 20 or November 1. The substance of this letter of the President Ellsworth sent at once to Pickering[4] — a procedure which shows clearly enough

---

[1] Flanders, 226–227.
[2] *Ibid.*, 226.
[3] Adams wrote on September 20. Gibbs, II, 265.
[4] Flanders, 228.

the peculiar relation between Adams and his own
cabinet members. October 1, Ellsworth wrote to
Wolcott [1] that as Judge Cushing had relieved him
from the Vermont circuit, and the President had postponed the mission for a month, he had time to sit
down and think; and he thought the distracted prospects of Europe, and of America also, had begun to
brighten — a view which he commended to his gloomy
correspondent. The cabinet, encouraged, perhaps, for
much the same reasons, urged the President to come
on from his home in Massachusetts for a conference at
Trenton, N.J., whither the government departments
had been moved, Philadelphia being threatened with
yellow fever. Pickering, who wrote for his fellows,
told Adams that Davie had already come to Trenton, and that Ellsworth would also doubtless soon be
coming, and would certainly be gratified to accompany the President. But when Adams, on his way to
Trenton, stopped at Windsor and called on Ellsworth
at Elmwood, neither guest nor host spoke of this
suggestion. Some years later, Adams wrote of the
interview: [2] " On my way I called upon Chief Justice
Ellsworth, at his seat in Windsor, and had a conversation of perhaps two hours with him. He was perfectly
candid. Whatever should be the determination, he
was ready at an hour's warning to comply. If it was
thought best to embark immediately he was ready. If
it was judged more expedient to postpone it for a
little time, though that might subject him to a winter
voyage, that danger had no weight with him. If it
was concluded to defer it to the spring, he was willing
to wait. In this disposition I took leave of him. He

[1] Gibbs, II, 266–267.   [2] Works, IX, 252.

gave me no intimation that he had any thought of a journey to Trenton." Yet two days later Ellsworth wrote to Pickering:[1] "I was, the evening before last, honored with a call from the President of half an hour; but nothing passed respecting my going to Trenton. I have, notwithstanding, presumed to write him by this day's mail, as follows: Since you passed on, I have concluded to meet Governor Davie at Trenton, which he probably will expect, and which, besides putting it in our power to pay you our joint respects, and to receive as fully any communication of your views as you may wish to make, may enable me to accompany him eastward, *should you continue inclined* to such suspension of our mission as, under present aspect, universal opinion, I believe, and certainly my own would justify. It is a matter of some regret, Sir, that I did not consult you on the proposition of this visit; but if I err, experience has taught me that you can excuse. Governor Davie will doubtless arrive before me, and I hope will be made comfortable and easy. It will be Thursday evening or Friday morning next before I shall have the pleasure of seeing you and him."

One may feel that Ellsworth's conduct at this point was a trifle disingenuous; but he committed no disloyal act, he broke faith with no one. Adams does not condemn him. On the contrary, he twice declares that Ellsworth's conduct throughout all this business was perfectly proper. His precautions were no more than so great a matter required.

At Trenton, Ellsworth found not only Adams, Davie, and the cabinet, but Alexander Hamilton, and the whole episode came at once to its crisis.

[1] Flanders, 229; Adams's Works, IX, 37.

The opponents of the mission drew strength from the news from Europe — that the British had landed in Holland, that the Dutch fleet had been captured, that the Russian general, Suwarrow, had won a victory over the French in Switzerland. From these portents they again augured the fall of the Directory and the restoration of the Bourbons. At any rate, they urged, we ought again to postpone action. It was the old Directory, not the new, that had given us the assurances we asked for. Talleyrand himself was out of power. This reasoning Adams heard from nearly all about him. Even Hamilton called to press it upon him. But he saw the European situation more clearly than any of his advisers, and he did not forbear to take account of considerations closer to his own dignity. " I transiently asked one of the heads of departments," he says,[1] " whether Ellsworth and Hamilton had come all the way from Windsor and New York to persuade me to countermand the mission." He accordingly held to his purpose. He invited Ellsworth and Davie to dinner, and they discussed the embassy with perfect freedom. " At table," he relates,[2] " Mr. Ellsworth expressed an opinion somewhat similar to that of the Heads of Departments, and the public opinion at Trenton. ' Is it possible, Chief Justice,' said I, ' that you can seriously believe that the Bourbons are, or will be soon, restored to the throne of France?' ' Why,' said Mr. Ellsworth, smiling, ' *it looks a good deal so.*' ' I should not be afraid to stake my life upon it, that they will not be restored in seven years, if they ever are,' was my reply. And then I entered into a long detail

---

[1] Adams's Works, IX, 299.   [2] *Ibid.*, 254.

of my reasons for this opinion. They would be too
tedious to enumerate here, and time has superseded
the necessity of them. The result of the conversation was, that Mr. Davie was for embarking immediately, as he always had been from his first arrival,
and Mr. Ellsworth declared himself satisfied, and willing to embark so soon as I pleased." [1]

At a cabinet meeting on October 15, the instructions
took their final shape, and early the next morning
the President gave order that the envoys should set
sail not later than November 1. November 3, Ellsworth and Davie embarked at Newport in the frigate *United States*, whose captain was ordered to
land them at any French port they might prefer,
and to touch previously at any port which they might
designate. They chose to touch first at Lisbon, and
on the 27th of November the frigate sailed into the
Tagus. Learning that Napoleon had overthrown the
Directory and made himself practically supreme in
France, they lingered a fortnight at the Portuguese
capital, and then set sail again, this time for L'Orient
in France. But a great storm drove the vessel far out
of her course, and after days and nights of terror and
suffering for all on board she finally put in at Arras,
on the coast of Spain, near Corunna. Sending forward the news of their arrival, and again requesting

---

[1] Works, IX, 254. One would infer that this was before Adams ordered the
departure of the envoys ; but Gibbs (II, 273) states that the dinner occurred
after the order had been given. October 24, Pickering wrote to Cabot :
" Some communication took place Thursday with the envoys, who dined
with the President (after the point had been decided), when many strange
ideas were broached. I heard Judge Ellsworth recite a part, but had no
patience to hear the remainder and went away. It was at Wolcott's the
same evening." Lodge's " Cabot," 249.

assurances concerning their reception, the envoys set off from Corunna overland to Paris.

Ellsworth emerged from the battered frigate a physically broken man. Seasickness and the other hardships of the two passages had permanently deranged his constitution. The land journey over a poverty-stricken region of Spain proved almost equally trying. He was never again to know his old strength and energy of body. But his intellect was still undimmed, his will unshaken. Fisher Ames was reckoning rightly when he wrote to Pickering, " I rely on Mr. E., as much as any man can, to watch the foe, and to parry the stroke of her dagger." [1]

[1] Nov. 15, 1799, Ames's Works, I, 261.

CHAPTER VII

At Burgos, Ellsworth and Davie met their returning messenger. He brought them their passports; and from Talleyrand, who was again at the head of the French department of foreign affairs, he brought a letter which assured them of a proper reception at Paris. Bonaparte, on coming into power, had at once decided in favor of seeking the friendship of America. Apparently, he was already planning to draw the United States into a commercial union with the northern states of Europe against Great Britain. Talleyrand accordingly wrote to the envoys that they were "expected with impatience, and would be received with warmth." Pushing on, therefore, with confidence, they reached Paris on the evening of March the second.

Oliver Ellsworth, Jr., a young graduate of Yale, who had come with the embassy as private secretary to his father, recorded in his diary some of the incidents of the mission and some of the impressions which the Paris of the consulate made upon these American visitors. The morning after their arrival, it seems, they had to endure the first ceremonial of their mission. According to the established custom in Paris, the young diarist relates, a deputation of the market women waited upon them. Warned by the *maître d'hôtel* that the women would make trouble if they did not receive a money present, Ellsworth and Davie consented to see them; and two of the sister-

hood were accordingly conducted to a hall where the
envoys, dressed in black, sat solemnly awaiting them.
One of the women presented a large nosegay, they
both offered congratulations, and for a climax of their
welcome they gave Ellsworth and Davie "the double
embrace on each cheek." This honor the two envoys
reciprocated with a gift of two guineas to each of
their visitors. As the women were middle-aged,
stout, and red-faced, the younger Ellsworth was quite
content that his private station permitted him to be
a mere spectator of the exercises.

Pages of his diary are given to accounts of the
places he visited and the entertainments he attended
— all set down in the most matter-of-fact manner, and
accompanied with observations that reflect a serious,
sensible, but quite unimaginative and unpoetical mind.
At the opera, the young man thought that only a
corrupted taste could relish what he saw and heard.
Attending a masquerade, he concluded that in such a
gathering "many intrigues are probably carried on."
With similar common-sense remarks he records the
celebration of the decade at Notre Dame, — an affair
of " music, marriages, and the covering of the heads
of boys and girls with garlands,"—the annual April
parade of the Parisians to Longchamp, and the exercises on the anniversary of the fall of the Bastille. A
fortnight after his arrival, he got his first glimpse of
Napoleon. There was a grand review of seventeen
thousand troops on the Champs de Mars. After describing it, the diary proceeds:

"Bonaparte himself reviewed them, attended by a
number of his generals; as well as I could judge from
a view of him riding on horseback, he is a middle-

sized man, thin, spare body, and pale face, dark eyes and short hair of black color; his dress and appearance were plain; two gentlemen (the American Ambassadors, who had seen him at an audience in the palace) thought he resembled Mr. Jay in appearance, one of them likewise observing he had much gravity in his face as well as covered cunning or sagacity."

The audience of the envoys with the young conqueror was on March 8, in the hall of the ambassadors in the Tuileries. Only tradition informs us of what occurred. Napoleon, it is said, fairly dazzled Ellsworth, who afterward declared that no other man ever had given him so vivid an impression of mental power. The first consul, as his wont was, discharged at the envoy a rapid fire of questions, which were so searching and intelligent, and showed such a clear comprehension of all the issues between the two countries, that Ellsworth, though himself a rapid thinker and talker, was hard put to it to frame suitable replies. Tradition also has it that Napoleon, on first catching sight of Ellsworth's grave, firm face, had said to some one, " We must make a treaty with this man." [1] But according to the secretary of Governor Davie, it was he — a man of fine appearance and courtly manners — with whom Napoleon was most favorably impressed; so favorably, indeed, that he treated Davie as if he, and not Ellsworth, were the real head of the embassy.[2]

Ill and worn as he was, Ellsworth took little pleasure in his sojourn in France. His life there was quite unlike the highly entertaining experiences of Franklin

[1] Wood and Jackson Mss.

[2] Fordyce M. Hubbard, " Life of Davie," in Sparks's Library of American Biography, XV, 124-125.

and of Gouverneur Morris. He had neither the inclination nor the strength for social distractions. There are no glimpses of him at fine parties or engaged in bouts of repartee with sprightly ladies. Doubtless, however, he did enjoy the opportunity to discuss with eminent Frenchmen those great problems of the right ordering of political societies with which the peoples of France and of the United States had both been wrestling. With Talleyrand, who had been in America, he had one day a long conversation on the subject of free government and the French experiment in democracy. In the course of it, Talleyrand asked the broad question, How France should proceed in order to develop stable republican institutions like those of the United States? Ellsworth's reply was what a chief justice might be expected to give. For a first step, he said, establish a supreme judicial tribunal, made up of the best and oldest judges to be found, and pay them salaries that will free them from all temptations to accept bribes and from all dependence on the government. Once it is known and felt that in that court all have equal rights, lower courts of a like character will be easily established, and other institutions will follow. Talleyrand agreed, but declared that his countrymen, always in a hurry, would never wait upon so slow a process.[1] To Volney, the philosopher, with whom also he had some talks about government, and who had worked out an elaborate system for France, Ellsworth presented the old objection to all Utopian schemes. " There is one thing," he said, " for which you have made no provision, — the selfishness of man."[2]

[1] Wood Ms. [2] *Ibid.*

Apart from such serious interchanges with the famous men whom he encountered, Ellsworth seems to have given his time and strength wholly to his duties. As he and Davie had found Murray awaiting them at Paris, the American envoys saw no reason why the negotiations should not begin at once; and Napoleon, far from following the tactics of the Directory, waived all objections to their letters of credence and promptly named three ministers on the part of France: his brother Joseph, Roederer, who was counsellor of state, and Fleurieu, who had been minister of marine. These appointments were regarded as decidedly complimentary to the United States. Joseph Bonaparte falling ill, the first meeting of the commission was not held until April 2, when powers were exchanged; but at this point Napoleon again showed a conciliatory disposition. As the powers of the French ministers seemingly extended only to a negotiation on the subjects of controversy, not to the conclusion of a treaty, the Americans thought them insufficient; and the First Consul at once issued a new instrument at which there could be no cavil. As he departed soon afterward for the second campaign in Italy, he can scarcely have found time for any further attention to America until, by a new series of victories in battle, he had won for France another interval of security from her European enemies. But his victories against Europe had also a potent bearing on the whole question of the relations between France and America. After Marengo, Ellsworth and his colleagues could no longer entertain the notion that they might soon see the consulate share the fate of the Directory, and perhaps the Bourbons restored. Deeply impressed, on the contrary, by the genius of Napoleon and the ever rising prestige of France, they became convinced that any arrangement not inconsistent with the honor of their country would be preferable to war. Perhaps it would be more accurate to say that they grew more than ever anxious to secure peace; for the relations between the United States and France had been for nearly two years little better than a state of undeclared war.

For this the United States could be held responsible only on the broad ground that they had no right to remain neutral while France was at war with England, nor to conclude the Jay treaty. Up to the summer of 1798, these two policies of the American government had constituted substantially the entire grievance of France. Congress and the President had then added the various measures of retaliation naturally provoked by the continued depredations of France upon our commerce and her contemptuous responses to our efforts for an understanding.

By the old treaty of alliance, we had promised France succor in war; and by the treaty of commerce, besides other favors and privileges, we had guaranteed all her possessions in America and bound ourselves, whenever she should be at war, to open our ports to her privateers and prizes, and close them to those of her enemies. These were the principal compensations, apart from the discomfiture of England, that France had received for the aid which she gave to America during the Revolution; and France held both Washington's proclamation of neutrality and the Jay treaty with England to be plain breaches of faith. If the agreements with her still held, then certainly we had no right to grant to England exclusively, as we did in

the Jay treaty, the freedom of our ports for her privateers and prizes. It was, in fact, impossible to justify
our course if we conceded that our promises of 1778
were still fully binding in 1793 and in 1796, and that
they applied to the war between France and England.
But the friends of England in America had argued
from the first that in this particular war France was the
aggressor, and that the old alliance bound us only in
case she were on the defensive. They might have
cited also a declaration made by Genet, immediately
after his arrival in America, and afterward confirmed
by Talleyrand, that France did not expect the United
States, in this instance, to execute the defensive clauses
of the treaty of alliance. To these excuses for America's neutrality, France herself had soon contributed
another. Even before the Jay treaty, and before the
Directory came into power, the Revolutionary government had entered on a policy quite inconsistent not
merely with the actual treaties between the two republics but with the ordinary obligations of belligerents to neutrals. By a succession of decrees, it had
endeavored to injure England, and to supply its own
needs, at the expense of neutral commerce. It had
treated as contraband all provisions and all enemy's
goods found on neutral vessels. It had authorized the
impressment and forced sale of such cargoes of neutral
vessels visiting French ports as the committee of public safety might desire. By declaring an embargo at
Bordeaux, it had detained there for a year a large
number of American merchantmen. It had caused
the seizure and imprisonment of many American seamen on the pretext that they were British subjects.
Moreover, its official agents had failed to pay for great

quantities of supplies purchased in America. In 1794, when Monroe went to Paris, he found pending a multitude of claims for damages to Americans inflicted in these various ways.

After the Jay treaty, the Directory had taken still more high-handed measures. One of these was to revive certain old Revolutionary ordinances treating as a pirate every neutral vessel not supplied with a *rôle d'equipage* — a ship's register of a form not known in America and countersigned by a public official who had no counterpart in our system — and requiring also a sea letter, which no American vessel carried. A thoroughgoing enforcement of these rules would have subjected to seizure the crew of every American merchant vessel afloat. The climax came with a decree that subjected to capture and confiscation all neutral vessels in whose cargoes there should be found anything whatever of British production. A declaration of war would hardly have given to the navy and privateers of France any greater freedom with the property of Americans on the ocean. And the practice of the navy and the courts of France had been even worse than the letter of the decrees.

The instructions to the American envoys bade them insist on some provision for reparation for these outrages as an absolutely indispensable condition of a peaceable agreement. Ellsworth, who had been consulted freely both by Adams and Pickering while they were preparing the instructions,[1] had approved this decision; but he had successfully opposed Pickering's

[1] "I am glad you have sent a copy to the Chief Justice. I had several conversations with him last winter on the whole subject. He appears to

apparent desire to put into the American contention so severe a reflection on the course of France that the French government could not with self-respect have entertained our proposals. What Pickering had designed may be inferred from this note of Ellsworth, written in September, 1799:[1]

" Having given your draught of instructions such perusal as the hurry and pressure of a court, crowding two terms into one, admits of, I remark, with all the freedom you invite, that to insist that the French government acknowledge its orders to be piratical, or, which is the same, *absolutely* engage to pay for the depredations committed under them, is, I believe, unusually degrading, and which would probably defeat the negotiation and place us in the wrong. The alternative of insisting that the fifth commissioner shall be a foreigner, is more than was insisted with Great Britain, and a ground, as I apprehend, hardly sufficient to risk failure upon, though an eligible arrangement to attempt. The style of the instructions is certainly nowhere heightened beyond the provocation received; yet in some few instances, which will readily occur to you on revision, is more spirited, as it seems to me, than can be necessary to impress the envoys, or than, in the event of publication, would be evidential of that sincerity and concilia-

me to agree most perfectly with me on every point of our policy towards France and England; and this policy was founded only in perfect purity of moral sentiment, natural equity, and Christian faith towards both nations. I am, therefore, under no hesitation in sending the draught to him. . . . Indeed, Mr. Ellsworth is so great a master of business, and his colleagues are so intelligent, that I should not be afraid to allow them a greater latitude of discretion, if it were not unfair to lay upon them alone the burden of the dangerous responsibility that may accompany this business." Adams to Pickering, Sept. 19, 1799. Adams's Works, IX, 31.

[1] Flanders, 236–237.

tory temper with which the business should appear to
be conducted."

Two weeks later, he wrote again in favor of modify-
ing the conditions in respect of the French decrees
and the fifth commissioner.[1] In their final form, the
instructions defined clearly those cases of captures and
condemnations of American property which were held
to be illegal and for which compensation was demanded,
and set forth in some detail the American view of the
conduct of France. At the end were seven *ultimata*.
There must be a board of claims to determine damages,
and France must bind herself to pay; there must be
no guaranty to France of any part of her dominions;
there must be no promise of a loan or of aid in any
other form; prior treaties with other countries, including the Jay treaty, must be fully respected; there must
be no grant of power to French consuls of a nature to
permit them to set up in America tribunals incom-
patible with the complete sovereignty of the United
States; the new treaty must not run for more than
twelve years.[2]

It required less than Ellsworth's ordinary shrewdness to perceive quickly that there was no hope of
securing a treaty which should meet all these requirements of his government. He and his colleagues, in their opening note, named two main
objects of the negotiation: to provide for the
claims of each party for damages inflicted by the
other, and to frame a new commercial agreement.
But the ministers of France, in their reply, held that
the first step should be to agree upon the principles

[1] Flanders, 237–238.
[2] For the instructions, see American State Papers, II, 301–306.

to govern the awards of damages, and the second, to secure the enforcement of the treaties already in existence. They also expressed surprise that France had received no assurance of the repeal of the retaliatory acts which Congress had passed in 1798. This first interchange disclosed clearly enough the true desires of both parties. Many other points were afterward taken up, but the Americans were always trying to secure damages without renewing the treaties; and the Frenchmen were trying to renew the treaties without any binding agreement concerning damages.

It has always been supposed that Ellsworth directed the negotiation for his side, and the style of the correspondence, grave, weighty, and condensed, with now and then a passage of dry humor or sarcasm, bears out the tradition.[1]   A clear contrast has been noted between the diplomatic methods of the Americans and that of the ministers of France.   The Americans took much pains to sustain all their specific contentions, and in general to prove their country in the right. They seemed at times to suppose that the justice of a claim sufficiently commended it.   One finds repeatedly in their communications a note of entire sincerity. They have been criticised, in fact, for trying to inject moral ideas into a discussion in which the other party kept in mind nothing but the main chance.   The French commissioners did not by any means neglect to argue their case or fail to dilate on the good faith and magnanimity of their country; they several times

[1] The entire correspondence is given in the journal of the embassy, in American State Papers, III, 307–345.   This is my authority for the present account of the negotiation, except as other sources are mentioned.   It seems hardly worth while to give page references to the journal for specific statements.

succeeded in this way in putting the Americans rather
absurdly on the defensive.   But they plainly regarded
the whole correspondence as a dicker.   The object of
it, they considered, was not to establish justice, but to
adjust interests; in a word, to strike a bargain.   It
would be absurd to suppose that the Americans, experienced men of the world, childishly ignored that point
of view.   The difference was only of degree.   But
they did endeavor to harmonize interests with morality
and law.   The Frenchmen, not, apparently, distracted
by any such desire, were superior in *finesse*, and in
turning to advantage every favorable factor in the
situation.   One of their devices was delay, for they
could not fail to note the eagerness and the growing
uneasiness of the other side.   About the middle of
April, Talleyrand fell ill, and for a month they made
this an excuse for dilatory tactics.

On April 9, the American commissioners, to expe-
dite the business, had submitted various specific
articles which they desired to incorporate in a new
treaty of commerce.   These included a provision for
a board of claims, all claims that had arisen before July
8, 1798, to be adjudicated according to the old treaties,
and all later claims to be adjudicated according to the
law of nations.   After a fortnight the Frenchmen
replied, again insisting that the old treaty of commerce
was still in force, and objecting to the distinction
between the two classes of claims.   The Americans
had already written home that they would be hard-
pressed to revive that treaty, at least so far as to concede its anteriority to the Jay treaty; but in their
next communication to the French ministers they
incorporated, nevertheless, the remaining heads of

their proposals. They waited in vain for any further answer until near the end of May. On May 23, they were informed at a conference that the negotiation on the part of France had come to a standstill. The First Consul's instructions having made the revival of the old treaties a *sine qua non*, nothing more could be done until he had passed on the American proposals. Fearful of his decision, Ellsworth and his colleagues quickly resolved to modify one of their articles. They proposed that in the future neither country should open its ports to the privateers and prizes of a third power unless they should first have guaranteed the same favor to each other. A month of silence followed. Early in June, Joseph Bonaparte slipped away to Italy to submit everything to Napoleon. On June 14 came the battle of Marengo.[1] July 3, Napoleon himself returned to Paris. Thereafter, the American envoys felt, behind every move of the other side, his controlling mind and purpose.

On July 11, Joseph Bonaparte, at a dinner at his own house, announced that the First Consul would never consent to pay indemnities on any other basis than the old treaties, nor make any new treaty that should not at least place France on a footing of equality with Great Britain. Four days later, the Americans proposed that indemnities be ascertained as in their project of a treaty, but that payments be withheld

---

[1] "A gentleman, who saw Mr. Ellsworth the end of June, informs me that he expressed an opinion that it was best he and his colleagues should be where they were; that Austria probably would make peace and England perhaps would not continue the war after the summer campaign ends; that if all others should adjust their differences, and our own remain unsettled, we might find it difficult to obtain terms that were just and reasonable." Cabot to Wolcott, Lodge's "Cabot," 290.

until the United States should offer France an agreement concerning privateers and prizes similar to that
of 1778 — a move which they saw plainly did not
produce a pleasant impression. The response to it,
delayed until August 11, on the ground that the other
side was still waiting for instructions, took the form of
two alternative offers. France would renew the old
treaties and provide for indemnities; or she would
consent to abrogate the old treaties, and make a new
one unattended with indemnities, insisting only that it
should place her on an equal footing with England.
Ellsworth and his colleagues, having pondered the
entire situation, now wrote to Pickering that they
must either abandon the negotiation or depart from
their instructions.

Believing, however, that if they failed to secure an
agreement for indemnities the failure would be final,
they tried their ingenuity on a series of proposals
looking to a modified renewal of the treaties. They
were met in every instance by counter proposals which,
however worded, always either left open a way for
France to escape from paying indemnities or else
coupled the payment with concessions which the
United States would find it impossible, or at any rate
extremely distasteful, to make. Seeing that the negotiation was again coming to a deadlock, the Americans then made up their minds to test the sincerity
of the original French offer to pay indemnities on
the renewal of the treaties. They considered carefully the extent to which their country was bound by
her engagements with England, and indulged themselves in what seems a bit of rather sharp casuistry.
Their reasoning, as set forth in their final report,

turned chiefly on the rule of priority in respect of conflicting international agreements, and moved in a kind of circle to the conclusion which they wished to establish. The rule being always understood, they argued, it could be no breach of faith to make with one power a treaty inconsistent with an existing treaty with another. The Jay treaty expressly bound both the contracting parties to forbear from making with any other country any engagement inconsistent with the mutual guarantee concerning privateers and prizes in time of war. If, therefore, the United States should now make such an engagement with France, it would be understood with the limitation that it did not extend to a case in which Great Britain should be the enemy. The instructions to the American envoys bade them make, if they should consent to renew that clause of the treaty of commerce of 1778 which bore on privateers and prizes, a special saving of Great Britain's rights; but the rule of construction would save those rights without any stipulation. Besides, it was a question of renewing old treaties with France, not of making new ones. Since such renewals constitute the usual method of terminating hostilities, no commitment with another nation could conceivably forbid them. The uniform usage in such cases implied that hostilities did not destroy preëxisting treaties, but only suspended their operation. The acts of Congress in 1798 had really brought about a state of war with France. The present negotiation ought, therefore, to be regarded as making peace by restoring the suspended agreements. Moreover, there should be no difficulty about Great Britain, for in 1792 Lord Malmesbury had offered France, in a project of a peace treaty, the same exclusive rights in British ports that France now demanded in the ports of the United States. " The foregoing considerations," the envoys wrote in their report, " induced the undersigned to be unanimously of the opinion that any part of the former treaties might be renewed consistently with good faith."

On September 6, they accordingly made their most advanced overture. They offered to renew the old treaties in full, on three conditions. For the mutual guarantee of succor in the treaty of alliance there should be substituted an agreement to furnish aid in a certain amount of money or provisions; indemnities should be provided for, and all captured property not yet condemned should be at once restored; at the exchange of ratifications, the United States should have the option, by giving up the provision for indemnities, to get rid of all the obligations of the treaties, save that each of the parties should continue to have, for its men of war, privateers, and prizes, such rights in the ports of the other as the most-favored nation might enjoy. At a conference on September 12, when the commission went over these proposals with the closest scrutiny, the ministers of France made an avowal which Ellsworth and his colleagues afterward dryly pronounced " quite unnecessary." They avowed that their real object from the beginning had been to avoid by every means the payment of indemnities. France, they confessed, was in fact unable to pay. Joseph Bonaparte went farther still, and declared that if his government should order him and his colleagues to make a treaty on the basis of indemnities and modified renewal of the old treaties, he would resign sooner than obey. The Americans, retiring for a few minutes, agreed that it was useless to make any more proposals. Their original mission had plainly ended in failure. They might at once have asked for their passports, gone home, and received an honorable discharge. But if they could not compass their errand, they could, they believed, serve their country in another way. If they could not secure reparation for past injuries, they could perhaps prevent a recurrence of like molestations in the future. Abandoning the project of a treaty, they decided to propose a temporary arrangement which should at least make an end of a state of affairs that could otherwise end only in war. The next day, accordingly, they wrote to the French commissioners:

" The discussion of former treaties and of indemnities being for the present closed, it must, of course, be postponed until it can be resumed with fewer embarrassments. It remains only to consider the expediency of a temporary arrangement. Should such an arrangement comport with the views of France, the following principles are offered as the basis of it:

" 1. The ministers plenipotentiary of the respective parties, not being able at present to agree respecting the former treaties and indemnities, the parties will in due and convenient time further treat on these subjects; and, until they have agreed respecting the same, the said treaties shall have no operation. In the meantime,

" 2. The parties shall abstain from all unfriendly acts; their commercial intercourse shall be free, and debts shall be recoverable in the same manner as if no misunderstanding had intervened.

" 3. Property captured and not yet definitely condemned, or which may be captured before the exchange of ratifications, shall be mutually restored. Proofs of ownership to be specified in the convention.

" 4. Some provisional regulations shall be made to prevent abuses and disputes that may arise out of future cases of capture."

The ministers of France responded with reasonable promptness. On September 19, there was a conference; and at conferences held from day to day the new proposals were carefully explored. Joined with certain articles of the treaty originally offered, they gradually took shape in a convention covering all fresh difficulties likely to arise.[1] Having for the time being escaped indemnities, the French ministers consented to leave the old treaties in abeyance, it being agreed that the two countries would again negotiate concerning indemnities and treaties "at a convenient time." They likewise accepted the American contention on various other important points that had been in controversy. The convention in fact secured for America much more than England had conceded in the Jay treaty. It rescued all the ships and other property that had been taken but not yet definitely condemned. It ended the old difficulty about the *rôle d'equipage* by providing for a uniform passport, to be used by both countries. It guaranteed all debts owed by the government or by individuals of either republic to the government or individuals of

---

[1] Napoleon himself insisted on calling it a convention instead of a "provisional treaty," telling Roederer that there were times to disregard forms but that this was a time to pay strict attention to them. "Œuvres de Roederer" (Paris, 1854, printed by his son, A. M. Roederer), III, 336.

the other. It secured freedom of trade between the contracting parties, and it freed the trade of America with Great Britain from all those irregular restraints with which France had hampered and harassed it. So far from assenting to the French contention about provisions and enemy's goods, it declared that only arms, ammunition, and implements fit for the use of troops should be treated as contraband, and that in the case of all other cargoes free ships should mean free goods. It carefully regulated the procedure of captures, so as to prevent wanton destruction of property. In a word, it accomplished the entire design of Ellsworth and his colleagues when they decided to stay in Paris and propose a temporary arrangement.

On October 3, this instrument was completed, and Ellsworth had finished his last great service to the United States. It had proved, doubtless, the most trying of them all. Apart from the tax on his waning strength, the long absence from his home, and the sojourn in a strange country which he did not like, he had the melancholy experience of Jay to warn him that he need not expect the gratitude of his countrymen. He also knew well enough that he was likely to disappoint and anger his closest party friends.

His letters home have a certain effect of resignation. The tone of them is that of a strong man, fearfully exhausted, but resolute and faithful. From Burgos, he had written to his son Martin:[1]

"Distant as you are from me, my dear boy, you are not a day out of my mind, nor can I ever think of you

[1] Feb. 10, 1800. For a copy I am indebted to Mr. G. E. Taintor of Hartford.

without the most ardent wishes for your welfare. I
hope and trust, that you make the best improvement
of your time, and that while you are preparing to live
and act your part well in this world, you will not forget that there is another to prepare for."

Two letters from Paris to his twin children, Billy
and Harry, aged eight, are, it is true, playfully affectionate. The first runs:

" Daddy is a great way off, but he thinks about his
little boys every day; and he hopes they are very good
boys, and learn their books well, and say their prayers
every night, and then God will love them as much as
Daddy does.

" There are a good many fine things here, and a great
many strange things. Oliver writes them down, and
he will have enough to tell the boys twenty nights.

" The Robbers came round the house where Daddy
lives the other night and the Gardener shot off his two
barrel gun and killed two of them. And Daddy believes, if the Robbers come into his room, they will get
killed, for he keeps a gun and two pistols charged all
the time. And when he comes home he intends to
give his gun to Martin, and his pistols to Billy and
Harry."

And in the second he actually drops into rhyme:

> " The men in France are lazy creatures,
>   And work the women and great dogs,
> The Ladies are enormous eaters,
>   And like the best, toadstools and frogs.

> " The little boys are pretty spry
>   And bow when Daddy's paid them,
> But don't think they shall ever die,
>   Nor can they tell who made them.

"But Daddy's boys are not such fools,
And are not learned so bad,
For they have Mamma and good schools,
And that makes Daddy glad.

"Daddy won't forget them pistols." [1]

But the only letter to his wife is as solemn as it is brief. "I shall leave France next month," he wrote, "let our business, which is still unfinished, terminate as it may. If it please God that I see my family and friends once more, I shall certainly love them better than ever." [2]

After the convention was signed, he wrote to his brother David : [3]

"Altho' our best and long continued efforts have not obtained all that justice required, yet enough is finally done, if our government should approve of and ratify it, to restore peace to our country, — to make some saving of the property which has been wrongfully taken from us, — to guard against further injuries, as well as they can be guarded against by engagements, and to disentangle our country from its former alliance and connections with France.

"I know you will be much disappointed at my not returning this fall; but the gravel and the gout in my kidneys, which constantly afflict me, forbid my undertaking a voyage in a cold and boisterous season of the year. I hope that by going to a mild climate in the South of France to spend the winter, and by being freed from the anxiety and perplexity of business,

---

[1] Neither of these two letters is dated. Both copied by Mr. W. Irving Vinal from originals in the possession of Mrs. Waldo Hutchins.

[2] Jackson Ms. Copied from the collection of Mr. Teft of Savannah. As the collector added the signature from another source, there may have been more in the original.

[3] From Havre, Oct. 10, 1800. Copy furnished by Mr. G. E. Taintor.

which has much increased my complaint, that I shall be able by the opening of the Spring to return without hazard. . . .

"I pray God to preserve your health, and that of your family, and to grant that in due time we may again meet and rejoice together."

And to Wolcott:

"You will see our proceedings and their result. Be assured more could not be done without too great a sacrifice, and as the reign of Jacobinism is over in France, and appearances are strong in favor of a general peace, I hope you will think it was better to sign a convention than to do nothing. Sufferings at sea, and a winter's journey through Spain, gave me an obstinate gravel, which, by wounding the kidneys, has drawn and fixed my wandering gout to those parts. My pains are constant, and at times excruciating; they do not permit me to embark for America at this late season of the year, nor, if there, would they permit me to discharge my official duties. I have, therefore, sent my resignation of the office of chief justice, and shall, after spending a few weeks in England, retire for winter quarters to the South of France.

"I pray Mrs. Wolcott to accept of my best respects, and shall ever remain, dear sir, your affectionate friend." [1]

---

[1] From Havre, October 16. Gibbs, "Administrations of Washington and John Adams," II, 434. To Pickering, probably at the same time, he wrote: "My best efforts and those of my colleagues have not obtained all that which justice required, or which the policy of France should have given. Enough is however done, if ratified, to extricate the United States from a contest which it might be as difficult to relinquish with honour, as to pursue with a prospect of advantage. A partial saving is also made for captured property, goods are provided against future abuses as well perhaps as they can be by stipulations, and our country is disentangled

Having heard, apparently, that Adams had dismissed Pickering, and that Wolcott had contemplated resigning, Ellsworth added a postscript, than which he never wrote or said anything more expressive of his own high standard of patriotism.

"You certainly did well not to resign, and you must not think of resigning, let what changes may take place, at least till I see you. Tho' our country pays badly, it is the only one in the world worth working for. The happiness it enjoys, and which it may increase, is so much superior to what the nations of Europe do or ever can enjoy, that no one who is able to preserve and increase that happiness ought to quit her service while he can remain in it with bread and honour. Of the first, a little suffices you, and of the latter, it is not in the power of rapine or malevolence to deprive you. They cannot do without you and dare not put you out. Remember, my dear friend, my charge — keep on till I see you."

To resign his own great judicial office must have cost Ellsworth a struggle. He took the step solely because of his broken health. The opposition at home criticised him for holding the place while engaged with other duties in a foreign land, but his predecessor, Jay, had done the same thing, and his successor, John Marshall, after accepting the appointment to the bench, continued to act as Secretary of State down to the very last moment of the Adams administration.[1]

from its former connexions. . . . I hope you will think it better to do this, than to have done nothing." Quoted in a letter of Pickering to Wolcott. *Ibid.*, 463.

[1] In the Pyne-Henry Collection in the Princeton University Library there is a letter from Ellsworth, dated March 17, 1802, which seems to

Ellsworth would doubtless have preferred to leave Paris as quietly and as quickly as possible. But the French government had no mind to let the long negotiation come to an end without making some sentimental use of the occasion. Napoleon was still bent on conciliating America; and it need not be doubted that the restoration of friendly relations appealed to a genuine sentiment in the hearts of many Frenchmen. The First Consul had remained uniformly gracious to the envoys. Besides other attentions, he made Ellsworth a gift of a costly piece of Gobelin tapestry, and with a truly French cognizance of his one vice presented him also with a gold snuff-box. Prompted, perhaps, by the government, Joseph Bonaparte now tendered the three Americans an elaborate entertainment. The occasion is thus described in the diary of Oliver Ellsworth, Jr.:[1]

"October 3d the American commissioners left Paris for Mortfontane, a village perhaps 18 miles north of Paris; to which village they with their suite had been pressingly invited by Joseph Bonaparte (one of the French ministers) to assist at a fête, before going to embark at Havre de Grace. To this village we

indicate that he was required to refund his salary as Chief Justice from the time of his appointment as envoy, and that he was allowed only three months to return home after signing the convention. He points out in this letter that after he accepted the appointment as envoy he travelled the southern circuit and performed other judicial duties out of his turn, that by arrangement certain of his associates performed his circuit duties in his absence, that the Supreme Court had a quorum without him, and that, as the signing of the convention was a preliminary step, unauthorized by his commission, it left the commission still unexecuted, and he might have been justified in waiting in Europe to see if his government would acquiesce.

For a copy of this letter I am indebted to Mr. W. W. Bishop of the Princeton Library.

[1] Flanders, 254–256, gives the extract, but not so nearly *verbatim* as in the text. See Thiers, "Consulate and Empire," II, 247–248.

arrived about two o'clock P.M., where we found a large number of the magistrates of the French government collected in Joseph Bonaparte's chateau. The First Consul Bonaparte arrived here about 4 o'clock P.M., cannon firing and music playing upon his entrance into the chateau. During the afternoon, the company amused itself in the gardens or parc attached to the chateau, which are in English style, affording picturesque views. Behind the chateau a canal, etc., etc.; in the front at a small distance a parc with rocky and barren hills topped by an ancient tower on one side, a large natural pond interspersed with islands in the bottom of the plot, and fine cultivated sides of hills in other parts.

"In the evening, after the final signature of the treaty by the French and American ministers, it was presented for ratification to the First Consul, upon which occasion, about 8 in the evening, cannon were fired to announce the ratification. About nine the company of perhaps 150 were conducted to a supper prepared in three *salles* or halls. The principal, called Union Hall, was superbly illuminated, hung with verdant wreaths and many inscriptions to the memory of the 4th of July, 1776, and other periods and places celebrated by important actions in America during the struggle for independence.[1] Among these inscriptions,

---

[1] "In the Hall of the Union shields placed over crossed swords were arranged at intervals. On one shield one read : *Lexington* ; on another, 4 *July*, 1776, *American Independence* ; on a flag folded under this last, one read : *Hancock* ; on another shield one saw two *fasces* united and the initials of France and of America, F and A ; on one of the flags, *Warcen* (Warren?). One shield bore *On the* 9 *Vendémiaire year IX* (date of the signing of the convention). A little farther on was written : *Putnam*. . . . One shield was consecrated *to* 9 *October*, 1781, *York Town*." *Journal de Paris*, quoted in Roederer, VI, 419.

besides frequently the letters F, A, *i.e.* France and America, were the views of the federal city of Philadelphia and Havre de Grace, the port from which the American ministers were to embark, and what is curious the representation of an angel flying with the olive branch from Havre de Grace to Philadelphia. The second hall, called *Salle de Washington*, was adorned with Washington's bust, the French and American flag side by side, etc. The third, *i.e. Salle de Franklin*, had Franklin's bust, etc. The intention of these decorations seemed to be the commemoration principally of the American independence, and, from the toasts given at the table, etc., at the same time the commemoration of the French liberty; for instance, the First Consul's toast, viz., to the memory of those who have fallen in the defence of French and American liberties, or something to this purpose. The toast of the second consul, Cambaceres, was ' The Successor of Washington.' [1]

"After the supper, about ten, were splendid and very ingenious fireworks in the garden, the chateau being illuminated during the evening. Next followed a fine concert. About twelve or midnight two short but interesting comedies were performed in the private theatre in the chateau, the actors being the best from Paris. At the conclusion of one of these pieces some-

---

[1] Lebrun, third consul, proposed "The Union of America with the Northern powers to enforce respect for the liberty of the seas," and he probably came nearer than the others to a correct expression of the true object of Napoleon's policy with the United States. Thiers ("Consulate and Empire," II, 247) remarks of the convention, "C'était donner sur les mers un allié de plus à la France, et un ennemi de plus à l'angleterre; c'était un noveau ferment ajouté à la querelle maritime, qui relevait dans le Nord, et qui de jour en jour devenait plus grave."

thing in verse was sung respecting the United States.[1] The plays ending about two o'clock in the morning, (of) the company some took soon to their beds, some taking a second supper, and some starting for Paris at three o'clock. In the forenoon of the fourth, I had leisure for walking again in the garden, and being in company with Mr. Roederer's son he informed me that Joseph Bonaparte proposed the raising of a marble monument in the garden to the commemoration of the signing of the treaty of F. and U.S.A."

The memoirs of Roederer add another incident.[2] The First Consul, it seems, had directed the minister of foreign affairs to present to each of the American ministers a costly gift. Moreover, the prefect of L'Oise having brought to the fête, as a present to the First Consul himself, a basketful of gold medals of different periods of the Roman republic, which had been found in his department, Napoleon remarked that the best possible disposition of these relics of a great republic was to present them to the citizens of the American republic. He accordingly gave a handful to each of the three. A few minutes later, the company observed the Americans retire into the recess of a window, and there engage in an animated controversy with their secretary, who, as it afterwards appeared, had reminded them that Americans employed in diplomatic offices were forbidden to accept gifts from foreign governments. Roederer was of opinion that the secretary, having been overlooked in the distribution

---

[1] The *Journal de Paris* of October 6 contains the verses, which are hardly worth quoting. Roederer, III, 420.

[2] *Ibid.*, 337–338. The passage in which Roederer gives his own recollections of the convention and the fête was translated and printed in the *National Intelligencer* of Aug. 22, 1855. Jackson Ms.

of the medals, mixed some personal pique with his constitutional scruples. The envoys, however, accepted
his view, explained their position to the First Consul
through the French ministers, and gave back the
medals. Napoleon, explaining that he had not meant
to make them an ordinary diplomatic compliment, and
that he had offered the medals, not as so much gold,
but as mementoes, persuaded them to retain this gift; [1]
but Talleyrand did not venture to offer them the other.
Roederer tells the story with an air of discontent, which
the sequel explains. Napoleon soon afterward said to
him: "I am vexed on your account. You lose a present of equal value which they would have made in
return." And by way of compensation the First
Consul himself presented to Roederer and Fleurieu
fifteen thousand francs apiece.

According to the *Journal de Paris*, the American
ministers had heard with much emotion the toasts of
the three consuls, and had expressed their appreciation
as well as their imperfect French permitted; and when,
the next day at noon, Talleyrand presented them to
the First Consul to take their leave, Ellsworth said:
"The convention which we have had the honor to
sign will indissolubly reunite the two nations. We
make no doubt but that it will produce that happy
effect." Murray added, "And the three American
ministers engage themselves to give all their attention to the attainment of that object." Whereupon
Napoleon declared that the misunderstanding between
the two nations would leave no more traces than a

[1] But this story of Roederer's is not confirmed by any mention of the
medals in any other account of the mission, nor by any tradition in the
Ellsworth family.

family quarrel, and predicted that the American people would soon learn, "from what was coming to pass in the North," the value of a union founded on liberal principles.[1]

Taking their departure in the afternoon, the Americans proceeded straight to Havre, and a fortnight later, having been detained only by the tides, Ellsworth and Davie passed over to England. After a farewell dinner at Weymouth on October 22, Governor Davie and Oliver Ellsworth, Jr., sailed for America, bearing with them the convention and Ellsworth's resignation of his judicial office. He himself remained in England, still designing to go to southern France for the winter. Meanwhile, though he awaited with a natural concern the judgment of his government, of his party, and of his countrymen in general, on the outcome of the mission, he could only leave the case as he and his colleagues had put it in their final letter to the Secretary of State: " If, with the simple plea of right, unaccompanied with the menaces of power, and unaided by events either in Europe or America, less is at present obtained than justice requires, or than the policy of France should have granted, the undersigned trust that the sincerity and patience of their efforts to obtain all that their country had a right to demand will not be drawn in question."

It is perhaps the strongest of all the evidences of Ellsworth's standing with his contemporaries that his sincerity and his integrity were not drawn in question, as Jay's had been. Long before the outcome was known, his political friends at home had been busy

[1] Roederer, VI, 420.

conjecturing what was going on at Paris. Pickering, Wolcott, Ames, and Cabot, in particular, had expressed in their correspondence an anxiety hardly less than that of Adams himself, who regarded the mission as the crucial episode of his administration. There is also reason to believe that in the autumn of 1800 a number of Federalists entertained a hope that the outcome might bring Ellsworth's figure into such distinct relief before the whole country that the party would turn to him as a fit man for the presidency or vice-presidency. It is said that a caucus of moderate Federalists actually resolved to bring him forward in case Adams should show a disposition to retire.[1] But if Adams had any disposition to retire, the opposition within his own party was enough to make him change his mind. The convention, though it was published in France in October, and soon afterward in England, did not reach America until December — too late to have any perceptible effect on the political situation — and when the anti-Adams Federalists learned its provisions they were inclined to consider it as a triumph for Adams, rather than for Ellsworth or themselves. It is possible to understand, but hardly possible to justify, the temper in which these men received the news that the envoys had made peace with France. Apparently, nothing that could have happened in our foreign relations would have displeased them more — except, perhaps, a disagreement with England. Their partisanship of

---

[1] Van Santvoord, 284. "It has been thought by some, that if *your* policy had been pursued, and Mr. Adams renounced absolutely by the Federalists, it would have been in our power to have carried Pickering and Ellsworth or Jay." Cabot to Wolcott, Nov. 28, 1800, Lodge's "Life of Cabot," 288. See also Wharton's State Trials, 39.

Great Britain had come to equal the Gallomania of
the Democrats a few years earlier; and their hatred
and distrust of France almost equalled the feeling of the French Jacobins toward "perfidious
Albion."

Their grief over Ellsworth's share in the business
was comical. Unable to suspect him of treachery,
they mournfully concluded that his illness had im-
paired his intelligence. Early in October, Cabot had
communicated to Wolcott his fears " that the high
and well-tempered mind of our excellent friend Ellsworth has been shaken perhaps by sickness in part,
but in part also by the events he has witnessed, and
by others which he apprehended, and all aggravated
by the acts and management of a set of people at
Paris employed for the purpose, as the Kosciuskos,
Barlows, etc." [1]   And when the first reports of the
convention reached America, Cabot wrote,[2] " If what
the newspapers represent with great appearance of
truth be correct, I should think the affairs of our
country are in the worst possible situation in regard
to foreign nations."   When the convention arrived,
Wolcott wrote to Hamilton : [3]   " You will be afflicted
on reading the treaty with France.   Mr. Ellsworth's
health is, I fear, destroyed."   And to Pickering : [4]

" You will read the treaty which was signed with
France with astonishment.   I can account for it only
on the supposition that the vigour of Mr. Ellsworth's
mind has been enfeebled by sickness.   The Senate
are, I understand, much embarrassed, though they will
advise a conditional ratification.   It is now certain

[1] Lodge's "Cabot," 204.   [3] December 25, Gibbs, 460.
[2] Ibid.   [4] December 28, Ibid., 461.

that the mission has proved as unfortunate as we considered it at the time it was instituted."

And Pickering replied: [1]

"The treaty with France as you suppose has excited my utter astonishment. Davie and Murray always appeared to me fond of the mission, and I supposed that they had made the treaty, but when informed that our friend, our highly respected and respectable friend Mr. E——, was most urgent for its adoption, my regret equalled my astonishment. The fact can be solved only on the ground which you have suggested."

The former Secretary of State then went on to criticise the convention more specifically. The envoys, he thought, never should have countenanced the notion that the old treaties could ever be revived, or consented to the coupling of indemnities in any fashion with the revival. The sixth article, granting the privateers and prizes of France the privileges of the most favored nation in our ports, he pronounced a plain violation of the Jay treaty. By engaging to give up captured ships, we admitted that we were wrong in taking hostile measures at all. Commerce with the colonies of France was silently denied us. A stipulation that the word of the commander of a convoy should exempt a merchant fleet from search also struck him as exceptional. Why not simply leave to each of the parties entire freedom of trade with the enemies of the other? If, as Wolcott had predicted, the Senate should ratify only conditionally, we should not be "extricated from our contest"— the great object that Mr. Ellsworth had had in view

[1] Jan. 3, 1801, Gibbs, 463.

when he decided to remain in Paris after the failure to conclude a treaty.

Sedgwick of Massachusetts also concluded that "the mind as well as body of Mr. Ellsworth are rendered feeble by disease."[1] Otis pronounced the whole business "another chapter in the book of humiliation."[2] Gunn of Georgia called the convention "detestable."[3] "We are, by treaty, to embrace France," wrote Fisher Ames, "and Frenchmen will swarm in our porridge-pots."[4]

Hamilton himself, the feud with Adams being now at its height, took in private a tone hardly less severe. Arguing against the proposal of certain Federalists to support Burr as against Jefferson when the contested election of the President should come into the House of Representatives, and describing Burr as a very Catiline, he cited in evidence toasts given at Burr's table to the French republic, to the commissioners on both sides, to Bonaparte, and to Lafayette.[5] The convention, he wrote to Sedgwick, played into the hands of France by conceding those principles of navigation on which she wished to build up a league of the northern powers against England.[6] He also regretted the free ships, free goods provision, because he thought England would object to it. But in public he defended the convention. Even in that unwise pamphlet on the public conduct and character of Adams which he published about this time, fiercely as he assailed the policy of the mission, he

---

[1] Hamilton's Works, VI, 491.   [3] *Ibid.*, 492.
[2] *Ibid.*, 490.   [4] Ames's Works, II, 289.
[5] Hamilton to Wolcott, Dec. 17, 1800, Gibbs, II, 459.
[6] Hamilton's Works, VI, 495.

pronounced the final issue of it "an honorable accom-
modation," and he advised his friends in the Senate
to ratify the convention.[1]

President Adams, on the other hand, found no
fault whatever with it. He wished it ratified uncondi-
tionally. " Had it betrayed a single point of essential
honor or interest," he afterward wrote, " I would have
sent it back, as Mr. Jefferson did the treaty with
England, without laying it before the Senate."[2] The
majority of the Senate, and perhaps the majority of the
Federalist senators, although they probably could not
agree entirely with the President, refused to follow
his enemies. The southern wing of the party, more
moderate in general than the northern wing, had been
for some time out of sympathy with what Adams called,
not without reason, the " British faction." They had
never joined in the attack on Adams and the mission;[3]
and if John Marshall, after his humiliating experience
at the French capital, could accept peace with France
on the proposed terms, other fair-minded men within
the party can hardly have had much difficulty with
the question. As Secretary of State and as the foremost southern Federalist, Marshall had at this time
a potent voice in his party's councils. He admitted
that he was very far indeed from approving the convention, but he advised that it be ratified.[4] Gouver-

[1] From a letter of Ellsworth to Rufus King it appears that he had
written Hamilton "a few observations respecting it (the convention),
intended to guard against surprise." Flanders, 264.

[2] Adams's Works, IX, 281.

[3] " Unhappily the Federalists of the North do not agree with those of
the South. The former have pretty generally expressed a disapprobation,
while the latter have as openly vindicated the mission to France." Cabot
to Gore, Jan. 21, 1800, Lodge's " Cabot," 268.

[4] Hamilton's Works, VI, 502.

neur Morris, who knew his France better perhaps
than any other American, and who was, moreover, an
excellent man of business, thought that with one or
two changes it would be "no bad bargain."[1] As the
Senate held it from the middle of December until
the beginning of February, it doubtless encountered
serious opposition. But at this session the House of
Representatives had to choose between Jefferson and
Burr, who had received the same number of electoral
votes for the presidency, and the contest absorbed
much of the passion that had so long embittered the
controversies over foreign affairs. Federalists as well
as Republicans were intriguing to influence the
choice of the House. Two letters from Rufus King,
minister to England, to the Secretary of State, must
have gone far to silence one contention of those
who opposed ratification. The convention had no
sooner been published in the English newspapers
than King set himself to learn how the English government regarded it. He sounded several of the ministers, and even found occasion to bring up the subject
with the king. So far from encountering protest and
remonstrance, he gathered from his inquiries an impression of complaisance bordering on indifference.
When he could report that England's minister of
foreign affairs, with whom he had had a long conversation, showed no signs of disappointment or discontent, it was absurd for Americans to argue, — as some,
however, did, — that good faith with England required
us to reject the convention.[2] In his second letter,

---

[1] Hamilton's Works, VI, 503.

[2] See Ellsworth's letter to King, *post*, p. 318. Hamilton did not at all
agree with this view. "In my opinion," he wrote to Gouverneur Morris,

King declared that England now desired to make peace with Bonaparte. Ellsworth's reception at court proved, he thought, that the government was without animosity or unusual prejudice against America.

On February 3, the convention was ratified with only one condition; but that condition was unwise. Striking out the entire second article, which contained the agreement to negotiate at some future time on the subject of indemnities and the renewal of the old treaties, the Senate substituted the words: " It is agreed that the present convention shall be in force for a term of eight years from the exchange of the ratifications." In this amendment, Adams reluctantly acquiesced. When Napoleon came to consider it, he at once discerned in it an unexpected opportunity to erect another barrier against the claim of indemnities. He gave his consent both to the time-limit and to the elimination of the second article, but with the proviso " that by this retrenchment the two states renounce the respective pretensions which are the object of said article." As this made another change, Adams felt bound to take the advice of the Senate a second time before proclaiming the convention. But the Senate resolved to consider it fully ratified, and it became the law of the land.

When Ellsworth learned of the Senate amendment, he wrote to his friend King at London:[1]

" The exception of the 2d article makes the instrument rather worse for us, as it leaves room for France

" there is nothing in it (the convention) contrary to our treaty with Great Britain." Works, VI, 496. It is rather curious that Jefferson, on the other hand, perhaps because he was soon to be the responsible head of the government, felt uneasy lest we compromit ourselves with England.

[1] March 17, 1801, Flanders, 264; Wood Ms.

to claim anteriority in the point of interference. And I think it most likely she will accede to the alteration."

Apropos of what was said in the United States about the convention and about himself, he had already written to the same correspondent:[1]

" I am very sorry to hear that his Majesty has been deranged, and still more so to learn that I am supposed to be in the same predicament. I devoutly hope that a similar imputation will not extend to our government; but that it will continue to have respect, though mine is lost in its service. What more is at present to be done with France will, at least, fall to the lot of some one not prejudged distracted for undertaking it.

" It is strange that after your letter to the Secretary of State (of which, if you see no impropriety, I hope you will favor me with a copy, or an extract) it could have been supposed that G. B. (Great Britain) had a right to complain; and even without that letter it ought to have been sufficient, that by an uncontested rule of construction there is implied and understood a saving for the operation of prior treaties.

" The 3d article, including a restoration of the frigate, had, as you know, its real reciprocity in that part of the 4th which secured the restoration of about forty valuable merchantmen, chiefly letters of marque, on such proofs of ownership as they were known to be furnished with. If the rights of war had attached, restoring the latter was a much greater sacrifice than that of the former; and if there had not been war there was nothing humiliating nor unusual in the restorations on either side.

" The 2d article was harmless; and by admitting

[1] Feb. 26, 1801, Flanders, 262–263.

the inoperation of the former treaties, silenced a claim which would have been continued, and might have become embarrassing.

" As to provisions respecting future captures and commerce, we might have been satisfied with them quite as long as France, by observing, would avoid an occasion to revise them. To have expressed a limitation of years to the convention was truly compatible with the idea of a further and definitive treaty, embracing the claims of indemnity which we were not at liberty to abandon. But I will not trouble you with remarks as obvious as they are now become useless."

An excellent temper, surely, in which to meet criticism. The poise and self-control, the modesty and good nature of " our excellent friend Ellsworth " make here a good contrast with the shrill carping of such a man as Pickering. And the " obvious remarks " are a really convincing answer to the principal strictures on the convention. On the whole, Ellsworth had done better with France than Jay had done with England. He had made the best of a difficult situation, and that best proved to be better than most observers thought. He and his colleagues had not merely extricated their country from an unequal contest; they had secured for her positive benefits and still more valuable immunities. They had also materially promoted a cause in which their country was not alone interested. The provisions of the convention concerning neutral commerce — that the flag covers the goods, that only material and instruments of war are contraband, that neutral vessels may pass from any port to any other port not actually blockaded, that searches and seizures shall be governed by rules — carried out the most advanced and enlightened views of the relations between neutrals and belligerents. They embodied, as Thiers remarks, the law of neutrals.[1] Ellsworth may have worked for these agreements only because his own country desired them. His merit may not have gone beyond patriotism. But of that virtue he had given a superb example. He had risen above personal ambition, above party, above the mere combativeness and truculence into which patriotism itself sometimes turns. He had sought nothing but the interest and the honor of his country. It would be hard to find in the political history of the time another public service that commands an approval so unreserved. Compared with any one of the party leaders at home, not even Hamilton or Jefferson excepted, the figure of Ellsworth during the interval of his exile in England rises into a superior dignity. It were well if we could steadily prefer such integrity, such singleness of purpose, such absorption in service, even to the surpassing genius and the monstrous self-assertion of that extraordinary creature whom this old-fashioned American statesman had recently fronted at Paris and at Mortefontaine.

Ellsworth enjoyed his stay in England, for he found there men and things that interested him deeply. To visit England at this period, when the passage of the Atlantic was still a matter of weeks and perhaps months, when memories of the Revolution still combated and heightened older loyalties and reverences, must have been a great experience to any thoughtful American. Ellsworth, moreover, was of pure English blood; he had been all his life a student of English

---

[1] "Constituent veritablement le droit des neutres." Thiers, "Consulate and Empire," II, 219.

institutions and English law; he was himself lawyer, lawgiver, and judge, and one of the framers of a free constitution of government. In his own character, and his ideals of life and conduct, he had followed, perhaps unconsciously, English models. He had left France with relief, so soon as his work there was done. Once in England, he found himself disposed to linger there longer than he had intended.

In London, he made a visit to Westminster Hall, where his reception probably gratified him even more than that he got at court. It does not appear that Jay had ever invaded the precincts of the King's Bench; and the judges and the bar of that ancient and famous court manifested much curiosity and interest at the appearance there of an American Chief Justice. Invited to a seat beside Lord Kenyon, the English Chief Justice, who was sitting with Judges Grose and Le Blanc, Ellsworth heard several of the most distinguished lawyers in England plead in a still famous cause. The case on trial was Rex *vs.* Waddington, and of counsel on one side or the other were such famous advocates as Law, Erskine, Garrow, and Scott. Such had been the keenness of the contending parties to retain Garrow that there had been a scuffle between rival emissaries before the door of his chambers. Lord Kenyon was an uncommonly awkward man, and Ellsworth's simple but dignified carriage shone by contrast. In spite of his broken health, he made an excellent impression on the English lawyers who saw him, and indeed greatly surprised them; for these learned gentlemen were not, it appears, superior to the mass of their countrymen in the knowledge of things American. When he came

down from the bench, a knot of them surrounded him,
" curious to know how the Common Law stood trans-
planting," and some of them asked questions that
threw a comical light on the notions of America which
prevailed in the mother country.   Thinking, doubtless,
that Americans were for the most part a kind of creol-
ish hybrids, a mixture of English and Indians, Judge
Grose inquired, with an air of great delicacy, "whether
the obstruction of the course of descent had not turned
fee simples into life estates."   Garrow's question was,
" Pray, Chief Justice, in what cases do the half blood
in America take by descent ? " [1]

Finding himself strong enough to travel, Ellsworth
made several brief excursions.   On one of them, he
visited a hamlet called Ellsworth, near Cambridge,
and learned also that a number of people living near
by, in Yorkshire, bore the same name.   Originally, he
was told, the hamlet had been called Eelsworth, from
the circumstance that it was situated on a small stream
famous for eels — the Anglo-Saxon terminal " worth "
signifying "place."   The explanation was doubtless
correct; and as the American Ellsworths had a tradition that their common ancestor came from that part
of England, and as a Mr. John Ellsworth of London,
a rich cheesemonger, told the Chief Justice of a great-
grand-uncle who had gone from Yorkshire "to foreign
parts," it is quite possible that the American Ellsworth
had discovered the original seat of his family as well
as the origin of his name.

The   circumstance   can   hardly   have   failed   to
strengthen   his   growing   attachment   for   England.
Even the climate had had an unexpectedly favorable

[1] Wharton's American State Trials, 40.

effect on his health. Abandoning his plan of going
to southern France, he proceeded, instead, to Bath,
whence he wrote occasionally to King at London.
These letters are nearly all about English and
American politics, and for a man suffering from so
cruel a disease he made them surprisingly cheerful.
One of them refers, with a mild jocularity, to his own
illness:

" As you have lived long and well enough to begin
to die, you should welcome the gout in your joints, as
the best means to protract the process, and give lucid
intervals. The Bath waters, I believe, seldom cure
this disease, though they mitigate and shorten its
paroxysms; and are also of great use when needed
to fix it to the extremities. This effect, however, is
more than they are likely to produce for me, while my
kidneys are weakened by the constant laceration of
sand. . . ."

Having learned that in the elections in the United
States the Federalists were defeated, he added:

" So the anti-Feds are now to support their own
administration, and take a turn at rolling stones up
hill. Good men will get a breathing spell, and the
credulous will learn the game of *out and in*."

All his allusions to the great political change of
1800 show the same good sense, and the same
balance and magnanimity, that he had displayed
under the criticisms of his course at Paris. He proved
a far better loser than some others of the group of
Federalists who for twelve years had held the chief
places in the government. Even as far back as 1796,
when most of his friends had contemplated the possibility of the election of Jefferson with the utmost

horror and dismay, he had taken a somewhat more charitable, if not more cheerful, view. A gentleman who was at that time a member of Congress afterward wrote : [1]

" I was one evening sitting alone with Mr. Ellsworth, when I asked him the question, why the apprehensions of Mr. Jefferson's being President should occasion so much alarm ? at the same time observing that it could not be supposed he was an enemy to his country, or would designedly do anything to injure the Government as constitutionally established. Mr. Ellsworth, after a short pause, replied : ' No, it is not apprehended that Jefferson is an enemy to his country, or that he would designedly do anything wrong. But it is known he is a visionary man, an enthusiastic disciple of the French Revolution, and an enemy to whatever would encourage commercial enterprise, or give energy to the government. It is apprehended that, if he were President, he would take little or no responsibility on himself. The nation would be, as it were, without a head. Everything would be referred to Congress. A lax, intriguing kind of policy would be adopted; and while arts were practiced to give direction to public sentiment, Mr. Jefferson would affect to be directed by the will of the nation. There would be no national energy. Our character would sink, and our weakness invite contempt and insult. Though Mr. Jefferson would have no thoughts of war, his zeal in the French cause, and enmity to Great Britain, would render him liable to secret influence, that would tend to the adoption of measures calculated to produce war with England, though it was not

[1] Flanders, 177–178.

intended, and the nation might be plunged into a war wholly unprepared.' "

This was a severe judgment; but it was a judgment, not a mere outbreak of partisan malice and fear, and it set forth correctly, though it may have exaggerated, the weakness of Jefferson's character. " A lax, intriguing kind of policy " is not an entirely unfair description of his ways in the presidency; and the more specific predictions of the results of his administration proved measurably accurate.

And yet, now that the great Republican theorist had triumphed, Ellsworth, disposed to make the best of it, could write to King:

" You do not surely mistake the fear of Jefferson for the gout; because you think as I do, that he dare not run the ship aground, nor essentially deviate from that course which has hitherto rendered her voyage so prosperous. His party *also* must support the government while he administers it; and if others are consistent and do the same, the government may even be consolidated, and acquire new confidence. It may be well however for your letters to guard against that despondency of some who, always believing that the government must soon die, will be apt to say, it can never die in better hands."

Unfortunately, the mass of his fellow-Federalists did not see their duty as he did. But for the patriotic stand by which Hamilton atoned for his recent far from admirable course in the quarrel with Adams, and which eventually cost him his life, the Federalists in Congress would have made Burr President — the first of the many spiteful acts of disappointment and chagrin that soon completed the party's ruin. " So then,

my dear sir," Ellsworth wrote to King, when he knew
that the scheme had failed,[1] "after thirty trials, fortune has given us the best of a bad bargain.   I think
the Feds have acquired less reputation by the contest
than the public would have lost had they succeeded."

In the same letter, he announced that he had
engaged passage from Bristol and would sail the
27th or 28th of March.   The Bath waters had merely
given him some relief from suffering; they had not
cured his malady or restored his strength.   The
return passage again taxed him sorely.   Landing at
last in Boston, he rested a little time with Cabot, and
then journeyed painfully on to Windsor.   The day set
for his home-coming, the members of his family were
gathered at Elmwood awaiting him; and when at
last they caught sight of his carriage, they all rushed
forth to greet him.   But instead of the robust, strong
figure of two years earlier, they saw a feeble, pale, fearfully emaciated old man step from the carriage.   Pro-
foundly affected, Ellsworth silently waved back the
eager greetings of his wife and children, tottered to
the gate, leaned over it, covered his face with his
hands, and bowed his head in a prayer of gratitude
that he had lived to see again his country, his home,
his family.[2]

[1] March 22, Flanders, 264–265.
[2] Mrs. Sigourney, in "National Portrait Gallery," IV, article on Ellsworth.

CHAPTER VIII

HOME

IT was from no unusual impulse that Ellsworth paused to offer thanks to God before he tasted the happiness of his home-coming. If in this account of his career any force that helped to shape his character has been hitherto neglected, it is religion. In the list of the principles that controlled his life, the religious ought perhaps to be put highest: above patriotism; even above that instinct and habit of complete devotion to the task in hand which he displayed in all his activities. When he turned away from the ministry in his youth, he did not abandon his interest in religious subjects, nor did he reject the particular creed in which he had been bred. He accepted it fully, and he took it as his fathers had taken it, — gravely and practically, for a rule of conduct as well as a creed.

The present generation, not perhaps less open to religious moods than any that has gone before, but in a strong revulsion against the forms and usages of piety, and inclining more and more to sublimate doctrine, can hardly appreciate the literal force of Christianity in the lives of educated men and women a century or more ago. But to understand a life like Ellsworth's we must take account of a well-nigh constant reference, in his own mind, of all his actions and decisions to a hard-and-fast moral standard, and of a steadfast acquiescence in all the main Christian tenets. He prayed to a personal God. He held to the hope of a future life, for which this earthly life should be but a preparation. On all questions in theology and church government, he was an orthodox Congregationalist.[1]

Human nature does not justify confident reasoning from men's beliefs to their conduct, but Ellsworth was a man who lived up to his professions beyond the ordinary standards of consistency. He kept the Sabbath holy, and went unfailingly to church. In the absences of the minister, he himself frequently served as a lay reader. He held prayers every morning in his own household, with lessons from Doddridge's "Expositor"; often read Tillotson's sermons aloud to his family; studied the Bible daily. When he came back from Europe, he brought several boxes of books, and most of them were religious. In the catalogue of his library which was made at the time of his death, more than half the titles are of works on religion. During his later years, he gave himself more and more to the study of theology. Now that, as he wrote to King, he had "begun to die," he turned with his old resolute concentration to a closer grappling with the great problem.

He took his full share of the work of his church and of other organized religious activities in his own community. In the middle of the eighteenth century,

---

[1] But quite probably called himself a Presbyterian. "The (Congregationalist) churches of Connecticut were often designated by their own pastors and members as 'Presbyterian.'" Williston Walker, "History of the Congregational Churches in the United States," 315. "They freely used the name Presbyterian as the briefest description of their ecclesiastical position." R. E. Thompson, "History of the Presbyterian Churches of the United States," 15.

the old "First Society" of Windsor had divided, the
seceders forming the Fourth Society. In 1792, joining
with several other men of influence, he worked for and
accomplished a reunion. The reunion made it possible
to build a new meeting-house, and he served on the
building committee, chose the plans of the new edifice,
and when it was finished helped to raise for the society
a money endowment.[1] Altered somewhat in 1745,
but not radically, the building still stands, a good
example of the dignified architecture of the period, on
the pleasant knoll on the north bank of the Farmington, where once stood the "palisades," built by the
first settlers for a defence against the Indians, and
where so many Windsor generations lie buried.

A few years later, he rendered what at the time
probably seemed a good service to his denomination
throughout the state. At the beginning of the nineteenth century, the Congregationalists of Connecticut
found themselves under fire. Their creed and their
organization kept still a strong hold on New England
society. The Unitarian revolt was not yet under way,
even in Massachusetts. But the other denominations
were growing restive under the long dominance of
Calvinism, and in the Connecticut laws concerning
religious societies they found much to complain of.
These statutes, they charged, violated the principles
of religious freedom. The Baptists were most ardent
in the agitation for reform, and in 1801 and 1802, in
a vigorous petition to the General Assembly, they set
forth at length the grievances of all the other Christians of Connecticut against the dominant church.
The act for the support of ministers, they declared,

[1] Ms. notes of Mr. W. Irving Vinal; Jackson Ms.

inured unfairly to the advantage of that church, since
it empowered the majority in any community — usually a Presbyterian majority [1] — to choose the minister,
and appropriated to his support all property devoted
in general terms to the maintenance of religion. Various other acts and parts of acts were cited as operating in similar fashion to take money from Christians
of other denominations to support Presbyterian ministers and build Presbyterian churches.

In May, 1802, the General Assembly set Ellsworth
at the head of a committee to report on this " Baptist
Petition," and the report, which he signed alone, reveals
him a decided conservative. He adopts the principle
that every member of society may be required to help
support religious institutions, and on that broad ground
justifies the laws attacked in the petition. One appreci-
ates the great advance in religious freedom which the
then dawning century witnessed when one reads, over
the name of a man who on other lines had served the
cause of free government so well as Ellsworth had,
such reasoning as this:

" This opinion, however, is founded on the principle
recognized, that every member of society should, in
some way, contribute to the support of religious institutions. In illustration of this principle, it may be
observed, that the primary objects of government are
the peace, order, and prosperity of society. By their
preservation, individuals are secured in all their valuable interests. To the promotion of these objects,
particularly in a republican government, good morals
are essential. Institutions for the promotion of good

[1] In the petition, Congregationalists are uniformly styled Presbyterians.
See ante, p. 328, note.

ELMWOOD, ELLSWORTH'S HOME AT WINDSOR.

From a photograph.

morals are therefore objects of legislative provision
and support; and among these, in the opinion of the
committee, religious institutions are eminently useful
and important. . . .

"The right of the legislature to oblige each individual of the community to contribute towards the
support of schools for the instruction of children, or of
courts of justice for .the protection of rights, is not
questioned; nor is any individual allowed to refuse
his contribution, because he has no children to be
instructed, no injuries to be redressed, or because he
conscientiously believes those institutions useless. On
the same principle of general utility, in the opinion of
the committee, the legislature may aid the maintenance of that religion whose benign influence on morals
is universally acknowledged. It may be added that
the principle has been long recognized, and is too
intimately connected with the peace, order, and happiness of the state to be abandoned."[1]

Ellsworth served on this committee as a member of
the council; for he had yielded to the wish of his
neighbors that he should again represent them in the
upper house of the legislature. He kept his seat as
long as he lived, and never neglected to attend the
sessions when his health permitted. The council was
still the judicial court of final resort, and its business
as a court was usually important. His own reputation
gave an additional distinction to his appearances as a
member of it. In Thomas Day's reports of its decisions, the only clew to those that are his is the style
and reasoning. One merely conjectures, for instance,

---

[1] Both the petition and the report are in the *Connecticut Courant* of June
7, 1802.

that it was he who, in Brainerd *vs.* Fitch,[1] again argued,
as in Adams *vs.* Kellogg, that a *feme-covert* cannot
devise real estate. But he is presented to us in this,
his last public character, in the admiring tributes of
several younger men who doubtless studied him keenly
as an example of conspicuous success in the law and
in statesmanship. Day, the reporter, was one of those
who left their impressions of the figure Ellsworth made
in the council. His manner in rendering opinions
Day thought greater and more majestic than any other
man's he ever saw. According to another observer,
a young lawyer who himself rose to judicial eminence,
when Judge Ellsworth spoke in the council, he always
held his listeners perfectly silent and attentive, not by
his reputation, but by manner, voice, presence, and
particularly by the extraordinary terseness and lucid-
ity of his expositions. These were compared by
another distinguished lawyer to the husking of an
ear of corn,— layer after layer of misconception peeled
off, until the true issue shone forth clear to every intelligence.[2] His opinions had an extraordinary weight
with his fellows in the council. One day, after a
brief discussion of an apparently simple case, the
second Governor Trumbull, who presided, put the
question to each member in turn, beginning, as usual,
on the right; and when a majority had voted, all on
the same side, he was about to stop and announce the
decision. But Ellsworth, who as the senior member
sat on the governor's left, advised him to keep on
around the board. Again no one dissented until
Ellsworth's own turn came. Calling attention, in a

---

[1] Day's Reports, 163–194; Van Santvoord, 288.
[2] John Allyn, quoted in Jackson Ms.

few brief sentences, to a principle in the case which no one else had discerned, he voted alone on the other side. Without a word more of discussion, the others all changed their votes.[1]

There is another story that exhibits a very amiable trait of his character. The senior counsel on one side in an important cause, disregarding the courteous usage of the bar, addressed the court without first consulting his associate, a young man just beginning practice, as to the line of argument they should follow. The junior counsel showed plainly that he felt the slight; and when his turn came, disregarding the lead of his senior, he coolly proceeded to argue the case on an entirely different line. The court took the unusual course of ordering the arguments repeated, and in the end based its decision solely on the younger man's. A few days later, Ellsworth called at the latter's room, had a look at his slim collection of law books, told him he ought to have more, and offered to lend him the money to buy them. The story has a proper sequel; for the young lawyer became Ellsworth's son-in-law, and rose in time to be Chief Justice of the state.[2]

Ellsworth, it appears, though he had sons of his own, was given to befriending young men of his acquaintance, particularly young lawyers. During the winter after his return from Europe, he invited five youths of his neighborhood into his office and library, and himself guided their studies. He took much interest in the whole subject of education. As a member of the council he had, *ex officio*, a seat among the governors of Yale, and he served his old college

[1] Ms. notes of Mr. W. Irving Vinal.   [2] Jackson Ms.

with a loyalty quite unaffected by any memories of
the strained relations of earlier days. All his sons
who lived to manhood were graduated there. The
college for its part had in 1790 bestowed upon him
the degree of LL.D., a rarer honor for laymen than at
present. Princeton, his other *alma mater*, gave him
the same decoration the same year, and Dartmouth in
1797. Had he desired any honor in the gift of his
state, Connecticut would gladly have given it. He
was but fifty-six when he left the service of the nation,
and though he once remarked, while in retirement,
that he saw nothing to envy, or anything to seek for,[1]
he would probably have preferred to remain many
years in harness. But his malady never left him, and
it granted him but few intervals of ease from pain. In
1807, the last year of his life, he yielded to the urgent
solicitation of the governor and the people of the
state, and consented to be its first chief justice, — the
legislature having reconstructed the judiciary, taken
away the judicial functions of the council, and set up
a new supreme court of appeals. But before the time
came to enter on his duties a savage seizure convinced
him that he ought not to take the office, and he withdrew his acceptance.

He kept an intense interest in national politics, and
sometimes, it is said, grew warmer in discussing them
than became his years or accorded with the dignity
of his retirement. But he was not, like some of his
fellows in political exile, continually writing bitter
and intriguing letters about them. For that matter,
he never lost his old dislike of the pen. " *Litera
scripta manet*," he was fond of repeating. He did not

[1] Ms. of Oliver Ellsworth, Jr.

spare ridicule of Fisher Ames, who could find no
other outlet but letter-writing for the wit and humor
and the keen interest in life that ill health forbade
him to exercise in affairs. " Always writing, writing,
writing," Ellsworth complained of him.[1] It would
have been well, however, for the good fame of the
defeated party, if none of its leaders had put into their
talk and their letters anything worse than the not very
rancorous satire that Fisher Ames put into his. The
latter end of Federalism makes an unpleasant and
an unpardonable chapter of our political history. By
having no part in it, Ellsworth avoided a damning
error, kept safe his fame as a patriot, and rendered a
real though negative service to his country.

There exists no evidence whatever that connects
him with any of the blameworthy doctrines or policies
of the Federalists in these years; and we can hardly
doubt that men like Pickering and Hillhouse, if they
could have drawn him into their intrigues, would gladly
have made use of his name. Beginning with a narrow
sectional opposition to the annexation of Louisiana,
an irreconcilable group of fallen leaders, chiefly from
New England, nursed their discontent into disaffection,
and came finally to designs and propaganda which we
should now certainly call treasonable. When even so
honorable a man as Gouverneur Morris — once so
strong a Unionist — could inveigh bitterly against the
Union as a failure and a positive evil, Ellsworth, who
had once stood for state-rights against the national
principle, might have been expected to share the
reaction. It was particularly strong in his own Connecticut. But he left behind him not one word in the

[1] Wood Ms.

slightest degree disloyal to the Union or the government. Only a student familiar with the history, and particularly with the political correspondence, of the period of his retirement can understand how, by reason of this mere innocence of disaffection, he again rose distinctly above the level of the wisdom and the patriotism of contemporaries otherwise quite as eminent as he.

Nothing in his life in retirement showed any lapsing from the good intention and performance of his active years. To the measure of his remaining strength, he still addressed himself to the service of the public. Certain books he had bought in England having aroused anew his interest in agriculture, he resolved to try to introduce better methods among his farmer neighbors, and to that end he began in August, 1804, and continued for two years, to publish in the *Connecticut Courant* brief essays and notes on agricultural topics. Many of his ideas he drew from the excellent agricultural writings of Arthur Young, better known for an unrivalled picture of French civilization under the old régime. The series appeared in a column headed " The Farmer's Repository," and under the title was a motto from Dean Swift, — " Whoever can make two ears of corn or two blades of grass grow on a spot of ground where only one grew before, deserves better of mankind and does a more essential service to his country than the whole tribe of politicians put together." Noah Webster, and perhaps others, made occasional contributions. Ellsworth's own papers are not signed, but he wrote many more than any one else, and it probably would not be impossible to distinguish all that are his by their style, which he made even more direct and unadorned than in his other writings. For the most part, he stuck close to his practical object. He discussed old and new ways of growing the crops that throve best in Connecticut, old and new styles of implements, the treatment of cattle, and the various means to restore worn-out soils. He dwelt longest on fertilizers, and may have been the first New England writer to explain the value of gypsum and to treat somewhat scientifically of the food of plants. Probably to enliven his subject, however, he also gave two or three papers to brief accounts of agriculture in early ages and in strange lands. Now and then, but not often, he enforced his contentions with illustrations drawn from his own keen observations in other parts of the country or in Europe. " The lowlands of Virginia," he thus finds occasion to remark, "fixed as it seemed in the garden of Eden, except that there is no account of the Lord ever walking there, after cultivating Indian corn and tobacco only, till a hundred slaves can scarcely support one master, are now beginning to *cow-pen* their fields for white clover." Still less frequently, he indulges in some terse reflection about politics; as when he moralizes: " Happy would it be if other good qualities could be as easily renewed as those of land. Would to God there were some kind of tillage also by which a republic that once loses its virtue might be restored to virtue again " — a sentence that is far from characteristic, and probably conveys, with its gloom and its note of passion, the severest view of politics and of life that he ever entertained.

These papers, much in advance of the ideas and the knowledge of even the more progressive farmers

of New England, do not seem to have had much immediate effect. " The Farmer's Repository " may in
time have earned for Ellsworth the dubious praise in
Swift's famous apothegm; but the farmers of the
Connecticut valley probably rated his statecraft
above his efforts to teach them other ways in their
own business than the good old ways they had learned
from their fathers.

But his neighbors at Windsor could never complain
of him for putting on airs of superiority. With his fel-
low-townsmen and old acquaintance, he was quite as unpretentious as John Marshall was with his. Tradition
whispered of him that in his youth he might often have
been seen eating apple-pie and cracking jokes with
other young fellows at Sergeant Sam Hayden's tavern
in North Windsor; and now that he was both rich
and famous, he passed along the streets of his native
town clad like a respectable farmer and greeting all
he met quite as his equals.[1] He preferred to walk the
mile or more from his house to his church, lest he give
rise to envy in the poor. When some one told him
that he ought, since he could afford it, to buy a new
sleigh, of a better kind than the old " pung " sleigh he
used, his answer was, " Well, well, Mr. H——, I suppose I might; but if I should get a new sleigh perhaps Mr. H——'s family would think they needed a
better one than they have ; and if you get one, some
other neighbor will want one ; everybody in town will
want a new sleigh." [2] Having bought a store and set

---

[1] " We ought not," he once said to his son, " to talk to people about
anything they do not understand, and if we feel our superiority to others,
not to display it in society." Ms. of Oliver Ellsworth, Jr.

[2] Jackson Ms.

up two of his sons as merchants, he was not ashamed
to superintend the business down to its minutest
details, and he went about it with as much energy and
system as if he himself had never had any other
ambition than to be a merchant.[1] Happily, there are
towns and villages in New England where equally
democratic social standards still prevail. In such a
community, the first citizen of the entire republic, if
he should happen to have been born there, would
stand, and doubtless prefer to stand, on a footing
of perfect equality with all his neighbors.

Ellsworth was quite probably the wealthiest man in
Windsor, as well as the most distinguished. Unlike
many successful public financiers, he had managed his
own affairs extremely well. One of his ventures in
business had been to build houses in Hartford to let
— a kind of investment not at all common in his day
— and it proved very successful. All his investments,
in fact, seem to have proved fortunate. Half a century
after his death, a competent authority declared that
his holdings were still excellent properties.

He had made Elmwood an attractive home.
Whether or not he himself built the entire house is
not certainly known. But he enlarged it, he filled it
with books and with the excellent furnishings affected
by the well-to-do of his times in New England, and he
planted about it thirteen elms, in honor of the thirteen
states that formed the original Union.[2] For many
years, however, he had spent there but a small part of
every year, and these intervals were not vacations.

[1] Jackson Ms.
[2] A family tradition has it that the day South Carolina seceded lightning
blasted one of them.

His winter in England was probably the first real vacation he had ever taken. He can hardly be said to have lived at his own home until his national career was finished. He and his wife were then elderly people, and several of their children were grown.

Four sons and three daughters had survived infancy and childhood. The eldest of the surviving sons, the second to bear the name of his father, and who had been his father's intimate companion on the mission to France, died in the summer of 1805. The loss of him greatly afflicted Ellsworth, deepened the gravity which had become his habitual mood, and probably weakened him in his own struggle with disease. He lived, however, to see his other sons and daughters well on the way to excellent lives. They all seem to have inherited strong family traits of body and of mind. One son, in particular, exhibited in very high stations — as congressman, governor, and judge — some of his father's best characteristics.[1] Another became the first commissioner of patents.

Ellsworth's domestic life, thoroughly New England in all its standards and ideals, probably differed little from that of his neighbors, or from that of his fathers before him. He took his duties to his family quite as he took his duties to the state. Provident and far-sighted, he taught all his children to work, and insisted that they should earn what they had for their pleasures. But he was never stern or forbidding with them, for he kept all his life the habit of playing with children for his own relaxation, and he had the happy gift of making them companions. While attending the council

[1] Ms. notes of W. Irving Vinal; Stiles's "Ancient Windsor," II, 219–225.

at Hartford, he would spend hours in intense thought, pondering out some decision, then suddenly, on making up his mind, dismiss the subject completely, and look about for some child to romp with. His own children did not stand in awe of him. He drew them pictures, talked with them, taught them, but left their mother to correct them.

His habit of complete absorption in whatever matter he might be engaged with had the effect of extreme absent-mindedness. He would stand for hours at the window of his study, his eyes fixed on a certain tree, or he would pace the room or the hall, taking innumerable pinches of snuff, utterly oblivious of everything but the subject of his thoughts. If at such times a meal were announced, he would sit through it in a silence which no one ventured to interrupt; for experience had taught his family that it was useless to try to break the current of his thought. If, on the other hand, he became much interested in conversation while at table, he would go on talking, consuming at the same time astounding quantities of food and countless cups of tea, until, perhaps, his wife remonstrated.[1]   A young man who called one evening at his request, finding him seated in deep meditation by the fire, greeted the other members of the family, and had spent half an hour conversing with them when Ellsworth, suddenly awaking to the presence of a visitor, welcomed him cordially and proceeded to present him to the rest of the circle as if he had just arrived.[2]   Taking snuff was the inevitable accompani-

[1] Ms. notes of Mr. W. Irving Vinal; Jackson Ms.; articles in *New York Evening Post*, March–August, 1875, and July, 1876, by O. E. Wood; article in *Hartford Courant*, April 5, 1880, by Rev. G. I. Wood.   [2] *Ibid.*

ment of these long intellectual wrestlings, and with all his will and prudence Ellsworth never overcame the habit. Once, thinking to diminish the number of his pinches, he deposited his snuff-box at the top of the garret stairs, so that he would have to climb two flights every time he used it. Victims of similar habits will hardly need to be told that he very soon abandoned this device and put his snuff-box back in his pocket.

Odd as his fits of abstraction sometimes made him, he was an agreeable companion, fond of conversation, and himself a good talker, with a great fund of observation and anecdote. Roger Minott Sherman, who studied law in his office, declared that when a subject thoroughly aroused him he talked with extraordinary brilliancy, pouring forth a perfect stream of terse, aphoristic wisdom. Dr. Dwight put him in the first rank as a conversationalist, and Dwight had a very wide acquaintance among men of parts. He himself, moreover, was one of the greatest talkers of his time: a daughter of Roger Sherman used to say that Dr. Dwight led the talk in every company in which she ever saw him, — and she saw him often, — unless Judge Ellsworth were present, but that then he became a listener. Democratic as he was, Ellsworth also knew how to suit dress and manner to the company and the occasion. He was by no means careless of his appearance, and he wore well the stately dress of his age, — always with a white ruffled shirt and silk stockings and silver knee-buckles. He was neither plebeian nor aristocrat. He had a social quality and a code of manners not known in countries where any kind of class system prevails, and doubtless commoner in New England than in any other part of America.

After disease had seized him, softening his perhaps too energetic manner, and age had wrought the mellowing effect it nearly always has with men of his strong type, he would have commended, to any company in the world, that new American standard of manners and of manhood.

He died in his own home at Windsor, close to the spot where he was born, on Nov. 26, 1807. The final ravages of his disease had caused him excruciating suffering, and at times deprived him of his reason. But he held fast to his religious convictions, and bore his agony with fortitude. A formal discourse, after the fashion of the time, was pronounced at his funeral in the church he had helped to build, and a crowd of mourners followed him to his grave in the old burial ground. It was universally considered that at the time of his death he was the first citizen of Connecticut. Had not John Adams been alive, he would have been the most distinguished survivor of the group of statesmen whom New England had contributed to the Revolution and the founding of the national government.

His entire character seems now to belong to a past phase of American life. His career has an effect of iterating lessons that most Americans have learned in their childhood. They are lessons which our national experience has never falsified, but which, unhappily, we sometimes find merely irksome, with their insistence on the elementary obligations of citizenship in a republic. Because his character was so free from intricacy, because the sources of his strength are so plain, his life is a particularly good instance of the truth that for the highest and most difficult tasks in

the service of a free people the really essential qualities
are such not uncommon qualities as energy, industry,
good sense, steadfastness, sagacity. These, rightly
devoted, he proved to be enough. Of them all, sagacity alone — practical wisdom, the judicial quality
in action — may perhaps be considered a special gift, a
natural endowment. He had always a quick sense of
the controlling factors in situations and problems, and
a keen instinct for the main chance. He knew when to
be cautious and when to be bold. He judged shrewdly
men, parties, causes, occasions. But the basis of this
accomplishment, and indeed of all his competence, was
that common sense which the people of his own New
England hold indispensable even to genius. The
furnishing of his mind was neither profuse nor rich,
but like the furnishing of the better New England
houses of his time. Many intellectual and emotional
experiences, now not uncommon among educated
Americans, he never knew. Many aspects of human
life he probably never contemplated. He had but
a slight sense of the beautiful in art and nature.
The formality of the age straitened him, as it did
Washington. The range of his tastes and sympathies, like that of most colonials, would to-day seem
narrow. But he lived a good life, and he did a man's
part in a very noble business.

He gave his whole strength to the hardest, most
prosaic work of an enterprise that has proved pro-
digiously successful: to the details of the task of
building up, out of a few struggling, loosely joined
English colonies, a free federal nation, which within
a century has many times doubled its area and its
numbers and its wealth, and is now fast swelling into

a mighty empire. His handiwork passed integrally into the structure of a political organism that endured, and took on life, and grew, so that it is become, to millions of human beings of all creeds and races, a bond of union, a shelter from oppression, an opportunity, an inspiration. Throwing himself in his utterly absorbed way into the responsibilities which confronted his generation, he helped to organize security and prosperity for multitudes of future generations. Having only the wisdom of his age, he shared in one great error, in that he consented to prolong the worst of our national offences. But in the avoidance of errors he was, on the whole, singularly fortunate. Our debt to him — to this old-fashioned patriot, to this exemplar of hard-working statesmanship — is real and enduring ; for we owe to him essential parts of the political system under which we live. His was not a career, nor were his the gifts or the personality, to bring his name often to men's lips, or keep his image in their eyes. But his hard-earned reputation is secure. It rests on the same foundations that uphold the strength and greatness of his country.

APPENDIX A

LETTER OF SHERMAN AND ELLSWORTH, MEMBERS OF THE CONTINENTAL CONGRESS, TO THE GOVERNOR OF CONNECTICUT

"PHILADELPHIA March 20, 1780.

"SIR: The President will transmit to your Excellency the resolutions of Congress for sinking the Continental bills of credit and issuing new bills on the credit of the several states, which we hope will be approved by your Excellency and the Honorable General Assembly.

"It was judged impracticable to carry on the war with the present currency, and no other plan has been proposed which appeared so likely to relieve us from the embarrassments of a fluctuating currency, as that which has been adopted by Congress. The depreciation here has been at the rate of sixty for one, and in the Southern states from forty to fifty. Neither the scarcity, nor collection of taxes has had any effect to appreciate or fix its value.

"'Tis apprehended that the new bills will be effectually secured against depreciation, from the smallness of the quantity to be in circulation, the funds provided for their redemption, the shortness of the period, and the payments of an annual interest.

"The preparing them under the direction of the Board of the Treasury, and the insurance of payment by the United States in case any state shall by the event of the war be rendered incapable of redeeming them, will give them a currency throughout the United States, and be a security against counterfeits.

347

"The emission of bills will not only introduce a staple medium of trade, but will increase the Revenue the amount of Five millions of Dollars equal to specie. The sixth tenths of the bills to be emitted will enable the states to purchase the specific supplies called for by the Resolution of the 25th of February last, and the remaining four tenths will supply the Continental Treasury for paying the army, etc., while the states are collecting the old bills by taxes, and although it is recommended to collect in the old Continental bills by monthly assessments, it may be expedient for the States to allow new bills to be exchanged for old, that the old may be drawn out of circulation as soon as possible, to prevent further counterfeits; and if there should be scarcity of money people might be allowed to pay their taxes in provisions delivered at the magazines, at the prices fixed by Congress.

" The new bills will be prepared and forwarded to the States as soon as possible.

" We hear that the honorable Assembly have ordered a new emission of Bills. We beg leave to submit to your Excellency whether it will not be expedient to stop the issue of them and adopt the plan recommended by Congress.

" We should be sorry to have that fail of the good effects expected from it, by any act, or omission on the part of the States.

" The same proportions are kept up in the present requisitions as in the Resolution of the 7th of October last, wherein Connecticut is rated much too high; but hope that won't prevent her compliance, at least to the amount of her quota. Perhaps her quota in present circumstances would be more than one eleventh part of the whole.

" Repeated assurances have been given by Congress that those States which do more than their proportion shall be equitably compensated.

" There is a Report before Congress for fixing the rate in specie, at which the loan office certificate will be paid.

" It is reported that a new regulation of the Quarter-Master's and other staff departments, will soon be established on the most economical plan, whereby much expense will be saved. They will be accommodated to the late regulation of making purchases by the States. The prices of the specific articles to be furnished by the States were estimated at about fifty per cent. above the prices of 1774. They include all expenses of purchasing and delivering them into the magazines. The motives for adopting the measure were, the rendering the supplies more certain and equable among the States, and to prevent fraud and abuses. And the aid of the States in procuring the supplies was (thought?) to be absolutely necessary.

" By the letter from General Lincoln of the 22d ultimo we are informed that part of the British forces that left New York, landed at St. John's and St. James' Islands near Charleston, the numbers not ascertained; but he thinks there is a good prospect of making a successful opposition to them.

" Mr. Laurens expected to sail for Europe the 26th of February.

" With the greatest Respect your Excellency's humble servants,

" ROGER SHERMAN,
" OLIVER ELLSWORTH.

" *His Excellency Gov. Trumbull.*"

APPENDIX B

MR. PRESIDENT: This is a most important clause in
the Constitution; and the gentlemen do well to offer
all the objections which they have against it. Through
the whole of this debate, I have attended to the objections which have been made against this clause;
and I think them all to be unfounded. The clause is
general; it gives the general legislature "power to
lay and collect taxes, duties, imposts, and excises, to
pay the debts and provide for the common defence
and general welfare of the United States." There
are three objections against this clause — first, that
it is too extensive, as it extends to all the objects of
taxation; secondly, that it is partial; thirdly, that
Congress ought not to have power to lay taxes at
all.

The first objection is, that this clause extends to all
the objects of taxation. But though it does extend to
all, it does not extend to them exclusively. It does
not say that Congress shall have all these sources of
revenue, and the states none. All excepting the impost shall lie open to the states. This state owes a
debt; it must provide for the payment of it. So do
all the other states. This will not escape the attention of Congress. When making calculations to raise
a revenue, they will bear this in mind. They will not

take away that which is necessary for the states. They are the head, and will take care that the members do not perish. The state debt, which now lies heavy upon us, arose from the want of powers in the federal system. Give the necessary powers to the national government, and the state will not be again necessitated to involve itself in debt for its defence in war. It will lie upon the national government to defend all the states, to defend all its members, from hostile attacks. The United States will bear the whole burden of war. It is necessary that the power of the general legislature should extend to all the objects of taxation, that government should be able to command all the resources of the country; because no man can tell what our exigencies may be. Wars have now become rather wars of the purse than of the sword. Government must, therefore, be able to command the whole power of the purse; otherwise a hostile nation may look into our Constitution, see what resources are in the power of government, and calculate to go a little beyond us; thus they may obtain a decided superiority over us, and reduce us to the utmost distress. A government which can command but half its resources is like a man with but one arm to defend himself.

The second objection is, that the impost is not a proper mode of taxation; that it is partial to the Southern states. I confess I am mortified when I find gentlemen supposing that their delegates in Convention were inattentive to their duty, and made a sacrifice of the interests of their constituents. If, however, the impost be a partial mode, this circumstance, high as my opinion of it is, would weaken my

attachment to it; for I abhor partiality. But I think
there are three special reasons why an impost is the
best way of raising a national revenue.

The first is, it is the most fruitful and easy way.
All nations have found it to be so. Direct taxation
can go but little way towards raising a revenue. To
raise money in this way, people must be provident;
they must constantly be laying up money to answer
the demands of the collector. But you cannot make
people thus provident. If you do anything to the
purpose, you must come in when they are spending,
and take a part with them. This does not take away
the tools of a man's business, or the necessary utensils
of his family: it only comes in when he is taking his
pleasure, and feels generous; when he is laying out a
shilling for superfluities, it takes twopence of it for
public use, and the remainder will do him as much
good as the whole. I will instance two facts which
show how easily and insensibly a revenue is raised by
indirect taxation. I suppose people in general are
not sensible that we pay a tax to the State of New
York. Yet it is an incontrovertible fact, that we, the
people of Connecticut, pay annually into the treasury
of New York more than fifty thousand dollars.
Another instance I will mention; one of our common
river sloops pays in the West Indies a portage bill of
£60. This is a tax which foreigners lay upon us, and
we pay it; for a duty laid upon our shipping, which
transports our produce to foreign markets, sinks the
price of our produce, and operates as an effectual tax
upon those who till the ground and bring the fruits of
it to market. All nations have seen the necessity and
propriety of raising a revenue by indirect taxation,

by duties upon articles of consumption. France raises a revenue of twenty-four millions sterling per annum ; and it is chiefly in this way. Fifty millions of livres they raise upon the single article of salt. The Swiss Cantons raise almost the whole of their revenue upon salt. Those states purchase all the salt which is to be used in the country : they sell it out to the people at an advanced price; the advance is the revenue of the country. In England, the whole public revenue is about twelve millions sterling per annum. The land tax amounts to about two millions; the window, and some other taxes, to about two millions more. The other eight millions are raised upon articles of consumption. The whole standing army of Great Britain could not enforce the collection of this vast sum by direct taxation. In Holland, their prodigious taxes, amounting to forty shillings for each inhabitant, are levied chiefly upon articles of consumption. They excise everything, not even excepting their houses of infamy.

The experiments, which have been made in our own country, show the productive nature of indirect taxes. The imports into the United States amount to a very large sum. They will never be less, but will continue to increase for centuries to come. As the population of our country increases, the imports will necessarily increase. They will increase because our citizens will choose to be farmers, living independently on their freeholds, rather than to be manufacturers, and work for a groat a day. I find by calculation, that a general impost of 5 per cent. would raise the sum of £245,000 per annum, deducting 8 per cent. for the charges of collecting. A further sum might be deducted for

smuggling — a business which is too well understood
among us, and which is looked upon in too favorable
a light. But this loss in the public revenue will be
overbalanced by an increase of importations. And a
further sum may be reckoned upon some articles which
will bear a higher duty than the one recommended by
Congress. Rum, instead of 4*d*. per gallon, may be set
higher without detriment to our health or morals. In
England, it pays a duty of 4*s*. 6*d*. the gallon. Now,
let us compare this source of revenue with our national
wants. The interest of the foreign debt is £130,000
lawful money, per annum. The expenses of the civil
list are £37,000. There are likewise further expenses
for maintaining the frontier posts, for the support of
those who have been disabled in the service of the
continent, and some other contingencies, amounting,
together with the civil list, to £130,000. This sum,
added to the interest of the foreign debt, will be
£260,000. The consequence follows, that the avails
of the impost will pay the interest of the whole foreign debt, and nearly satisfy those current national
expenses. But perhaps it will be said that these
paper calculations are overdone, and that the real
avails will fall far short. Let me point out, then,
what has actually been done. In only three of the
states, in Massachusetts, New York and Pennsylvania, £160,000 or £180,000 per annum have been
raised by impost. From this fact, we may certainly
conclude that, if a general impost should be laid, it
would raise a greater sum than I have calculated. It
is a strong argument in favor of an impost, that the
collection of it will interfere less with the internal
police of the state than any other species of taxation.

It does not fill the country with revenue officers, but is confined to the sea-coast, and is chiefly a water operation. Another weighty reason in favor of this branch of the revenue is, if we do not give it to Congress, the individual states will have it. It will give some states an opportunity for oppressing others, and destroy all harmony between them. If we would have the states friendly to each other, let us take away this bone of contention, and place it, as it ought in justice to be placed, in the hands of the general government.

" But," says an honorable gentleman near me, " the impost will be a partial tax; the Southern states will pay but little in comparison with the Northern." I ask, What reason is there for this assertion? Why, says he, we live in a cold climate, and want warming. Do not they live in a hot climate, and want quenching? Until you get as far south as the Carolinas, there is no material difference in the quantity of clothing which is worn. In Virginia, they have the same coarse clothing that we have; in Carolina, they have a great deal of cold, raw, chilly weather; even in Georgia, the river Savannah has been crossed upon the ice. And if they do not wear quite so great a quantity of clothing, in those states as with us, yet people of rank wear that which is of a much more expensive kind. In these states, we manufacture one-half of our clothing, and all our tools of husbandry; in those, they manufacture none, nor ever will. They will not manufacture, because they find it much more profitable to cultivate their lands, which are exceedingly fertile. Hence, they import almost everything, not excepting the carriages in which they ride, the hoes with which they till the ground, and the boots which they wear. If we doubt of the extent of their importations, let us look at their exports. So exceedingly fertile and profitable are their lands, that a hundred large ships are every year loaded with rice and indigo from the single port of Charleston. The rich return of these cargoes of immense value will be all subject to the impost. Nothing is omitted; a duty is to be paid upon the blacks which they import. From Virginia, their exports are valued at a million sterling per annum; the single article of tobacco amounts to seven or eight hundred thousand. How does this come back? Not in money; for the Virginians are poor, to a proverb, in money. They anticipate their crops; they spend faster than they earn; they are ever in debt. Their rich exports return in eatables, in drinkables, and in wearables. All these are subject to the impost. In Maryland, their exports are as great in proportion as those of Virginia. The imports and exports of the Southern states are quite as great in proportion as those of the Northern. Where, then, exists this partiality, which has been objected? It exists nowhere but in the uninformed mind.

But there is one objection, Mr. President, which is broad enough to cover the whole subject. Says the objector, Congress ought not to have power to raise any money at all. Why? Because they have the power of the sword; and if we give them the power of the purse, they are despotic. But I ask, sir, if ever there were a government without the power of the sword and the purse? This is not a new coined phrase; but it is misapplied; it belongs to quite another subject. It was brought into use in Great

Britain, where they have a king vested with hereditary power. Here, say they, it is dangerous to place the power of the sword and the purse in the hands of one man, who claims an authority independent of the people; therefore we will have a Parliament. But the king and Parliament together, the supreme power of the nation, — they have the sword and the purse. And they must have both ; else how could the country be defended? For the sword without the purse is of no effect; it is a sword in the scabbard. But does it follow, because it is dangerous to give the power of the sword and purse to an hereditary prince, who is independent of the people, that therefore it is dangerous to give it to the Parliament — to Congress, which is your Parliament, to men appointed by yourselves, and dependent upon yourselves? This argument amounts to this: you must cut a man in two in the middle, to prevent his hurting himself.

But, says the honorable objector, if Congress levies money, they must legislate. I admit it. Two legislative powers, says he, cannot legislate in the same place. I ask, why can they not? It is not enough to say they cannot. I wish for some reason. I grant that both cannot legislate upon the same object at the same time, and carry into effect laws which are contrary to each other. But the constitution excludes everything of this kind. Each legislature has its province ; their limits may be distinguished. If they will run foul of each other; if they will be trying who has the hardest head, it cannot be helped. The road is broad enough ; but if two men will jostle each other, the fault is not in the road. Two several legislatures have in fact existed and acted at the same time in the same territory. It is in vain to say they cannot exist, when they have actually done it. In the time of war, we have an army. Who made the laws for the army? By whose authority were offenders tried and executed? Congress. By their authority a man was taken, tried, condemned, and hanged, in this very city. He belonged to the army; he was a proper subject of military law; he deserted to the enemy, he deserved his fate. Wherever the army was, in whatever state, there Congress had complete legislative, judicial, and executive powers. This very spot where we now are is a city. It has complete legislative, judicial, and executive powers; it is a complete state in miniature. Yet it breeds no confusion, it makes no schism. The city has not eaten up the state, nor the state the city. But if there be a new city, if it have not had time to unfold its principles — I will instance the city of New York, which is and long has been, an important part of the state — it has been found beneficial; its powers and privileges have not clashed with the state. The city of London contains three or four times as many inhabitants as the whole state of Connecticut. It has extensive powers of government, and yet it makes no interference with the general government of the kingdom. This constitution defines the extent of the powers of the general government. If the general legislature should at any time overleap their limits, the judicial department is a constitutional check. If the United States go beyond their powers, if they make a law which the constitution does not authorize, it is void, and the judicial power, the national judges, who, to secure their impartiality, are to be made independent, will declare it

to be void. On the other hand, if the states go
beyond their limits, if they make a law which is an
usurpation upon the general government, the law is
void, and upright, independent judges will declare it
to be so. Still, however, if the United States and the
individual states will quarrel, if they want to fight,
they may do it, and no frame of government can
possibly prevent it. It is sufficient for this constitution, that, so far from laying them under a necessity
of contending, it provided every reasonable check
against it. But perhaps, at some time or other, there
will be a contest; the states may rise against the
general government. If this do take place, if all the
states combine, if all oppose, the whole will not eat
up the members, but the measure which is opposed to
the sense of the people will prove abortive. In republics, it is a fundamental principle that the majority
govern, and that the minority comply with the general
voice. How contrary, then, to republican principles,
how humiliating, is our present situation! A single
state can rise up, and put a veto upon the most important public measures. We have seen this actually
take place. A single state has controlled the general
voice of the Union; a minority, a very small minority,
has governed us. So far is this from being consistent with republican principles, that it is, in effect,
the worst species of monarchy.

Hence we see how necessary for the Union is a
coercive principle. No man pretends the contrary;
we all see and feel this necessity. The only question
is, Shall it be a coercion of law, or a coercion of arms?
There is no other possible alternative. Where will
those who oppose a coercion of law come out?

Where will they end? A necessary consequence of their principles is a war of the states one against the other. I am for coercion by law — that coercion which acts only upon delinquent individuals. This constitution does not attempt to coerce sovereign bodies, states, in their political capacity. No coercion is applicable to such bodies, but that of an armed force. If we should attempt to execute the laws of the Union by sending an armed force against a delinquent state, it would involve the good and bad, the innocent and guilty, in the same calamity.

But this legal coercion singles out the guilty individual and punishes him for breaking the laws of the Union. All men will see the reasonableness of this; they will acquiesce, and say, Let the guilty suffer.

How have the morals of the people been depraved for the want of an efficient government, which might establish justice and righteousness. For the want of this, iniquity has come in upon us like an overflowing flood. If we wish to prevent this alarming evil, if we wish to protect the good citizen in his right, we must lift up the standard of justice; we must establish a national government, to be enforced by the equal decisions of law, and the peaceable arm of the magistrate.

INDEX

Active, case of the, 68–70, 188.
Adams, Andrew, 51.
Adams, John, 57, 210, 343 ; and matters of state etiquette, 182 ; signs judiciary bill, 197 ; notes of Ellsworth's speeches, 202 ; praise of Ellsworth by, 231–232 ; Ellsworth administers oath to, at inauguration as President, 242 ; weak points of, 264 ; lukewarm loyalty of Federalists to, 264–265 ; foreign affairs during presidency of, 266 ; sends Marshall, Pinckney, and Gerry to France, 267–268 ; gains temporary popularity by stand regarding French treatment of American envoys, 268–269 ; growing feud of, with Hamilton, 269–270, 272–273 ; appoints Ellsworth, Davie, and Murray envoys to France, 273 ; calls on Ellsworth at Elmwood, 277–278 ; Ellsworth visits, at Trenton, 278–280 ; effect of Ellsworth's convention on interests of, 311–312 ; feud of, with Hamilton reaches its height, 314–315 ; acceptance of convention by, 315, 317.
Adams's Works cited, 202, 277, 278, 279, 290, 315.
Adams, Samuel, 57, 59.
Adams *vs.* Kellogg, case of, 332.
Addison, Judge, 270.
Agriculture, Ellsworth's efforts to promote, 336–338.
Alien and Sedition acts, Ellsworth's defence of, 265–266 ; provisions of, 270.
Allegiance, Ellsworth's ruling concerning perpetual, 257–262.
Allen, Ethan, 47.
Allyn, John, 26 n., 332.
"American Revolution," Trevelyan's, 82 n.

American Whig Society, debating club at Princeton, 19.
Ames, Fisher, 209, 311 ; member of first Congress (1789), 178 ; quoted, 195, 196 n., 281 ; oration by, defending Jay treaty, 222 ; opinion of, of Ellsworth, 230–231 ; letters of, 237, 335 ; on result of Ellsworth's mission to France, 314.
Ames's Works cited, 195, 196, 209, 230, 281, 314.
"Ancient Windsor," Stiles's, cited, 9, 10, 11, 118.
Andrews, W. G., cited, 36 n.
Annapolis Convention, the, 117.
Appeals, Committee of, and Court of, appointed by Continental Congress, 58–59, 65–66, 70–71.
Aristogiton, *nom de plume*, 259.
Army, question of payment of Continental, 56, 63, 90, 102–103.
Arnold, Benedict, 47, 50, 60, 69, 83.
Articles of Confederation, before the states, 56, 62, 64 ; put in force, 84 ; matter of revenue under, 87 ff.
Assumption of state debts, question of, 204–207.
Avery, Waightstill, 16, 18.

Baldwin, Abraham, in Constitutional Convention, 144.
Baldwin, Simeon, 171 n.
Bancroft, cited, 97, 103, 123, 127.
Bank, national, 207–208.
"Baptist Petition," 329–330 ; Ellsworth's report on, 330–331.
Bassett, Richard, 181.
Beardsley, E. E., cited, 36 n.
Bedford, Gunning, 18, 143, 144.
Bellamy, Rev. Dr. Joseph, 12–13.
Benjamin, Judah, 111.
Benson, Egbert, 196.

Bishop, W. W., 305 n.
Blair, John, 197.
Bland, Theodoric, 103.
Bliss, William, cited, 22.
Blue Laws of Connecticut, 109–111.
Bonaparte, Joseph, 286, 294, 297–298, 305, 308.
Bonaparte, Napoleon, American envoys and, 283–284, 294 ff., 305–310.
Boutell, L. H., cited, 45, 123, 170.
Brackenridge, Hugh H., 18.
Brainerd vs. Fitch, case of, 332.
Brearly, delegate to Constitutional Convention, 139.
British-debts cases, 248–250.
Brother Jonathan, origin of sobriquet of, 46.
Brown, messenger, 65, 78.
Brown vs. Barry, case of, 250–251.
Burke, Ædanus, 196.
Burr, Aaron, student at Princeton, 18; in second Congress (1791), 209; opinion of Ellsworth, 225; Hamilton's opposition to, 314, 325; ties Jefferson for presidency, 316.
Butler, Daniel, cited, 13.
Butler, Pierce, 185, 192.

Cabot, George, fellow-senator of Ellsworth, 209, 212, 215, 222, 227, 231; letters of, 237; attitude of, during Anglo-French complications, 273, 274, 275, 311; quoted on result of Ellsworth's mission to France, 312; Ellsworth visits, on return from abroad, 326.
"Cabot," Lodge's, cited, 280, 294, 311, 315.
Calhoun, John C., praise of Ellsworth by, 164–165, 176.
Capital, location of, 204–205.
Carson, H. L., cited, 71 n.
"Castle Rittenhouse," 70.
Censuses, question of, in Constitutional Convention, 147.
Chase, Samuel, 239, 240, 241, 249, 257; Jared Ingersoll incident, 243.
Church at Windsor, 328–329.
Clap, President Thomas, 13, 14, 15, 16.
Clark vs. Russell, case of, 250–251.

Cliosophic Society, the, 19–20.
College of New Jersey, in Ellsworth's youth, 17–20; degree conferred on Ellsworth by, 334.
"College of New Jersey," MacLean's, cited, 17 n., 19.
Committee of Appeals, Continental Congress, 58–59, 65–66, 70–71.
Committee of the Pay Table, 48–50.
Committee to report a constitution, chosen by Constitutional Convention, 158.
Committees of Continental Congress, 55, 58, 59, 60, 67–71, 73–74, 79, 96, 97, 101, 102, 103.
Committees of first Senate (1789), 181–182.
Connecticut, effect of position of, on historical importance, 5–6; in the Revolution, 44–50; Western claims of, 63–64; quota of, in establishment of Continental treasury, 65; agreement of, concerning laws limiting prices, 72; courts of, 108–109; attitude of, toward common law, 109–111; Blue Laws of, 109–111; delegates of, to Constitutional Convention, 118; the so-called "plan" of, in Constitutional Convention, 123, 127; ratification of Constitution by, discussed, 171–175.
Connecticut convention of 1788, 171–175; Ellsworth's speech in, 350–360.
Connecticut Courant, speech of Ellsworth incorrectly reported in, 171–172; Ellsworth's agricultural contributions to, 336–338.
Constitutional Convention, call for, 117; meeting of, 118; various plans for improved mode of government, 121 ff.; politics in, 129; discussions and debates, 130 ff.; compromise effected, 148–150; development of the Constitution, 158 ff.; return home of Connecticut delegates, 168–170.
Consular service, acts bearing on, 201, 209.
Continental Congress, delegates to, from Connecticut, 51; Ellsworth's irregularity in attendance at, 53; char-

acter of membership of, 54–55; committees of, 55, 58, 59, 60, 67–71, 73–74, 79, 96, 97, 101, 102, 103; matter of army supplies in, 56, 69, 73, 75, 85; notable members of, 57; question of finances in, 62–63, 65, 72, 75–79, 84, 85, 87, 88, 89–97, 102–105; hesitation of, to establish a federal court, 66–67; case of the *Active* before, 68–69; Court of Appeals in Cases of Capture appointed, 71; Hamilton and Madison potent forces in, 86, 91–93; peace treaty before, 98–102; mutinous troops menace, 102; removal of, to Princeton, 103; end of Ellsworth's service in, 103.

Court of Appeals in Cases of Capture, appointment of, 71.

"Court of Assistants" in Connecticut, 108.

Courts, of Connecticut, 108–109; establishment of federal, 184–199; maritime authority of, 254–256. *See* Superior Court.

Currency, question of, in Continental Congress, 62, 65, 72, 73, 75–77, 79, 84.

Cushing, William, 197, 249, 261; offered Chief Justiceship, 239.

Dartmouth College, degree conferred on Ellsworth by, 334.

Davie, William R., in Constitutional Convention, 142, 152; member of embassy to France, 273, 277, 278, 279, 280, 310, 313; Napoleon's impression of, 282.

Davis, J. C. Bancroft, cited, 67, 71 n.

Day, Thomas, court reporter, 331–332.

Deane, Silas, 60.

Debating clubs at Princeton, 19–20.

Debt, national, in first Congress, 204–207.

Debts, suits dealing with, owed to Britons, 248–250.

Degrees conferred on Ellsworth, 334.

Denning, William, 105 n.

Dexter, F. B., cited, 13, 14, 15.

Drayton, William Henry, 57.

Duties, question of, in first Congress, 202–204.

Dwight, Dr. Timothy, quoted, 36–37, 41, 342.

Dyer, Eliphalet, 51, 60, 64.

Edwards, Jonathan, 9, 13.

Edwards, Pierpont, 18, 191 n.; on Ellsworth's eloquence, 174–175.

Ellsworth, English hamlet, 322.

Ellsworth, Abigail (daughter of Oliver Ellsworth), 235, 236.

Ellsworth, Abigail Wolcott (wife), 23–24.

Ellsworth, David (father), 11, 12.

Ellsworth, David (brother), Oliver Ellsworth's letters to, 53 n., 54 n., 60–62, 74, 76, 213–214, 302–303.

Ellsworth, Henry, 301.

Ellsworth, John, of London, 322.

Ellsworth, Jonathan, 10–11.

Ellsworth, Josiah, 9–11.

Ellsworth, Martin, 235, 300, 301.

Ellsworth, Oliver, causes of neglect of, 3–5; family of, 9–11, 322; boyhood of, 12; at Yale, 13–17; at Princeton, 17–20; theological and legal studies of, 20–23; farming and law practice of, 24–29; personal appearance of, 28; attains first successes, 30; member of General Assembly, 30–31; acquires reputation and means, 32–34; oratory of, 35–37, 40, 142, 174–175, 331–332; member of Committee of Pay Table, 48–50; letters to Governor Trumbull, 49, 54; member of Council of Safety, 50–51; chosen state's attorney, 51; elected to Continental Congress, 51; in Continental Congress, 53–106; member of committees of Continental Congress, 58–59, 60, 67–68, 70–71, 73, 97, 101, 102–103; style of letters of, 60–62, 237; delegate to Hartford convention (1779), 72; member of governor's council, 83; first reported speech of, in Continental Congress, 91–92; member of Connecticut Superior Court, 108–116; in Constitutional Convention, 118–168; Major William Pierce's impression of, 119–120; "the government of the United

States" named by, 128–129 ; speeches of, in Constitutional Convention, 130–133, 136–143, 151, 154–155, 159–164, 166–168; work of, compared with Roger Sherman's, 150–151 ; opinions of, on slavery and representation, 152–157; member of committee to report a constitution, 158 ; Calhoun's eulogy of, 164–165 ; work of, in Hartford convention to ratify Constitution, 171–174 ; Webster's tribute to, 175–176 ; elected to first Senate, 177 ; services of, in Senate, 181–222 ; monumental work of, on judiciary bill, 184–199 ; letters of, to Judge Law, 188–191, 213 ; Rhode Island forced into the Union by, 200–201 ; speech of, on President's power of removal of officers, 202 ; attitude of, on French question, 212–214 ; interview of, with Washington concerning mission to England, 215–216 ; anxiety over Jay treaty, 219–221 ; appointed Chief Justice, 222, 238–240 ; John Taylor's interview with, 228–230; decisions of, on Supreme Bench, 248–265 ; ruling of, bearing on naturalization, 257–265 ; attitude toward Alien and Sedition acts, 265–266, 270–272 ; named member of embassy to France, 273 ; stay abroad, 282–326 ; effect of Napoleon on, 284 ; Napoleon's impression of, 284 ; talks with Talleyrand and Volney, 285 ; visit of, to England, 310, 320–326 ; last years of, at Windsor, 327–343 ; religious life of, 327–329 ; report of, on so-called Baptist Petition, 330–331 ; member of state legislature, 331 ; edits agricultural column in *Connecticut Courant*, 336–338 ; children of, 340 ; death of, 343.

Ellsworth, Oliver, Jr., 11 n., 12, 169, 235 ; secretary to embassy to France, 282, 308, 309, 310 ; French notes by, 282–284, 301, 305–308 ; Ms. of, cited, 334, 338 ; death of, 340.

Ellsworth, W. W., 175, 176 n., 301, 340.

Ellsworth family, origin of, 9, 322.

Elmwood, Washington visits Ellsworth's home at, 232–234 ; John Adams at, 277–278 ; Ellsworth's last years at, 339–340.

England, relation of United States to contest between France and, 211–214 ; Jay's mission to, 215–222 ; Ellsworth visits, 310, 321–326.

Erskine, Thomas, 321.

Evarts, Jeremiah, cited, 168.

Everett, Edward, 185.

"Farmer's Repository" column in *Connecticut Courant*, 336–338.

Farrand, Max, cited, 7 n.

Few, Congressman, 181.

Finances, matter of, in Continental Congress, 62–63, 65, 72, 75–79, 84, 85, 87, 88, 89–97, 102–105.

Finley, President Samuel, 18.

Flanders, Henry, cited, 23, 26, 35, 43, 113, 171, 172, 186, 200, 213, 243, 250, 265, 270, 276, 279, 291, 305, 317, 318, 324, 326.

Fleurieu, M., 286, 309.

France, complications of United States with, over Anglo-French contest, 211–212 ; popular sympathy with, 215 ; trouble with, caused by Jay treaty, 267 ; Pinckney rejected as ambassador by, 267; Marshall, Pinckney, and Gerry sent to, 276–268 ; Adams's firm stand with, 268–269 ; Ellsworth, Davie, and Murray appointed envoys to, 273; arrival of envoys in, 280–283 ; various attempts at an understanding with, 284–298 ; contrast between methods of American ministers and those of, 292–293 ; convention with, completed, 298–300; Ellsworth's letters home from, 300–304 ; festivities in, on conclusion of convention, 305–310; departure of envoys from, 310 ; ratification of convention with, by the United States, 317.

Franklin, Benjamin, 57 ; in Constitutional Convention, 134, 145.

Freneau, Philip, 18.

Gallatin, Albert, 209.
Galvez, expedition of, against West Florida, 80.
Garrow, English barrister, 321–322.
Genet, " Citizen," 211, 213, 288.
Gerry, Elbridge, 57, 146, 148, 161, 192; member of embassy to France, 267–268.
Gibbs, cited, 206, 211, 214, 216, 223, 227, 271, 277, 280, 303, 312, 313.
Gladstone, W. E., comments on remark of, 58 n.
Glass vs. the Sloop Betsy, case of, 255.
Goodrich, Professor, cited, 26, 32 n.
Gore, Christopher, 230.
Gorham, delegate to Constitutional Convention, 135, 157, 158.
Grant, Roswell, 15.
Green, Dr. Samuel A., 54 n.
Griswold, Governor Roger, 21.
Grose, Judge, 321, 322.
Gunn, Senator, 227, 314.

Hamilton, Alexander, in Continental Congress, 86, 88–89, 91, 92, 93, 96, 97, 98, 101, 102, 103, 105 ; Madison complementary to, 93 ; in Constitutional Convention, 118, 122, 125, 127–128, 131, 133–134, 135 ; contempt of democracy of, 122, 183 ; Secretary of Treasury, 203–204 ; counsel in Hylton vs. United States, 248 ; many Federalists regard, as leader rather than President Adams, 264–265 ; feud of, with Adams, 269–270, 272, 278–279, 314 ; supports Ellsworth's convention with France, 314–315 ; attitude of, after Republican triumph (1800), 325.
Hamilton's Works cited, 314, 315, 316.
Hamilton, J. C., cited, 214, 216.
Hartford, convention held at, in 1779, 72 ; convention at, for ratification of Constitution, 171–175.
Hart vs. Smith, case of, 112–115.
Hayden, Jabez H., cited, 24 n.
Hayden, Sergeant " Sam," 338.
Henry, John, 18, 19.
Henry, Patrick, 57, 170 n., 249, 273.
Hillhouse, James, 335.

Hoar, George Frisbie, cited, 151, 165, 223.
Hoar, Samuel, letter of, quoted, 236.
Holcomb, Elizabeth, 9.
Hollister, G. H., 41–42, 45 n.
Holton, Samuel, Ellsworth's letter to, 117 n.
Hopkinson, Judge Joseph, 227 n.
Hosmer, Titus, 33, 51, 71.
Hubbard, Fordyce M., cited, 284.
Hunt, Gaillard, 228, 230 n.; citations of, see " Madison's Writings."
Huntington, Benjamin, 52, 103.
Huntington, Samuel, 51, 52, 103, 170.
Hutchins, Mrs. Waldo, 237 n., 302 n.
Hylton vs. United States, case of, 248.

Ingersoll, Charles Jared, 243.
Ingersoll, Jared, 44–45.
Iredell, James, 239–240, 249, 251, 254.
Irvine vs. Sim's Lessee, case of, 251.

Jackson, Representative, 196.
Jackson, Rev. Abner, cited, 9, 19, 30, 171, 237, 245, 284, 302, 308, 329, 338, 339, 341 ; quoted, 26 n.
Jameson, J. Franklin, cited, 67, 71 n., 168.
Jay, John, 57 ; named first Chief Justice, 197 ; mission of, to England, 211–212, 215–222; governor of New York, 222; opinion of, concerning Ellsworth, 230; utterances about Supreme Court, 241.
Jay treaty, 217–222, 296, 299, 300, 319 ; difficulties with France over, 267, 287–289, 293, 296 ; Ellsworth's convention with France compared with, 319–320.
Jefferson, Thomas, 57, 183 ; Ellsworth's severe judgment of, 324–325.
Jennings vs. the Brig Perseverance, case of, 253.
Johnson, William Samuel, 33, 35–36, 118, 135, 157 ; elected senator from Connecticut, 177 ; becomes president of Columbia College, 177; on Ellsworth as a senator, 223.
Johnston, Alexander, opinion of, concerning Connecticut, 6–7 ; on Connecticut Blue Laws, 109.

Journal de Paris, quoted, 306 n.; cited, 308 n., 309.
Journals of Continental Congress, comments on, 58; Madison's notes supplement, 86.
Judiciary bill, Ellsworth's, 181, 184–199.

Kenyon, Lord, Ellsworth and, 321.
King, C. R., cited, 131, 136, 141, 217, 275.
King, Rufus, in Constitutional Convention, 143, 144, 148; senator from New York, 179, 185 n., 209, 215, 217, 222, 274; John Taylor's interview with, 228–230; minister to England, 231, 316–317; Ellsworth's letters to, quoted, 317–319, 323, 325–326, 328.
Kirby, Ephraim, 111–112, 113.

Langdon, Senator, 209–210.
Lansing, delegate to Constitutional Convention, 118, 134, 136, 149.
Laurens, Henry, 57.
La Vengeance, case of, 255–256.
Law, English jurist, 321.
Law, Judge Richard, 257; Ellsworth's letters to, 188–191, 213.
Lawrence, Representative, 196.
Laws for limiting prices, 72.
Leavitt, Jemima, 11, 12.
Lee, Arthur, 60.
Lee, Charles, 56.
Lee, Henry, 18.
Lee, Richard Henry, in Constitutional Convention, 57, 59; in first Congress, 178; and judiciary bill, 186, 192.
"Letters of a Federalist Farmer," R. H. Lee's, 192.
Liancourt, Duc de, 244.
Libraries, beginning of history of Congressional and State Department, 97.
Lincoln, Abraham, Ellsworth's style compared with that of, 264.
Linn, John Blair, quoted, 225 n.
Livermore, Representative, 195, 196.
"Lives and Times of the Chief Justices," etc., cited, 23 n.

Lodge, H. C., cited, 16, 151, 214, 216, 273, 275, 280, 294, 311.
London, Ellsworth in, 321.
Lusk, Moses, 110–111.

McDonough *vs.* Delancey, case of, 255.
Maclay, character of, 179–180; diary of, 180–181; quoted on judiciary bill, 193–195; on Ellsworth, 224, 225.
Maclay's Journal cited, 179, 180, 182, 183, 185, 192, 193, 194, 195, 200, 201, 203, 205, 208, 212.
McRee, Griffith J., cited, 239, 248, 251, 253.
Madison, James, at Princeton, 18, 19; in Continental Congress, 74, 84, 86, 89, 90, 101; notes of, in Continental Congress, 86; talents of, complementary to Hamilton's genius, 93; misspelling of New England proper names by, 94 n.; in Constitutional Convention, 122, 128, 133, 134, 135, 141, 145, 147, 167; notes on Constitutional Convention cited, 126, 129, 167–168; in first House of Representatives, 179, 183–184, 196; quoted concerning judiciary bill, 185; first tariff bill originates with, 202; quoted concerning Ellsworth, 226; John Taylor's report to, on King and Ellsworth interview, 228–230.
"Madison's Writings" cited, 17, 19, 76, 78, 89, 92, 93, 94, 97, 98, 99, 101, 102, 103, 118, 136, 141, 226; quoted, 93, 94, 98, 99.
Marshall, John, 2, 69, 247–248, 261, 304; argument of, in British-debts case, 249; comparison of Ellsworth and, 263–264; member of embassy to France, 267–268; advises ratification of Ellsworth's convention with France, 315.
Martin, Luther, 18, 20, 129, 134, 147, 149, 153, 192; cited, 126, 144, 147.
Mary Ford decision, 255.
Maryland, importance of delay of, in subscribing to Articles of Confederation, 64.
Mason, George, 146, 154, 155, 159, 163,

165, 167, 192; quoted regarding Constitutional Convention, 169.

Military establishment, the, 201, 210.

Mills, W. Jay, cited, 20.

Mitchell, Stephen Mix, 178 n.

Monmouth, battle of, 56.

Monroe, James, 216, 266–267, 289.

Moodie vs. the Ship Phœbe Ann, case of, 256.

Morris, Gouverneur, in Continental Congress, 57, 61 ; in Constitutional Convention, 122, 145, 147, 148, 152, 164 ; on result of Ellsworth's mission to France, 315–316; inveighs against the Union, 335.

Morris, Robert, member of Continental Congress, 57 ; investigation of army purchases of, 59 ; Continental finances and, 76, 79, 84, 87, 102, 105 ; letter from, to Franklin, 87–88; no speech credited to, in Constitutional Convention, 129 ; in first Congress (1789), 179, 185 n.

Morrison, John H., cited, 230 n.

Murray, William vans, 272, 273, 286, 309, 313.

Napoleon. See Bonaparte.

Naturalization, question of, in United States courts, 257–262.

Navigation acts, discussion concerning, in Constitutional Convention, 153–157.

Negro slaves and estimation of population, 147, 152–153.

New Jersey, Washington's requisitions on, 73, 75.

New York, Congress meets at (1789), 178.

New York resolutions, the, 88, 97.

Nicholas, George, 259–260.

Offices, President's power of removal from, 201–202.

Olmstead, Gideon, 68, 188.

Otis, H. G., 45 ; on result of Ellsworth's mission to France, 314.

Parker, Alton B., 260 n.

Parker, Moses, 110.

"Particular Court" in Connecticut, 108.

Paterson, William, 18, 20, 126, 148 ; plan of, in Constitutional Convention, 123–124, 127–128, 130 ; in first Senate (1789), 181 ; associate justice of Supreme Court, 241, 249, 253.

Pay Table, Committee of the, 48–50.

Pickering, Timothy, 264, 273, 274, 275, 278, 281, 289, 304, 311, 319, 335 ; letters from Ellsworth to, 266, 270–271, 276, 278, 290, 303 n.; on result of Ellsworth's mission to France, 313.

Pierce, Major William, quoted, 118–120.

Pinckney, Charles, 144–145, 157.

Pinckney, Charles Cotesworth, 144–145, 147, 155, 157, 266–267.

Plain Speaking Club, the, 19.

"Plan of Connecticut," the so-called, 123, 127–128.

Porter, J. A., cited, 20.

Prices, limitation of, by law, 72.

Princeton, American victory at, 56; Continental Congress temporarily at, 103 ; Ellsworth's relations with the college at, see College of New Jersey.

Privateering, matter of, in Continental Congress, 66–69, 70–71 ; jurisdiction of courts in cases concerning, 254–256; treated by Ellsworth embassy to France, 287–289, 291, 293–297, 297, 299–300, 317.

Putnam, Israel, 45, 46, 47, 50.

Randolph, Edmund, in Constitutional Convention, 121, 148, 158, 192; Secretary of State, 217; dealings with French minister, 219.

Read, George, 122.

Reeve, Tapping, 18, 20.

Rex vs. Waddington, case of, 321.

Rhode Island forced to join the Union, 200.

Rittenhouse, David, 69.

Roederer, M., 286, 306 n., 308–310.

Roosevelt, Theodore, 155, 260 n.

Root, Jesse, 21, 60, 64, 108, 113.

Rowland, Miss, cited, 169.

Rush, Benjamin, 18.
Rutledge, John, 57, 85, 86, 89, 91, 94, 98, 125, 153, 158, 192; becomes associate justice of Supreme Court, 197; attacks Jay Treaty, 218–219, 238; named Chief Justice but not confirmed by Senate, 238–239.

Salaries of government officials, 201.
Scott, English jurist, 321.
Sedgwick, Theodore, 196, 314.
Sherman, Roger, 5, 45; appointed delegate to Continental Congress, 51; Ellsworth claims, as his model, 57; reports of, with Ellsworth, to Governor Trumbull, 60, 67, 75, 76, 78, 83–84; member of Connecticut Superior Court, 108; elected to Constitutional Convention, 118; William Pierce's description of, 119; services in the Convention, 120, 123, 125, 126, 127, 128, 139, 150–151, 152, 161; work of, in the Convention, compared with Ellsworth's, 150–151; represents Connecticut in the House and in Senate, 177–178, 196; death of, 178.
" Sherman," Boutell's, 45, 123, 170.
Sherman, Roger Minott, 342.
Sigourney, Mrs., cited, 30, 326.
Slavery, discussions regarding, in Constitutional Convention, 147, 152–153, 153–157.
Smalley, Dr. John, 21.
Smith, Jeremiah, 230.
Smith, Samuel Stanhope, 19.
Smith, William, 196.
Snuff-box presented to Ellsworth by Napoleon Bonaparte, 225.
Snuff-taking, Ellsworth's habit of, 225, 305, 340–341.
Spaniards on Gulf Coast during Revolution, 80.
Stiles, Henry R., cited, 9, 10, 11, 118.
Stiles, President Ezra, 168.
Stone, Congressman, 196.
Story, Judge, 261.
Strong, Caleb, 148, 181, 194, 209, 215, 222, 231.
Stuart, Mrs. Geneve, cited, 17.

Sumner, W. G., cited, 87.
Sumter, Thomas, 196.
Superior Court of Connecticut, 108.
Supplies, matter of, in Continental Congress, 56, 69, 73, 75, 85.
Supreme Court of United States, Committee of Appeals a forerunner of, 58–59; Ellsworth's appointment to Chief Justiceship of, 222, 238–240; early character of, 241; work of, 244–245; noteworthy cases before, 247–267. See also Judiciary bill.
Susquehanna lands, the, 63, 66.

Taintor, G. E., 60 n., 300 n., 302 n.
Taintor, Mrs. Henry E., 234 n.
Talleyrand, American envoys and, 267, 268, 272, 282, 285, 309.
Tariff, first bill on, 202–204.
Taylor, John, 227–230.
Teft, Mr., of Savannah, 302 n.
Thiers, cited, 305, 307, 320.
Thompson, R. E., 328.
Titles, Congressional committee on, 182.
Tracy, Uriah, 243 n.
Trenton, American victory at, 56; seat of national government temporarily at, 277; meeting of statesmen at, 278–280.
Trevelyan, Sir George Otto, cited, 82 n.
Trumbull, Dr. John, quoted, 35.
Trumbull, Jonathan, governor of Connecticut, 46, 47, 48, 50, 59; Ellsworth's letters to, 49, 54; letters to, from delegates to Continental Congress, 54–55, 57, 60, 62, 64, 73, 75, 76–77, 78, 79–82, 83, 96, 99, 101, 102, 103–104, 347–349; charge of disloyalty against, 85–86.
Trumbull, Jonathan (second), 178 n., 332.
Trumbull, Colonel Joseph, 59, 65.
Trumbull, J. Hammond, cited, 21.
Trumbull Papers cited, 62, 64, 73, 75, 76, 78, 80, 84, 96, 99, 101, 103, 108.
Tucker, Congressman, 196.
Turner vs. the President, Directors, and Company of the Bank of North America, case of, 254.

United States *vs.* Henfield, 258.
United States *vs.* Hudson, 260 n.
United States *vs.* Peters, 69.
" Universities and their Sons " cited, 17, 19, 20.

Van Santvoord, George, cited, 30, 55, 84, 110, 112, 113, 116, 258, 311, 332.
Verplanck, Gulian C., 37 n.
Vinal, W. Irving, 9, 11, 237 n., 302 n., 328, 333, 341.
Virginia, debts owed to Britons in, 248–250.
Virginia plan, the, 121 ff.
Volney, Ellsworth and, 285.

Wadsworth, Colonel, 6, 174.
Walker, Williston, cited, 328.
Ware *vs.* Hylton, case of, 248–250.
Washington, Bushrod, 241.
Washington, George, 2, 4, 32, 41, 56, 57 ; letter to Continental Congress regarding establishment of a prize court, 66–67 ; letter to Hamilton on Constitutional Convention, 146–147 ; opinion of work of Constitutional Convention, 169 ; Ellsworth's remark on small part taken by, in Constitutional Convention, 169–170; inauguration of, 179 ; and matters of state etiquette, 183; signs judiciary bill, 197 ; and the Jay mission to England, 215–219 ; Ellsworth's relations with, 232–233 ; New England homes distinguished by visit of, 233.
Washington's Diary cited, 232.
Washington's Writings cited, 66, 67, 146.
Webster, Daniel, on Ellsworth, 175–176.
Webster, Noah, 32–33, 116, 336.
" Webster (Noah)," Scudder's, cited, 32.
Well Meaning Club, the, 19.
Western Reserve lands, 63–64, 97.
Wheaton *vs.* Peters, case of, 260 n.
Whiskey Rebellion, 204, 210.
Williams, Isaac, ruling in case of, 257–259.
Wilson, James, delegate to Continental Congress, 89, 91, 94, 97; figures in Constitutional Convention, 124, 125, 127, 133, 139, 145, 147, 158, 166 n.;

associate justice of Supreme Court, 197, 239, 249, 252, 254 ; bankruptcy and death of, 240.
Wilson, Woodrow, cited, 17, 18.
Wilson *vs.* Daniel, case of, 253–254.
Windsor, Conn., description of, 8 ; family names in, 8–9 ; Washington's visit to, 232–234 ; President Adams at, 277–278 ; Ellsworth's arrival at, from abroad, 326 ; church society and meeting-house in, 328–329.
Wingate, Congressman, 181.
Wiscart *vs.* Dauchy, case of, 252–253.
Witherspoon, John, 17–18, 57.
Wolcott, Abigail (Mrs. Oliver Ellsworth), 23–24.
Wolcott, Erastus, 118.
Wolcott, Frederic, 206.
Wolcott, Oliver, delegate to Continental Congress, 51, 94 ; Ellsworth's letters to, 100, 102, 213–214, 216–217, 222–223 ; governor of Connecticut, 222.
Wolcott, Oliver, Jr., auditor of Treasury, 206 ; quoted, 206–267 ; Ellsworth's letters to, 210–211, 220–221, 303–304 ; Secretary of Treasury, 219; attitude of, in Anglo-French complications, 264–265, 273, 274, 311 ; on result of Ellsworth's mission to France, 312–313.
Wolcott, William, 23–24.
Wolcott family, 8, 9, 23–24.
Wood, Rev. G. I., cited, 341.
Wood, Joseph, 9 n., 32, 333.
Wood, O. E., cited, 216, 341.
Wood Ms. cited, 19, 22, 23, 25, 26, 30, 33, 100, 171, 175, 213, 243, 245, 265, 270, 284, 285, 317, 335.
Wyckoff, Mrs. Alice L., cited, 17.

Yale, Ellsworth's student career at, 13–17 ; Ellsworth a governor of, 333–334 ; degree conferred on Ellsworth by, 334.
" Yale Biographies and Annals," Dexter's, cited, 13, 14, 15.
Yates, delegate to Constitutional Convention, 118, 149; cited, 130, 131, 136, 142, 143.
Young, Arthur, 336.